WHILE I REMEMBER

Ian Dormer, CBE

Copyright © 2024 Ian Dormer

All rights reserved. No part of this publication may be reproduced, distributed or transmitted in any form or by any means, including photocopying, recording or any other electronic or mechanical methods, without prior written permission of the author, except in cases of brief quotations embodied in critical reviews and certain other non-commercial uses permitted by copyright law. For permission requests, write to the author at ian@rosh.co.uk.

*For Emily and Mark.
The greatest gifts I have received*

"The rung of a ladder was never meant to rest upon, but only to hold a man's foot long enough to enable him to put the other somewhat higher."

Thomas Henry Huxley

"You miss 100% of the shots you don't take."

Wayne Gretzky

CONTENTS

Introduction	3
The Beginning	5
The Move North	48
16 Plus	73
Hitching with Richard	90
University	139
Leatherhead & Wallington	188
Flight International	194
Domestic Life	231
Julia Newton	237
Emily Dormer	249
Mark Dormer	274
Family Holidays	291
Rosh Engineering	340
Opportunities	369
Institute of Directors	380
Moving On	434
Eating Cake with Chop Sticks	437
After the IoD	480
While I Remember	492

militaristic with explosions and shooting. I am sure any psychologist or psychiatrist looking at this would have been worried. Now, the prospect of young men going to war and dying upsets me. I respect their courage and bravery but see no glory anymore.

Huw Williams and Phillip Riley both lived nearby on Moat Road. Phillip was one of four children… and lived in the big house at the end of Moat Road. His parents were doctors. Say no more.

A playground was built during our time there at the end of Moat Road, probably around 1972 or 1973.

Beyond my infant school, and still by the brook, was another playground we called The Reck (as in recreation ground). While the Moat Road was a more rustic timber affair, The Reck was a Wicksteed Park metal collection. I did go to Wicksteed Park – not sure how they made their own branded equipment but they did. It is near Kettering, so I must have gone during a visit to Uncle Derek and Aunt Gladys in Higham Ferrars.

Derek had his own stock-taking and book-keeping business, mostly for Working Men's Clubs. They were rich. Tom let it slip 30 years later that his dad was able to start his own business because he found some money under Jack's bed after he died. Jack had been running an illegal bookies and kept his earnings there. All the brothers and sister had inherited an equal share of £295/9 shillings of

CONTENTS

Introduction	3
The Beginning	5
The Move North	48
16 Plus	73
Hitching with Richard	90
University	139
Leatherhead & Wallington	188
Flight International	194
Domestic Life	231
Julia Newton	237
Emily Dormer	249
Mark Dormer	274
Family Holidays	291
Rosh Engineering	340
Opportunities	369
Institute of Directors	380
Moving On	434
Eating Cake with Chop Sticks	437
After the IoD	480
While I Remember	492

IAN DORMER CBE

INTRODUCTION

The 2020 COVID Pandemic confined us to our homes as work places and leisure activities were closed and travel was near impossible. With time on my hands, I decided to start writing the memories of my life so far. I had given my father a similar task when he was 75 as I loved his stories of growing up in the 1930s and during the Second World War. To him his life was normal. To me, and his grandchildren, it was an alien world of food rationing, German bombing raids, and only having a bath every few months... in a tin tub in the kitchen.

I am glad I made him write it all down. My father's death at the age of 91 two weeks into the Lockdown started my own memories of childhood and times gone by.

Figure 1: Ian Dormer, with sister Lisa and parents Sheila and Roy

It started with writing up my diary from a trip to North Korea with Emily and then extended to all my other stories. Only time will tell whether my life was an alien world compared to that of my grandchildren.

I finished the last chapter exactly one year after starting. A total of 160,000 words before final edits.

Some memories are strong and others faded and yellowed with time. I have remained true to events and people encountered throughout my life. There may be omissions – not every happening is significant – and sometimes memory is frustratingly elusive. So I thought I had better write it down *While I Remember*. But this is my truth and my lived experience. Here it is, all me.

Ian Dormer

THE BEGINNING

I was born on Easter Monday 30 March 1964 - two days early - at 6.30 in the morning, at 14 Oaklands Ave in Loughborough, Leicestershire. I was just over 8lbs.

My sister Lisa had been born in a nursing home but my mum thought it better to have a home birth for me as mothers were often hospitalised for a week or two after giving birth. This way, at least, she could look after Lisa and my dad a bit better.

We had no phone, so dad had to use a neighbour's to call the midwife and tell her that I was on my way. Because it was a home birth, he was there when I entered the world. That was unusual; he had not been allowed to be present when mum gave birth to Lisa.

By all accounts, Lisa was a poor sleeper and had never slept through the night. Except this one night, when it was my turn to keep my parents up all night.

Grandparents

My father, Roy Leonard Dormer, was an electrical engineer – or, more accurately, Chief Test Engineer and Quality Manager at Brush Transformers – and was the youngest of 12 children.

My mother, Sheila Ann Dormer (nee Bennett), was an only child and housewife.

Dad's mum, Grandma Dormer, died within my first year so although she did meet me, I never knew her. I was the last of her grandchildren. Grandpa Dormer, had died many years before, when dad was just 19 years old.

Mum's parents both lived nearby (a bungalow at 26 Linford Road) having moved to Loughborough from Derby to be near their only daughter.

I was born in a 1930s semi in a cul-de-sac but by the time I was one year old, we had moved to 90 Valley Road; a new three-bedroom, detached Dutch bungalow, only a short walk from my grandparents.

This was the first house that I remember.

Figure 2; Ian and his sister, Lisa

Mum and dad had a bedroom on the ground

floor next to the bathroom, while Lisa and I were upstairs – Lisa's room to the left, mine to the right across a balcony that looked over the stairs. The drop from the balcony later came in very handy for toy parachutists...But, I must admit, I was very jealous that Lisa's room had a hand basin and a small box room/walk-in cupboard.

My memory makes it seem like a huge house. But then I was small, so everything seemed big. There was a large lawn at the back, a big vegetable patch, and good size garden at the front. The front was enclosed with horizontal white fence panelling and gates at the bottom of the drive.

I once managed to escape. Dad used to come home from work for lunch – or a proper dinner in those days. I had been allowed out into the enclosed front garden to wait for him but managed to climb out. He was driving up the road, spotted me, and stopped. "Where are you going?" he asked. "Down there," I said pointing. Fortunately, he was not a kidnapper and I got in and went home....

Our telephone was in the hall at the bottom of the stairs. Many people used what was known as a "party" line, which meant that two or more houses in the same road shared the same line. If a neighbour was on their phone, then you could not use yours and it was possible to listen in if you picked up the receiver while they were on a call.

We didn't have a party line because dad's work sometimes required testing through the night, and school (Limehurst) by then and had to get a bus back, so was later than me.

Mum finished work at 5.30pm, and dad would collect her. She also had to work every Saturday. The money from this job paid for our first foreign holiday to Benidorm.

School

My first school was Lodge Farm School on Outwoods Drive, now a housing estate.

At the back were playing fields used by the University. One Saturday I was walking along the adjacent path, probably with mum on the way back from town, and there was a football game on. When we got home, dad was watching a football match almost certainly the FA Cup as that was the only football on TV in the 70s and I asked if it was the game down on the fields.

My first teacher was Mrs Tranter and she drove a Chrysler Sunbeam (Chrysler became Talbot in 1979). My next teachers were Mrs Plumb then Mrs Walker: I was never the brightest kid, just average.

You progressed through Wide Range Reader reading books, and I was never in the lead and very jealous of those children who seemed to have more interesting reading books. My first friend was Andrew Rawlinson, but he moved away within a year. I must have told my parents about him after school, saying he lived at 50 Hoult Drive. Before I knew it, dad was driving me down. I was shy at the best of times but desperately did not want to knock on the door.... But my dad did. Hey presto, there was Andrew. Too scared to stay at Andrew's house, he came up to our house to play, and we went down by the brook (more later) before taking him back.

I also met lifelong friend Richard Lambley at this time.

Richard lived right beside the school. Once, I learned that he went back to school after lessons and helped Mrs Walker do jobs, so after I got home and changed, I raced down on my bike to do the same. We once went to her house – again very near the school, on the same road to see a trout or maybe a perch in a pond they had in the garden.

I could not have been much older than six years old when I started walking to school without mum. It was just under a mile from our house and Lisa recalls walking with me more than I remember being with her.

The route was along the Brook Path before popping out near Valley Road. I remember having some friends back for my birthday when I was seven or eight, after school, and as they had not necessarily walked up the path before, we became distracted in the trees, and I got in trouble for being back so late.

I always went home for lunch throughout my schooldays – I was a fussy eater at best and was too nervous and unadventurous to stay at school to eat, so I did the journey back and forth four times a day.

I was always a good kid and only once was I told to stand in the corner at school, probably for talking. And the shame of that.

Mum always made sure we were smart and well-presented, and I never felt as if I went without. She used to quiz us on our times tables and spelling and we were also tested on capital cities, presidents, and prime ministers. I always remember the chuckles around French President Pompidou. It was not that the school wanted these latter tests, just the drive of my parents for us to do well - that working-class-going-on-middle-class aspiration.

Dad had a bit of a chip on his shoulder, feeling he had been passed over for things because he was not a member of the golf club and the like. True or not, I do not know, but he took me to the "Pitch & Putt" in Loughborough to get me acquainted with the game.

When we later moved to the North East, we joined the local golf club. He was never very good, never really felt comfortable in that atmosphere (we never went into the club house after a round), but he wanted me to feel at home in this next tier up the social ladder. And it worked, I do.

They also always wanted me to have opportunity, and never feel excluded or singled out. Dad once told me a story about when he was a kid (and very poor) and he went on a Cub Scout camp. All the kids had a knap-sack, of some description or another, to carry their things in to the camp. He had an old coal sack. He was ridiculed and never wanted the same to happen to his children.

The Boy's Brigade

I had wanted to join the Boy Scouts but there was a long waiting list. However, when I was eight, I went up to the Junior School and my teacher, Mrs Pickford, was a Boy's Brigade Leader. Close enough. So, me and some chums joined them.

We met at the Methodist Church Hall in town. 'Sure & Steadfast' was the motto. Not sure if we were meant to be steadfast Methodists or not. We were not. CofE and Emanuel Church for us.... Well, occasionally. mum had tried to get me to go to Sunday School there, but I was never happy so our attendance at the main church dwindled too.

The Boy's Brigade had an inspection parade at the start of each session and we had to get a card signed-off to earn points for our team. One year, I was a Limpet (groups named after seashells) then Trafalgar.

Throughout the evening, various competitions and races gave your team points. An eventual winner was then calculated as the year went on.

One point I always failed on was, of course, the church attendance. I had got dad to sign-off the relevant parts on my card. Some points were earned on the night, such as polished shoes and cap on straight, but I still scored 9/10 every session due to my lack of religion. Then, one day, I saw a kid who had his card with ticks in the boxes - it was not signed by a parent…. No need to get my dad to lie, I could just tick the boxes and get 10/10. So, I did.

We did not do much in the form of camps, fires, and knots, but learned things – from positions on a cricket field, to how to march in step.

We got badges (I managed to get everyone before I left Loughborough) that were studded into an arm band. Gold was the top badge. We had races and competitions and in the summer term, these were down in Southfield Park rather than in the hall.

We also went up into the woods for a session, one year. We played a form of hide and seek where you hid in the woods but also meant you could win if you got back to base camp without being caught. I decided to bury myself under leaves on one round. Staying stationary worked. The next round, I climbed way up into the top of a tree. I watched the other boys running around below looking. Sometimes a simple solution is the best.

We also put on an annual theatrical production.

One year we put on "Snow White & The 40 Thieves". The combination of themes ensured we all got a part. It was a mashed-up plot with singing and laughter. I played Dopey. So, I had no lines but a solo starring spot.

We had an upright vacuum cleaner with a

cardboard plaque as an "On & Off" button – but the On and Off were slip-in cards. I went on stage and mischievously switched them round, so Off became On, and vice versa. I am not sure what mayhem ensued, but it was part of the ribaldry.

Mum had to make me large velvet ears to play the part; a packed house and much laughter - it was to be my one and only stage performance.

The Brook

The stream that ran from school all the way up to within a couple of hundred yards of our house and beyond was my primary playground from a very young age. It was a gently flowing brook with occasional big pools in which trout and perch could be caught, but much of the length was no deeper than three-quarters of the way up your wellies.

We would go fishing with little nets on bamboo canes for everything from tadpoles to sticklebacks. Bigger boys had fishing rods for the trout etc.

On my walk to and from school over the years I saw all manner of wildlife. I saw my first kingfisher and was surprised how small it was. I had seen pictures in books but nothing that scaled the bird – and with a name like KING fisher I imagined it was the size of an owl not smaller than a sparrow. I saw nuthatches, water voles, and many more.

We climbed trees, built dams and dens, floated

boats of sticks or cans, threw stones and got wet...

The times that I was chastised when I went back home having fallen, or put my foot in the brook and had wet socks, were too numerous to count.

I was familiar with the area towards the school even before I started, as grandpa and dad had an allotment there. In my pre-school years I would accompany grandpa. While he was digging / tending the veg, he would set me up fishing in the brook. He made a rod with a bamboo cane, a bit of string and a plastic curtain hook. Guess what? I caught no fish. I remember complaining, as a four-year old would, about my lack of success. Grandpa laughed about this with another chap passing on the path, and my grandpa joked about how you needed a lot of patience to catch fish. In my case, I would still be sitting there now without a bite...

I was playing down the brook one Saturday when two older boys started fighting. I think I knew at least one of them as a neighbour. The other had a sharp stone in his hand that he was trying to hit our neighbour with. They were wrestling and holding wrists. Pleas of, "put it down" did not work from our neighbour's boy, so a compromise of, "give it to Ian" was suggested. The "give" launched it onto my head, which promptly spurted several gallons of blood over my white T-shirt. I ran home in tears. Mum must have been at the shops as dad was home alone. I was fine and easily mopped up, but the shock for him must have been dreadful.

The brook path in the other direction went up by Moat Road, and some fields that on one side were almost brownfield land, or at least waiting to be built on. Beyond these fields was farmland – growing wheat and barley, etc. These "brown" fields and the brook area became an area where many a WWII battle was enacted with friends, running around with our plastic guns and my camouflage beany hat (I was very proud of that hat). It was the only army type thing I had.

I was pretty obsessed with the Second World War as a child. Partly because my father grew up through this era, and he had brothers and brothers-in-law who fought during the conflict. Stories were in abundance. Also, many of the films coming out of Hollywood, or available on the two channels of TV, were about this period. I was, therefore, also going to be a soldier. Having a camo beany and a plastic M16 was one step on the way.

I later got a bolt-action rifle – the shell ejected as you used the bolt action. It also had a place to put caps (that went bang... or pop) but that was it. Yet, when running around the fields and trees, we would shout out the rat-a-tat-tat of a machine gun to floor our opponents, regardless of the equipment we carried.

I very much aspired to be in the army at this age. It was glamourous and exciting. At school, you would draw a picture and write about it each day as a regular exercise. Mine were all militaristic with explosions and shooting. I am sure any psychologist or psychiatrist looking at this would have been worried. Now, the prospect of young men going to war and dying upsets me. I respect their courage and bravery but see no glory anymore.

Huw Williams and Phillip Riley both lived nearby on Moat Road. Phillip was one of four children... and lived in the big house at the end of Moat Road. His parents were doctors. Say no more.

A playground was built during our time there at the end of Moat Road, probably around 1972 or 1973.

Beyond my infant school, and still by the brook, was another playground we called The Reck (as in recreation ground). While the Moat Road was a more rustic timber affair, The Reck was a Wicksteed Park metal collection. I did go to Wicksteed Park – not sure how they made their own branded equipment but they did. It is near Kettering, so I must have gone during a visit to Uncle Derek and Aunt Gladys in Higham Ferrars.

Derek had his own stock-taking and book-keeping business, mostly for Working Men's Clubs. They were rich. Tom let it slip 30 years later that his dad was able to start his own business because he found some money under Jack's bed after he died. Jack had been running an illegal bookies and kept his earnings there. All the brothers and sister had inherited an equal share of £295/9 shillings of it. I was duly asked to prove it, and of course could. First Certificate, in a plastic bag to protect it, I proudly presented the following day.

Over the coming years, I went up through the certificates and badges until I was eventually swimming seven days a week – Saturday just for fun. The highest personal survival badges, Bronze, Silver, Gold and Honours, involved variously swimming, first in pyjamas, through to fully dressed. You made a float out of pyjama bottoms, tying knots in the legs and then wafting overhead to fill them with air.

The fully dressed bit was a real trial. Especially as the only jumper we could spare to get soaked in the chlorinated water was a thick woollen jumper that soaked up a couple of hundred kilos of water. I then had to swim two lengths in 60 seconds. Other kids seemed to have much lighter weight attire.

After these badges, I started doing lifesaving and distance swimming – mostly on a Sunday morning. I was the youngest by far – and the other boys called me "Titch". Two were brothers and lived the other side of Forrest Road from the end of Valley Road. I visited their house once and was shocked, or at least surprised, that they shared a bed. One brother also had a bottle of beer (half full) under the bed. Bearing in mind he was 12 at best, this was alarming.

During the Sunday sessions, I learnt everything from rescuing a drowning person to mouth-to-mouth resuscitation. There was a dummy... well, a head and set of lungs to practice on. They could add weights to the rising lungs to make it harder. Tough, for a little one like me.

I swam one mile, then progressed and made my two-mile distance badge, all the time swimming continuously without touching the sides. And all by the time I was 10.

The swimming club continued through this period. Galas were the target of training, both in-club and travelling, although I recall travelling to watch Lisa compete more than I travelled.

In my first year, I won everything. Including the butterfly... but then again, I was the only entrant in the butterfly at that age group, so not a big ask. I just had to avoid getting disqualified and get to the other end.

As the overall winner, I also took home an extra trophy. As the years went by, though, others started to excel, and I started coming second, third, and then off the podium. Some of those boys at 10 had muscles and moustaches. I started to lose interest.

After training on a Thursday, we would stop by the fish and chip shop. Not liking fish, I had sausage and chips. The swimming pool had no facilities, apart from a vending machine that produced orange or lime cordial (even though the picture on the front showed it sparkling) and a wall-mounted vending machine with a rotary handle on the side that had Crunchy chocolate bars.

Mother & Father

Mum was a housewife and she took the role very seriously.

She had worked before getting married (at 20), until Lisa was born. She had done general admin at Corah's the printers, but once babies arrived, she was a full-time mum and wife.

She later admitted to me that her mum had given her little love and affection through her childhood. I do recall grandma saying how giving birth nearly killed her, so maybe there was some resentment? But my mum was the opposite. Absolute devotion, love, and care - more than you could ever ask for.

While our income was modest, Lisa and I were spoilt rotten. Or, as spoilt as we could be. This was manifested in our getting whatever food we liked, through to always being well-turned out.

She always made a huge effort to look smart and always has done.

She took her household chores seriously. Hoovering every day, dusting, and keeping the house spick and span. Before dad came home from work in the evening, she always changed out of her housework clothes and put on something better and did her make-up and hair. I asked her once, "why?" She replied, "Your dad has made an effort all day to provide for us, the least I can do is make an effort for him for when he comes home".

It was not a time of consumerism, nor was there social media pressure to have things.

There was fashion of a sort; I supported Arsenal football team because my dad did. So when the time came to get me a replica football kit, the shop assistant asked, "what team?" "Arsenal", I replied, but mum cut in and said just a red and white one. Of course, a proper Arsenal strip would be pricey, so I got as close as they could.

Mum seemed to manage the budget. While they always had a joint account, and Dad earned the money, mum was the one who had to make sure we ate well, dressed well, and had what treats we could afford.

She was also probably the more aspirational for us. While dad had a very poor background and had worked his way up the corporate ladder, mum was an only child, and had tasted privilege (albeit on a low bar) a little more.

During WWII her father had been medically unable to fight, and, due to the shortage of staff at the railway works, he had had lots of opportunity to earn overtime pay in the wages office where he worked. This led to them buying their own home. Proper rich. Mum also went to Notre Dame Convent (private) school in Northampton, from 11 years old, to 14, or 15..

Aspirational experience, so aspirational for us.

But mum was also the nervous type; she had learned to drive, but rarely did. When the first cheque books were issued, it was quite a challenge for her to master this new form of payment, although master it she did. She needed looking after by dad, and he took that hunter-gatherer role seriously and looked after us all.

Dad's childhood was tough, although he never actually thought that it was.

To him, it was normal. His friends and neighbours all had similar experiences. He was living hand-to-mouth with an unloving father, who did nothing in terms of childcare or a domestic role; sharing a bed with two brothers (one who got tuberculosis); having boils; rarely bathing and having few expectations or really achievable aspirations in life except getting a good trade or job.

But mum motivated him, and the 1960s were a time of opportunity, even though he was not comfortable within this aspirational world, as much as he tried. It was not his natural drive, but he did it for his children.

Figure 3 Christmas 1971 in Valley Road. Ian, Lisa and our mother

Mum and dad provided whatever they could for us. As mum made dresses for Lisa, he built a fort for my toy soldiers. One Christmas, I got a train set. It was second-hand, although I did not realise it at the time. But it was what little boys should have. So, I did.

He spent hours building Airfix models with me; well, he assembled them and I watched. Action Man became a must-have toy for boys, and I was desperate but dad resisted; dolls are for girls; such very traditional views, in that respect. But mum did not want me to be left out from playing with other boys, and so he relented.

Mum recalled how she has never seen a group of eight-year-olds playing for so long, and so well together, than when we had Action Men. We dug trenches in the vegetable patch, we hid them in the rose bushes, and re-enacted more battles than ever took place between 1939-45.

Mum and dad were both completely and utterly dedicated to each other, and to us. They always seemed old. They did not do pop music, they did not play sports, and in fact they did not have any hobbies apart from family. Their idea of a wonderful Saturday night was cuddled up on the sofa watching television, with us, as kids. And that continued after we had left home, and there was just the two of them.

That love and devotion to each other remained until my father died, just short of their 65th wedding anniversary.

Holidays

My first holidays were in Looe in Cornwall. Dad would drive through the night and we would all sleep and the journey was long because the M5 through the South West wouldn't open until 1971.

We followed the old Roman Road, the Fosse Way, across country. When we got to Cornwall, we decamped to the beach and mum would promptly fall asleep and, despite being fit to drop, dad had to stay awake to keep an eye on me and Lisa.

We became friendly with a couple in Looe - Claude and Pamela, and he had a collection of little motorboats that you could rent and pootle about on in the bay. Claude's Cornish accent was so strong I could hardly understand a word he said. Over the next 12 or 13 years we had two weeks each year in Newquay. Once at a flat where the bed was hinged and pushed up vertically against the wall, not a rare feature in its age, a sofa bed but not being a sofa.

Then we found Mr and Mrs Morris's flat where we

stayed up until I was 12. They had a B&B upstairs, which was accessed from Belmont Place, and our entrance was round the back by the garage. Two bedrooms and a living/diner, plus kitchen, bathroom, and a small yard. The squawking of the seagulls was something we never heard in land-locked Loughborough. I can still recall the ozone smell of the sea.

Mr Morris had a mackerel fishing boat that took tourists out. He and his wife were very small, and seemed so even when I was a child, but lovely people. The flat was near the harbour which also had a small beach. Our daily ritual involved going down the high street in the morning to buy fresh food and this gave us an opportunity to buy our one and only holiday treat. After shopping we would head down to the harbour beach for an hour or two. The water was very still and I had a go at snorkelling for the first time - my holiday treat being a mask and snorkel, and later, flippers.

We then went back to the flat for lunch, before heading off to Fistral Beach in the afternoon, walking across the golf course on a public footpath and on more than one occasion, we had an issue with golfer's balls coming a bit close.

Fistral had great waves and we had our own surfboard – or, more accurately, body board dad had made it from a piece of plywood, and painted yellow. We spent hours surfing. If the tide was out I would dig pools in the shallows with my trusty spade.

Mid-afternoon, we went up to the lifeguard hut where there was an ice-cream stand. Milk choc ice for me and Lisa, dark chocolate ones for mum and dad. The same every time, every year. While waiting in the queue we used to look up to the Headland Hotel, an impressive stand-alone mansion overlooking the bay. We dreamed of going there, imagining how rich you had to be: would the Rolls-Royces that went there have to have a roof rack with their luggage on, like we did on our car?

The evenings in Newquay occasionally involved a trip to the pub, where dad would have a rare and deserved pint and we would have a lemonade and pack of ready salted crisps. Kids were not allowed in the bar, so while dad was buying the round, I stood at the door waiting, hopping around as kids do. One year I tripped and fell against a small wall, splitting my head open. Head wounds bleed dreadfully of course, so off I was rushed to the cottage hospital. The mask of blood over my face raised concerns that I had taken my eye out in the process. Fortunately, a butterfly plaster was all that was needed.

Other evenings, we played a game of crazy golf and I managed to give Lisa a black eye swinging my club one year.

As the years passed, a roller blading rink was built further up the road. This caused much hilarity for mum, as Lisa just clung to the edge and crawled all the way round. To enter the rink, she would sink to her knees and crawl across, but dad did not try it: not the sort of thing they were adventurous enough to do. I'd had ice skating lessons with school and I managed with no problems.

Sometimes, we would head out for a walk up to the headland and once every holiday we would go to the small theatre. It was a variety show with magicians, singing, and audience participation. I would never go on stage but dad did once, and we came away with a tin tray and four cans of stout. While the sun always seemed to shine on our holidays, there were days when we did not go to the beach.

One rainy day in 1974, we went to the pictures and saw Towering Inferno, the blockbuster of the year. Other days, we would have trips out to Looe or local country homes and beautiful Cornish villages.

We went to Lizard Point one year, and to Land's End another. Once, as we had walked up Newquay High Street, several £1 notes were blowing down the road. There was no one around, and no one chasing after them, so we gathered them up. Being good people (and more as a lesson for me and Lisa), we took them to the police station. The desk sergeant said to keep them, but he would send anyone round to the flat if they came asking. Of course no one did so we spent it on a dinner in a restaurant.

As the years passed, we started heading down to Cornwall a day earlier, on the Friday lunchtime. This involved a stopover in a farmhouse B&B in Devon. We would drive to Tiverton in Devon where we would have tea with some old friends and neighbours; Barbara and Arthur Clarke, and their daughter Lisa. Barbara was being treated for depression and was prescribed Valium. Arthur worked in government communications - very secret and he could not say what. They were stationed in Cyprus when Turkey invaded in 1974, and Barbara and Lisa stayed with us a few nights after evacuation. Arthur had to stay behind.

After eating with the Clarke's we went on to a B&B. We stayed in some lovely old places. One was Barn Park which broke-up the journey and meant we arrived at lunchtime in Newquay. It was the biggest day of the year – who could spot the sea first? It was t only time in the year we would see the sea.

One year, dad managed to get a business meeting in Devon on the way down and this meant he could put one room on expenses, so we stayed in an hotel. We just stopped where vacancies were showing, he checked how much and, if it was within budget, we checked in. The excitement was huge - the first hotel I had ever stayed in.

It had colour television! It was in a resident's lounge and I wrote a postcard to my friend to tell him all about it. It also had a swimming pool and I went for a swim and came out with frostbite, but I still wanted my picture taken, as this was high living!

By 1976, dad had been promoted and was running Washington Engineering in the North-East. We then had the means to stay in an hotel - The Melanvrane Hotel on the Trevemper Road, by the boating lake.

There were suddenly other families to interact and play with. It had a small snooker table, and dancing in the ball room, meals were at set times but a fussy eater like me was more than satisfied. The owners were an odd Yorkshire couple who did not have the welcoming demeanour one expects and the old man did not seem to like kids at all.

We made some good friends and kept in touch with Mavis and Pete Waters, and their son Darren, from Grimsby. They were all regulars at the hotel and went to Crantock Bay. So, we started to do the same. Cousin Linda Dormer also came a couple of times to keep Lisa company.

Once, we went to Great Yarmouth for the night. It was in the summer holidays and dad had to be at the Birds Eye Pea factory when they turned on a transformer before the harvest. It had failed several times after installation and this time Birds Eye wanted him on site when they flicked the switch. Mum, Lisa, and I spent the day on the beach and I got badly sunburnt to the point of sunstroke.

The transformer switched on without an issue this time, of course.

We also had day trips to country parks and stately homes from Belvoir Castle to Chatsworth, where we were exposed to the culture and heritage of England. We would visit relatives and they visited us – mostly for the day, as I rarely remember staying overnight except at Uncle Reg and Aunt Dorothy.

Mum only had one relative who we kept in touch with; a cousin, Pat, who was about her age too. Big shopping trips were few, but when we went, we always went to Nottingham and not Leicester – even though it was equidistant to either. This involved a stop at a café, where mum and dad would share a cream cake or chocolate éclair. A real treat. As a fussy eater, I just had a bread roll and butter, which was perfect.

During these years, dad travelled on quality or technical issues to a number of countries to resolve issues on transformers.

International travel was a rare and exceptional activity in those days. There were currency controls, so you had to get permission to take money out of the UK, even for hotel and food expenses. Dad had these slips of paper in the back of his passport. Credit cards were unheard of. The rest of us did not have passports.

The first trip I remember him going on was to Newfoundland, Canada in winter. He had his photograph taken with him standing on the frozen sea, shivering in his English overcoat – hardly sufficient for a Canadian winter. Lisa was given a sea lion paperweight covered in real sea lion fur. I got three Airfix-type airplanes to build.

Other trips to Libya, Zambia, Saudi Arabia, and Bahrain all followed. None could be regarded as tourist destinations then. He came back with the tales of the markets, and trinkets as gifts for us, ranging from a wooden lion spear for me, to carvings of animals. But we also learned how some simple things were precious - such as Biro refills in Zambia, through to water in Saudi.

One of these trips, he went on a helicopter out to an oil rig. And on another, his flight was diverted somewhere and the only air-conditioned space was a customs and immigration building, which he was ushered out of, so he just squatted in the shade of a building. I remember him describing how it felt like walking into an oven as the aircraft door opened and he stepped out. It would be many years until I experienced that sensation, but how true it was.

Politics

A Labour Party jumble sale was my earliest memory of politics in the family.

Dad must have been a member and activist, as we were manning a stall in the hall. I remember having to draw a picture and adding some words about, "what I did at the weekend," as you do, although I did not understand that the Labour Party and a jumble sale were separate things. I thought a jumble sale *was* a Labour Party...

Mum was a bit embarrassed, I think, that I declared their politics at school.

The local MP was Labour – a chap called John Cronin, who represented Loughborough from 1955 until 1979, when he was beaten by the Conservative candidate, Stephen Dorrell. The Conservative candidate allegedly lived in a house just outside the town centre, at the bottom of Beacon Road. It was painted blue. Dad scorned this.

Dad's sister, Olive, was equally scathing of their sister, Eileen. Eileen lived in Surrey, and was rich. But, as Olive said with distaste, she was now a Tory.

As the years went by, activism dropped-off but the loyal, hard-core socialist beliefs never really did. Mum was less hard-core, and just voted the same way as my dad, I am sure. She even joined the Conservative Ladies afternoon tea set for a while when we lived in Whickham. It was not very political, just a social gathering, invariably with a non-political speaker. She enjoyed that social element.

But they always held their voting line.

During the Iraq war, which was justified on the basis of Saddam Hussein having Weapons of Mass Destruction (WMD), each night, mum prayed before bed that they would find the WMD. This would then vindicate Tony Blair's decision to attack. WMD were never found.

For all their socialist beliefs, they were actually Tories at heart.

I say this because when I went to University, I was very much expounding dad's beliefs. I was labelled a Tory. Dad believed in hard work being the route of success and he believed in freedom and free enterprise. Ironically, he believed he should be able to give me opportunities and advantages in life, although, he was not so keen on the rich, or the gentry, doing the same.

Mountfields School

Aged eight, I moved up to Mountfields School, only a few hundred yards further down the flow of the brook across some grassed areas with, most importantly, some horse chestnut, or conker trees.

Conker fights were an important game as a child.

Long before electronics, we would take the conker (or nut) out of its shell when it fell to the ground…. Actually, we spent a good deal of time throwing sticks up into these great trees to dislodge the conkers. Being small, we did not get our sticks up high, but I remember, one time, a man walking his dog came past and threw his dog's ball up into the tree - and down came our prize. What a day that was.

Figure 4: The Conker King+-

Having a good source of conkers was amazing. Later, after we had moved to the North East, there was not such a ready supply. In fact, one of my first businesses was selling conkers. We used to head back from Newcastle each month, for the weekend, to visit my grandparents, giving me the opportunity to get stocks in from these trees in Loughborough. The pricing was 1p per conker, 2p with a hole in it, and 3p for a conker including string. I learned at an early age about supply and demand.

The first class was in an old house that the school was built around. Mrs Pickford seemed about 90 years old, but was a kindly lady. Her husband was a teacher at Garendon Senior School, and they both ran the respective Junior and Senior branches of the Boys Brigade. They had lived in Africa – Kenya I think – for many years, doing missionary or charity work.

We were lucky to have lovely grounds around the

The school got an oven during this time, so we could all have a go at cooking. The oven – just a regular domestic cooker - was in a corridor (not a kitchen or classroom) where they set-up tables. A handful of us would have a turn each week. My week was scones. Not that I ate scones, but I baked them. I had obviously not fully written-out the ingredients we had to bring, much to the displeasure of Mrs Weston. I had no butter or margarine to grease the tray, but fortunately there was some left from someone else's. I rarely got in bother, so when I did it hurt and it stayed with me.

Every Saturday morning, the school had a football club that I went to.

We mixed with other boys, learned new skills and played little games. Some dads helped out with the running and coaching. Not mine- which I privately wanted - but he never seemed young and fit enough to do it. Not that he was old and decrepit... just from a different age or different background.

After a while, I began to cycle there. One day, I came back in the snow. I was so cold, I cried. I could not hold the handle-bars, and the journey seemed to take for ever. When I got home, mum was out (either shopping or at Grandma's, I imagine) so I only had dad to care for me and try and warm me up.

At times like that you need your mum. I vowed never to go outside again... as 8-year-olds do.

There was a real mixture of kids at the school. Over

the years, they seemed to come and go, or at least come and go from my circle.

There was an overweight smelly kid who sat by me once who had poor attendance, farted a lot, and when he brought in some homework, it was obvious an older brother had done it. We did not get homework as such, but I think he got it as he was so rarely in class.

Another chap was into ballet and quite proud of it, in a day when sexist stereotypes abounded. Then there was a chatty and opinionated girl called Hazel Brown who insisted her eyes were hazel brown, and not just brown.

It was during this time that we also had the influx of Ugandan Asians as Idi Amin expelled the Indian, Pakistani, and Bangladeshis from the former British Colony in 1971.

Our classes swelled to 42 or 43 pupils per class, from the 38 or 40 pupils that was standard.

As an area with light industry, like textiles, many settled in Leicestershire. Prejudice was certainly in the air, and while I never recall having any of them as friends, equally I never recall being hostile.

Girls never featured as friends, during these years. A strange race of human that was not to be encountered unnecessarily. Teachers would sit boys and girls next to each other in classes to maintain order, as you would not be with your chums and unable to cause mischief.

The neighbours to one side of us at Valley Road, going up Springfield Gardens, were the Easons. The daughter, Penny, was my age but while I had played with her as a young child, she did not exist in my universe during the following years. Her mum and dad were teachers, and her dad had started to drop us off at school at Mountfields. He had an old Austin Seven, which he started with a cranking handle on cold days. But it was so uncool to have this lift that, after a while, I built up the courage to suggest I walked instead.

Other friends during this time included Martin Thurston and Jeffery Dixon. Jeffrey's dad was a policeman and lived in the Avenue where I was born. Richard Lambley was a constant chum, who came into his own in the last few weeks of my time at Mountfields.

I supported Arsenal, just like dad, but the local football team was Leicester City. Football is tribal, and it was no different at age 10. I was not going to drop my principles to be part of the gang, but in my last year at Mountfields, it started to get increasingly hostile.

One lunchtime in the playground, a group were chanting at me while I was pinned in a corner of a building. This escalated to a challenge to a fight after school by one ringleader – Roy Ilston. I could not back down, and we duly assembled outside the school gates at 4pm. Encircled by other boys, he started to come for me, but I went at him full force.

His bravado and confidence evaporated, and he ran. I chased, but he kept running, so I let it pass.

But that was not the end. Jeffery Dixon was next, and that ended when an adult broke it up.

Huw Williams lined up a few days later. We just stood there thumping each other in the face for ages... to the point that the crowd had all gone home. Except one. Richard Lambley had never taken sides and was there supporting me. I went back via his house where I cleaned the blood off from my face.

I was so late that Dad was driving down the road looking for me. It must have been a Friday as he was working in the North East, prior to our move a few weeks later. Mum went up to school the following week, and the fighting and intimidation stopped. We moved house shortly after.

Boys will be Boys

Although I was a good kid, polite, well turned-out, and rarely in trouble, boys will be boys.

Apart from running around fields and shooting each other in WWII re-enactments, we built dens. We would cut sticks with my trusty penknife, and I developed a system of bending over tree branches or saplings, and tying them down to help make the den. I tied them down by cutting a strip of bark off the tree to make a strap/-string. Someone must have noticed this vandalism to tree trunks and the police came by once to ask if we had done this cutting of the trees. We denied it and blamed it on bigger boys.... A close brush with the law.

We also built traps to prevent invasion. We dug holes and covered them with light sticks and leaves. Anyone approaching would fall in and we would be safe. The reality was, they would probably only go ankle-deep... but the principle was sound.

Matches and fire always fascinated me. I once managed to get hold of some matches from the kitchen and, one dark winter night, set fire to some newspaper in the front garden flower bed with a friend. Before I knew it, as it was such fun, we had a whole line of newspaper strips burning away across the front of the house... A neighbour reported it to mum as it was like the Blackpool Illuminations.

Another time, we decided to build a bomb. Gossip and chatter amongst us came up with a myriad of fables and proposals. I had an old Airfix paint bottle. A small, thimble-size bottle. This was the casing. We knew that toy gun caps had explosive in – they went pop/bang. We also knew that white spirit or turpentine burnt. We put all this together then headed off to the fields. A safe distance from people and homes as we were surely going to have an explosion to rattle windows. We set the touch paper alight, and Roy Ilston ran to take cover the second it was lit. Me, Huw, and Richard back tracked a little slower, but we all took cover. Twenty seconds past and we lifted our heads. We could see a flame and hear the odd pop, pop, pop. No explosion. Not really a bomb.

Mum and dad's primary hobby was the garden. They spent hours making it look lovely. I was allowed to play football and cricket in the garden, but once I had obviously taken a few too many flowers out with a ball. Under strict conditions not to damage any more, I was allowed to play cricket with friends. Alas, a ball took the head off a daffodil. In an attempt to cover the crime, I stuck it back on with Bostik glue. Clear of blame for another day.

Action Men became a key part of playing during these years. I eventually had five in total. Tom and Jerry were first, followed by Bill and Ben. Jim completed the line up. Jerry was the only one without "realistic hair" as he was attained by collecting stars from the outfits you bought and sending them off to Palitoy. I later got a Brutus the bulldog this way too. Only Jim had "gripping hands".

An armoured car, jeep, assault craft and even a Scorpion tank joined the regimental line up. I also made many things from an assault course through to a tent. Mum also made a few dozen sandbags, which were much better than the commercially produced insipid things in the shop. Many an hour passed enacting battles and digging trenches for them in the vegetable patch. Mum said she had never seen young boys be so happily occupied for so long.

World Events

Between 1964 and 1975 a few world events took place, and one or two stick in my mind.

The oil crisis, where OPEC flexed their muscles, was one that stretched over 1973-1974. Dad received his petrol-ration coupons – issued as he needed them for work, as much as anything – but I think they were never needed as oil supplies started flowing and petrol pumps were back in action. The miners also went on strike in 1974, and we had power cuts and the Three Day Week and had to have candles: businesses and factories could only operate for three days a week to save energy. Of course, there was a shortage of candles then too.

In 1973, there were two mining disasters. The Markham Colliery disaster was when a lift cage crashed to the bottom of the shaft killing 18 men. Another was the Lofthouse disaster when a seam was flooded, trapping men underground. It was the main feature on the news as they tried a rescue over several days, hoping they had found an air pocket. Just seeing the rescuers going down and crawling through three-foot gaps underground scared me. No one was saved in the end.

We didn't see the first landing on the moon. It was shown on television, but it was the middle of the night and my parents probably thought a night's sleep was more important to a five year old. It was during the summer holidays but, when we went back to school, we found out that some children had been woken-up by their parents to watch it.

Later, at Mountfields Junior School, a teacher said she had some moon rock to show us. I think it was through a connection with the University. But disappointment dominated. It was more a large bit of grit than a rock. I suppose they rationed out what the rest of the world was given, and it was a privileged that our school got to see a bit.

Arsenal winning the Double in 1971 - the League and the FA cup - was momentous, and Charlie George scoring the winning goal with a scorching shot from 20 yards out in the Final was live on television. Around 2013, Mark and I did a tour of Arsenal's Emirates Stadium. Part of the appeal was having an "Arsenal Legend" as the guide. We had Charlie George. He did a great tour, telling of how different football was in his day – he used to go home on the bus after a game—great if they won, but he hid behind a newspaper if they lost.

The Cold War was ever present, and the conflict in the Middle East came into my consciousness. As did The Troubles in Northern Ireland. Bombings, shootings, and tension in the province dominated the news. Dad once had to go to Belfast on business, but told mum, Lisa and me that he was on a trip to Washington in the North East, so we would not worry until he safely returned.

THE MOVE NORTH

In late 1974, Dad was offered a promotion to be General Manager of a factory that Hawker Siddeley Group had bought, which manufactured cooling radiators for transformers. He was told he did not have to take it as other opportunities would arise, but we were all excited.

Several weekend trips were made, looking at potential new homes. We stayed at the Washington Forte Post House Hotel – at the junction of the A1 to Washington by the motorway services. It was all-expenses paid, so I had my own room - which had a TV (black and white) - and we ate in the restaurant.

Very posh, this "moving north" idea.

Eventually, we found a four-bedroom detached house – 2, The Cedars, Whickham. The garden was small, but it was near fields and countryside so a new area for me to explore.

This was a good street to live in, at the upper end of this suburban Newcastle town, although the shops in Whickham were known as the "Village" and the City of Newcastle was the "Town". All highly confusing.

Someone from Hawker Siddeley Group in London (A PR / marketing woman) called by our house once. She was very "rah," or had a "plumb in her mouth," as mum would say, but she described our home as a nice "little" house. Lisa and I were most put out. This was "The Cedars", didn't she know....

Dad started his new job in January 1975, but our house move did not happen until after Easter. So, dad lived at the Washington Post House hotel, from Monday through Thursday.

I had visited Washington Engineering before. One of the half-term holidays at Mountfields School was a day longer than Lisa's school, and mum was working at the shoe shop that day.

Not old enough to be left alone, I went with dad on his business trip north.

I sat in our Ford Cortina while he went in. A while later, a knock on the window and a man was inviting me in to give a tour of the shop floor.

The factory was noisy, felt dirty, smelly, and scary. The process was shown to me from the uncoiling of sheet steel, cutting, pressing, seam welding the panels, through to welding them onto header pipes, before water tank testing to look for leaks, and onwards to the paint shop.

The noise of banging and crashing, the welding flashes, the smell of oil, and paint solvents was a real insult to the senses of a sweet and innocent little boy. To top it all, I could not understand a word this Geordie chap was saying to me, even when the noise abated.

The factory had a large number of women welders - who were widely regarded as more productive and accurate than the men. Seeing this blond-haired little kid must have sparked something in them as one came across with a sweet in a wrapper for me. I put it in my pocket (after saying thank you, of course) It was a Locket – a cough sweet -probably all they had.

The factory had something like 200 staff at this point, working over two shifts. By the time dad had brought in efficiencies etc, they were closer to 100.

On this trip, the Works Manager, Tom Cook, took us to a very novel restaurant for lunch: The Marsden Grotto. We took a lift down the side of the cliff and ate overlooking the sea. A fascinating experience for this land-locked lad.

The factory ran a shift on Saturdays. Dad used to regularly go across on a Saturday morning to show his face and I would often go too, although I would spend my time playing in his office and nosing around the drawers.

He had a drinks cabinet, cigarette box (although he only had an occasional cigar), and all sorts of treats. Once, I noticed the cigarette box was gone. He decided the cleaners were taking them more than they were given away to visitors, so stopped that.

Dad eventually stopped having a cigar when I was probably in my twenties. He usually had half of a small Manikin or Hamlet after lunch, and half after dinner. One Sunday after dinner when we were round, mum asked if he was having a cigar. "No," he said, "I stopped a few weeks ago." Why? Well mum had commented she did not like the smell, so, he stopped. No fuss, no great announcement. Just did it, as mum did not like it.

On one of our Saturday morning forays to Washington

Engineering, it was chucking it down with rain. We went over Silver Hills from Sunniside to Lamesley – a country back-road. As we were going down the hill, we saw a man out running. What an absolute idiot, we said, in this weather. As we went passed, I looked back. It was North-East hero, Olympic medallist, and founder of the Great North Run, Brendan Foster.

Although my dad had been given a company car a couple of years earlier, they were small and average – a Ford Escort Estate and then a Ford Cortina. With the new job was the former General Manager's Fiat. A fancy Fiat... but still a Fiat.

Shortly after, we were given a new car – a Triumph 2500 TC. This was much better and, later, when dad was made Managing Director of the plant, he was allowed a three-litre car (this size of engine was reserved for Directors), and we got a Ford Granada Ghia.

The Cedars

Most of Whickham was a Bellway housing estate. Very similar boxes with very little character.

Our garden was much smaller than we were used to and, although we were a corner plot, most of the grass was around the front and side and not a private space. We had no vegetable patch here, but we had a downstairs toilet in addition to the upstairs family bathroom.

Mum and dad obviously had the largest bedroom, Lisa the second largest, and number three was for guests so that a double bed could be fitted. As the smallest person in the house, I got the smallest - and very small it was - fourth bedroom.

Our move there was quite eventful. After the removal truck was loaded, we had lunch with grandparents and headed north after the lorry, expecting to catch them up by Scotch Corner. We got to the house but there was no sign of the lorry for ages. Eventually it arrived, having broken down several times with fuel line blockages. The removal men's hands were black. Mum was worried about a chest freezer in the back that would be defrosting, so off it came and was plugged in. We then let the lads set up their sleeping bags in the house before we went off to stay in the Post House Hotel. We woke them the next morning; they had been out on the tiles in Newcastle, so seemed a bit groggy..... Of course, their lorry would not start the next day and they had to get towed....

A few days later, we had another incident. Noticing an upstairs floorboard was loose and squeaking, I hammered-in a nail to secure it (under the supervision of dad) before the carpet went down. The next morning, we woke up to a scream from mum. I had put the nail through a copper pipe and water was pouring into the living room below, with half the ceiling following it.

Our first experience in the North was fantastic. The day after we moved in, while we were unpacking and sorting, the doorbell rang. It was a neighbour, Trisha Kidd. "Has anyone welcomed you to The Cedars?" No. Well, that was unexpected and a taste of the friendly and warm feeling we were to have, going forward. It made mum's day.

Over the following weeks, she then became involved in a couple of different women's coffee mornings and a network of friends developed like she had never had before.

The move was a success. Mum was happy, so dad was happy. We were all happy and had a new-found wealth (relatively so). Although we had booked the flat in Newquay for that summer, subsequent trips would be to a small hotel.

First Foreign Holiday

My first flight in an aeroplane, my first trip out of the Country, all coincided with the move North. We moved to Newcastle two days after we got back. Mum's job at the shoe shop was mostly driven by the desire to give us enough money for a foreign holiday. This culminated with a long weekend (something like 4 nights) in Benidorm in a 2 star hotel. We flew from East Midlands Airport on a Britannia flight. The hotel food was rank. The best option I could see was liver and onions one night. It was greasy and awful. Mum said the cottage pie on the flight out was the best meal we had. She was right, and even that I thought was marginal. The sun was bright and I needed sunglasses, and we took a train trip excursion to the countryside and saw lemons growing on trees. Free fizzy wine was available on the way back on the train and lots of people got drunk. Something I had not seen before. All in all, a simple trip, and the only foreign holiday I ever had with my parents.

School in the North

My dad told me I had two choices of junior school in Whickham: Washingwell School or Parochial School. I suggested Washingwell, as it would be the only one I could spell.

So, I went to Whickham Parochial.

I would only attend it for the summer term before heading up to secondary school.

Our neighbours had three boys – all younger than me, two of whom went there – Richard and Matthew Armitage. Their younger brother, Patrick, was only about four years old. Their father worked for British Telecom, and later became UK Managing Director.

Richard took me up to the school during the Easter Holidays to show me where it was – it was only a short walk, and I walked there daily (including back for lunch).

I had always worn shorts as part of my school uniform in Loughborough. Richard said that was fine. But on my first morning there, all the boys in my year had long trousers on. Mum and dad were happy to take me back to quickly change, but I did not want to be late.

It was a very embarrassing and humiliating morning, though, as I felt like a little boy. I changed into long trousers for the afternoon.

It was a small school, which meant I even made the football team, despite neither me, nor the team, being any good. We played Crawcrook and lost 13 – 0, which was brilliant apparently, as the previous encounter we lost 25-0.

Whickham Comprehensive

My secondary school was a different scale.

It had opened the year I was born and had 1,200 students. Due to the baby boomers and growth of Whickham, the school used a number of prefabricated buildings (or Nissen huts) for classrooms to accommodate everyone.

We were spread across six Houses. Not quite Eton, or *Tom Brown's School Days*, but the principle was the same.

They were each named after local historical spots. I was in Axwell, as was Lisa. They kept siblings together to reduce rivalry, I imagine. Others were Beamish, Ravensworth, Tanfield, Hollinside, and Gibside.

Apart from inter-house sport (a once-a-year competition) we did little as a House group apart from daily class registration, and twice a week House assembly. Also, the head of House taught you one class in your first year – in my case, Mr Laverick taught us Religious Knowledge. Even though he was a Biology Teacher, but it was the way he got to know us. I got to know him well over the years, as he opened many opportunities for me.

John Laverick was a keen hill walker, skier, and adventurer. He gave up weekends and holidays to give us the opportunity to experience what he enjoyed. Over the years, I hiked up most of the major peaks in The Lake District; Scafell Pike, Skiddaw, the Langdale Pikes, were among those on the list.

My parents would never have given it a second thought, but I loved it. Even in atrocious weather.

We once scaled Helvellyn in early March. The fell top was still snow-covered, and we roped together for the final ascent. I was probably about 14 or 15 years old then and went behind John to help chisel-out better footings as we scaled the last 100 – 200 metres.

On the way back down, we had the brilliant idea to get our big orange survival bags and sledge on them down towards the tarn. Four students per bag, and off we went. The speed we reached was terrifying, so we dug our heels in. Snow was splattering into my face as I sat in third spot. Then we hit a mound. Number four flew off the back. Then another bump and I hit the snow. Looking down, the other two eventually fell off or rolled over. I was grateful I came off when I did, as rocks were increasingly peering up through the snow.

We were lucky to all escape injury-free. But what fun.

Whickham School Culture

Whickham was a decent area to grow-up, and generally regarded highly. But, being a comprehensive, it did take all sorts and had a mixture of cultures.

Not cultures as in in different ethnic backgrounds; it was pretty much 100% white, Anglo-Saxon Protestant (WASP). In fact, during my time there, I only recall a couple of Indian/Asians, two Afro-Caribbeans (a brother and sister), and that was it. Maybe one Chinese? This, in a school of 1,200+ students.

The "cultures" were split between the clever or nerdy types, the sporting types, the dim and thuggish, and the plain simple thickos. Occasionally, someone straddled between groups. I was more of the clever type who wanted to be cool, and was neither.

There were some thuggish rituals which haunted me. Slaps: If you had had your hair cut, everyone would slap you round the head. Not pleasant. Coming back after holidays and half-term meant that hair-cuts were not noticeable, so mum cut my hair the day before. Mid-term was the issue.

Bumps on your birthday was horrific. You would be grabbed by each limb and launched up and down in the air, banging your back on the ground on the downward drop, with the number of bumps equalling your age. It was not just me this happened to, but it was still brutish. If anyone found out that it was my birthday, then I would go into hiding at break times.

A couple of times in the run of my school life, a "hard" lad would try and push me around. Having learned well from my earlier experiences, I was not going to let this happen.

Nicky Swinhoe tried once. A small, but thick-set, lad who was popular and sporty. Fortunately, as I hit him back, he stumbled back over a table. It looked like I did the knock-out punch, so I was elevated for a while.

Similarly, Stephen Brown tried one evening when we were skate-boarding near our house. When I hit him, he fell back over a low wall.

My reputation climbed, and I never had any more bother.

During this era, boys did metalwork and woodwork, while girls did domestic science (cooking and needlework). There was no crossover.

Once in metalwork, four of us were using the forge with our four respective bits of metal stuck into the red-hot coals. As I moved mine about, another lad's steel bar dropped out onto the floor. "Pick it up" he said, aggressively. Leather gloves were in short supply, so we had one each. Foolishly, I went to pick up the metal bar, fresh out of a red-hot forge, with my un-gloved hand. I probably had a left-handed glove on my right hand and went with the hand that I knew had some dexterity. But, wow, did it hurt as I picked up the bar.

The teacher came across, sat me down, and cold-sprayed my fingers. My head went dizzy, and I passed out.

Friends & Activities

My first senior school friend was Mark McGovern who lived nearby in Ladyhaugh Drive. His mum had dreadful arthritis and was a switchboard operator at the Danish Bacon Factory, right by dad's work. His dad worked in administration at Jackson the Tailors in Newcastle.

Mark's dad died of a heart attack when we were 12 or 13 years old. He was a smoker, but very young.

I used to call by Mark's on the way to school and, that lunchtime, a strange woman answered the door. "Mark is not coming in this afternoon," she said. No explanation and quite stern in her dealing with me.

Confused, I headed off, but looked back at the house and saw Mark's little brother in a bedroom window. It looked like he was crying.

Mark was a great artist. He could sketch an elephant, or a hand, or a building, with such ease. No matter how I tried to emulate. I would fail. We have all encountered these naturally talented people – whether it is art, singing or sport. Mark was one. We drifted apart as the years went by and I wonder whether he ever used these skills.

Mark was also the first to get into skateboarding, which

was a massive craze in the mid- to late 1970s. Dedicated skateboarding shops were opened on the high streets of Britain, while zoos closed in order to become skateboarding parks, and the media was full of "the scourge of skateboarders on pavements".

I never went to a skateboarding park. The Cedars was on a hill, so we used the path down it because it was quite smooth.

My first board was cheap. Basically, a bit of plywood on a couple of roller-skate wheels. I got a better one, but it was nothing like top of the range model that Mark had.

You could customise them with super-grip wheels. I did not customise mine and, one evening, when I was doing a slalom around beer cans down the path, my board went from under me. I banged my head badly, and a huge lump formed. Mum bought me a helmet after that fall.

Money-Making and Businesses

I have no idea why I became entrepreneurial; it was not something that was in the genes but I saw neighbours, friends, or relatives, with their higher standard of living and that must have sparked my drive.

First, I started selling conkers; I could sell them for 1p each. If they had a hole, it was 2p, or with a hole and string, 3p.

It is amazing that people would pay for things I could get for free.

Beer-mat collections also become a fad. I would collect other boys' surpluses and occasionally someone would launch one in the air for a scramble. I gathered 100 in total and sold them to Philip Riley for £1.

I also set up a stamp-collecting business. My dad had collected stamps as a boy and I had his album, all beautifully laid out. I added a few and started my own. I borrowed a Stanley Gibbons stamp valuation catalogue from the library to see if any of dad's were valuable. They were not. However, I also sent off for a free bag of 100 world stamps from a company, who enclosed with them a catalogue for buying more. I assembled these free stamps into little paper booklets and wrote a bit about them – country of origin, date etc., with a price per page, or a discounted price for the whole book. I sold these around the school to stamp collectors.

As I got older, I secured a job delivering newspapers. These jobs were precious and were never advertised but came up through the network of friends. Stephen Brown tipped me off about a morning round at George Bailey's on Oakfield Road. I went round once with the existing paperboy before he quit, and then it was mine: I earned £2.10/week. And I delivered the school staffroom newspapers during term time, bagging another 20p/ week. Easy money, as I was already going in.

All told, I had 32 papers during the week, which was regarded as quite a lot. But the round started right by the shop, then down Warwick Ave and the few short cul-de-sacs off it. When I started, the layout of the newspapers I carried in my bag was not ideal for delivery, so I managed to convince the shop-owner that

I could write out the book again, so I had a more logical route for the deliveries. I used to get to the shop about 7am – mum never needed to wake me – and was back by 7:30am, for breakfast, change, and off to school by 8am.

I hated going down Birchwood Ave. I had a delivery at the bottom and the house opposite used to let out their dog, who would lie in wait. When I came out and got on my bike to cycle up the hill, he would chase after me, barking, and snapping at my heals. I tried to kick him away, but he was too quick, and hindered me getting back up the hill. The days when he was not outside were heavenly.

For a short while, I had a paper to deliver to a small semi with a dog the size of a horse. It was a white Pyrenean Mountain Dog who would leap towards the glass-fronted door as I pushed the paper through, barking like mad. Once, he ended up pushing the paper back through the letter box onto the path (I did not retrieve it). Another day, I arrived and the glass panel was smashed and taped-up..... Soon after, the delivery was cancelled. I have not been keen on dogs ever since.

A few months into working on the round, the job of writing out the papers on a Sunday morning fell vacant, and I took it. I would bring-in the paper bundles at 6:30am and write -out the addresses for the paper boys, and help serving at the counter. We had more papers on a Sunday, and there would be evening and morning paper boys, each with a round, weighed down with all the supplements etc. I completed my round at 9am after I had finished in the shop.

I also started a window-cleaning business. One half-term holiday, mum asked if I would clean the upstairs windows. She showed me what to do downstairs, and I got the ladders out and up I went. I had to wipe all the window-ledges too. A neighbour saw me doing it, and asked how much for their house too? I replied £1. Before I knew it, I had four or five houses each Saturday, rotating each month – and the ledge-cleans went down a treat.

All this work meant that I was "loaded". I bought a small black and white TV, an SLR camera with interchangeable lenses, a record player.... and I saved plenty of money too. The trappings of wealth.

Photography

My first proper camera was a Ricoh XR1. This was a single lens reflex (SLR) which produced very good photos.

Any special occasion, I was there – from the Whickham Chase Park summer fayre when parachutists dropped into a small arena, through to school events.

I entered a local inter-school photography competition, and mounted a few shots I had taken to illustrate school-life. I was then called to the Headmaster, Max Williams' office. I had never been there before, and with some trepidation he advised me that I had won. The prizegiving was that afternoon, in Gateshead somewhere - would my parents like to go too? Well, yes, I suppose. Mum and dad both came and I was presented with a Pentax K1000; another SLR. I sold it to my dad for £100... (it retailed at £110, so he got a bargain....)

Thanks to this success, I was given one day's work experience on the photo-desk at the Newcastle Chronicle & Journal. I went out with the photographers, taking shots of Royal Marine abseilers from the Tyne bridge, through to Malcolm MacDonald; a Newcastle United star striker, who was in the area promoting some venture with pre-school kids. I learned an important lesson when I got back and they developed my film with twelve shots taken on the 36-shot film... "What happened to the other 24 photos?" You get one chance, so take lots. But, as film was an expensive a precious commodity to a teenager, it was an alien extravagance.

I enjoyed my day, never knowing that journalism would one day be my profession.

Over time, I built-up a bag of detachable lenses, tripods, and trinkets. Although I learned how to develop black-and-white photos at school in their dark room, I did not have my own set-up until I was in my mid-twenties. Taking photos that were not just the Victorian parlour shots but had an element of creativity from shooting from different angles, or with different setups appealed to me.

Over time, I did a couple of weddings for friends, although I never charged as the responsibility would have been too great. I just enjoyed the hobby.

Golf

Dad had always felt that he had been left behind for promotions because he was not a member of the golf club. As he was now managing director of a factory, and had new wealth, this became a mission in the North-East - although, to be truthful, it was more for me than himself, I am sure.

Whickham Golf Club was a good suburban club, and we

applied and were granted membership.

Dad never played without me; he never really seemed comfortable, and although we were occasionally joined by other players for a few holes, he would not venture out at any other time.

Getting a handicap never happened. He had a second-hand set of clubs, bought via an advert in The Newcastle Journal and I had some clubs donated to me by Tom Cook, dad's works manager. But it was not the equipment, as much as the petty little managers that seemed to haunt the course. We were out there having fun, and golfers are quick to come and tell you if you are not following the rules correctly…. Whose "honour" it was… Do you take the flag out when putting, or not… Lots of ways to trip up.

Even now, I love playing golf but I am not so keen on golfers.

I had a few friends who also played: Stephen Storey (now a pilot after serving in the RAF), Damon Hill, Stephen Jacques, and others. I would often cycle up to the club after school with my clubs on my back (quite hazardous at times) to get in a few holes with a chum, before racing back for dinner at 6pm. Summer holidays had us playing more during the day, but I was never that good. I played a few junior competitions, but no trophies ever came home, even with a 36 handicap. Finding golf balls, or not losing many, was as much a victory as anything else.

After a couple of years, Dad let his membership lapse; he just did not have enough time to play.

School Ski Trip

Amazingly my mum nearly went on a school ski trip in the late 1940s possibly early 1950. They were going by train to Switzerland. But for some reason it fell through. When I came home after the school meeting with the information slip about the trip they were supportive. Mum & Dad were always keen for us to have opportunities and if we could do something, we did. We arrived home from the ski trip on my 14th birthday.

I think it cost about £45 for a week in Andalo, Italy. All in. I got a new anorak for the trip but just had my regular gloves and waterproof over trousers. Ski fashion, and especially cheap and readily available ski wear, was not available in 1978. Interestingly, many years later we met the owners of Trespass (The Kushi family) while on holiday in Mauritius who made their fortune capitalising on the boom in skiing to the masses during the 1980s.

We flew Dan Air from Teesside into Venice and stayed at the Hotel Margareta. I took a photo of this crumbling hotel to the surprise of my chums. They were too embarrassed to show their parents the state of our accommodation. The food was cafeteria style, and my fussiness meant I thought it was poor. Italy had a liberal attitude to alcohol and you could drink at 13 or 14. Some of the students went out on the first night and Stephen Banks managed to throw up everywhere from beer. School then banned us from drinking. No beer for me that trip.

We had 4 per room – Andrew Griffiths, David Gibson were two room mates. We had a little lesson on a dry ski slope near Morpeth before going but it was literally one run. But I took to snow, and proudly did not fall the whole trip. After a few days John Laverick took me and a few others who were doing well to the top of the mountain into lovely crisp snow and bright sunshine. We then skied the 3 miles down the mountain – although some bare spots meant we had to side step down some sections. I was hooked.

Skiing in Bulgaria

The Dyson family were part of a group of families that had a little tug motor so they could ski in a local field when it snowed. A couple of times I was invited out – once to a field in Burnopfield and once up near Alston. They also invited me on a group holiday to Borovets in Bulgaria. We had two weeks at Easter in 1983. I shared a room with Ian and Andrew Dyson in a classic communist hotel. There was a huge basket of bread buns for breakfast when we arrived with an old lady sat guarding it. We were allowed one each. The basket depleted over the first week, and was then re-filled. No fresh buns every day. The food was basic. We had mushed and compressed pork wrapped in bread crumbs a couple of times. The second time our rep had announced we were having a special meal that night to celebrate the end of our holiday. It would be Veal. One woman in our party said she did not eat veal so wanted an alternative. Out came the plates and everyone got the same. Our woman tried to point out she was not having veal. The rep looked at it… "that is ok, yours is not veal". Or more likely none of ours was.

There was another old lady sat outside the hotel lobby toilets. Which in principle you had to pay her to use. We just went to our room. It was a great eye opener to the communist world. They had a job for everyone regardless how mundane or pointless. The waiter tapped us up the first night wanting to exchange hard currency (good old £ sterling) for Lev the local currency. He offered a much better rate than the officials. We had a day trip mid holiday into the capital Sofia where we were soon approached to exchange money. Here we were more careful and declined. The underlying fear of the state pervaded, and we had no idea who he was and whether he was a Government Agent ready to catch us out. In the hotel and resort environment we felt more secure and relaxed.

Sofia was spotlessly clean and also very quiet for a capital city. Outside on the US Embassy wall there were newspaper pages on display – giving the "truth" about the world. On display stands opposite the Embassy was the Bulgarian newspapers of the same.. It showed riots in western cities, with police aggressively arresting people. It is not all sweet smells & roses in the west. But while there were dozens of people reading the Embassy walls, none looked at the Bulgarian stands.

While the food was marginal the skiing was pretty good despite being late in the season. It even snowed mid holiday giving us some fresh powder, and as I had paid for a few lessons I got to really have a go off piste. Andrew and Ian were much better skiers than me having been going with their family for years.

We went to a neighbouring hotel a few nights as they had live music. The husband and wife duo performed in English and did a reasonable set. We ended up chatting with them and I corresponded with them for a couple of years. They had performed all over Europe and I was fascinated why they went back to the Communist regime. It was simple. All their friends and family were there and that was their home. They had to send some of their earnings from abroad home as they toured but had enough to buy a western car – a Renault and have a better life than the average. The actually drove us back to the hotel one evening. I noticed they had taken the windscreen wiper blades off. A rare commodity, easily taken, so removed as a precaution.

One evening a Bulgarian guest approached us to see if we had any branded clothes we wanted to sell. He was obviously a dealer and inspected and bartered for what we offered. I had a pair of Addidas Trainers, but they had a bit of trim missing so it was a no. Anything obviously western was a real prize.

8, Woodmans Way

When I was 16, we moved to a new house on Fellside Park on the other side of Whickham. This was a big executive house with a one-third of an acre of land.

The back garden was an old spinney – with large oak and beech trees. Set on the side of the hill looking over the valley, it had four bigger bedrooms. I had bedroom three, mum and dad had bedroom one with an ensuite bathroom. The unusual feature was that the downstairs was upstairs, so we slept downstairs. It meant that you went out on the level into the back garden at the rear from the lounge. But if you welcomed visitors to front door for the first time, you had to explain why you were taking them upstairs. We were not being weird.

We were very close to farmland and the countryside, so the woodland encouraged lots of wildlife. We saw red squirrels, woodpeckers and hedgehogs. I often helped in the garden and enjoyed it immensely but, to begin with, it was often back-breaking because there was so much to clear-up.

One summer, Richard came to visit and we were tasked with trimming and felling a couple of trees. I was high in the branches of a small oak with a bowsaw taking the tops off before the trunk was felled. Richard was on the ground with a rope attached to the branch I was cutting, so he could pull it away from me as it fell. It did not quite go to plan. As I cut through it, it swerved into me. I hung-on for dear life but in the process the bowsaw lacerated my hand. When I looked down, my middle finger was almost detached, yet the fingers either side were hardly touched. I snatched my hand in a fist and scrambled down one-handed. I opened my hand up in the kitchen and realised I was in a mess, so I grabbed some kitchen roll and squeezed it hard to stem the flow of blood.

Richard then drove me to hospital. On the way, I started to feel faint and gave him a quick set of directions in case I passed out on the way, but we made it, and I was stitched-up. The finger healed well… although the tree-felling was paused.

Remrod Engineering

When I was 15, Hawker Siddeley Group decided to close Washington Engineering, as big corporates do. They offered my dad a job in a different industry within the group in Nottinghamshire, but we were settled in the North East and were not keen to move.

As part of my dad's plans to save Washington Engineering, he had started Sundwel Ltd, manufacturing solar panels using the big presses within the factory to stamp out the copper back-sheet for the thermal reception area. This back-sheet then heated the water that circulated through tubes into a domestic water system. While Sundwel did not save Washington Engineering, it led to the start of Remrod Engineering; "Remrod" was Dormer backwards... and my idea.

Sun Harvester had been a customer of Sundwel and the owner, Ron Aylward, helped start Remrod, putting in sufficient initial capital to became a 50% shareholder.

They were very exciting times. I worked on the factory floor in the Team Valley during the holidays too, although the soldering station - where the copper pipe was affixed to the copper sheet - was my least favourite. The fumes were awful, and an open window was the only ventilation, which wasn't great health and safety.

The press for the copper sheet was ok... although I managed to slice my finger open on a sheet once, pulling it out of the press. A couple of stitches were need at Gateshead's QE Hospital.

The bit I liked most was securing the frame and glass in place at the end. I always made sure I was first to start back after breaks and last to leave my station to set an example to the other staff. I did not want them thinking I was on a cosy number as the boss's son.

There were only about a dozen staff, but I got a good all-round experience. I even learned how to do the wages and took sole charge of this whenever the accounts clerk was on holiday. There were no computers it was all done in ledgers and by hand.

The business had its challenges, mostly because Ron Aylward was a fly-by-the-seat-of-his-pants "flash" salesman. Based in Knutsford, but operating nationally, in some respects they were the archetypal door-to-door rogue traders.

Ron had a flash car, sharp suit, a couple of racehorses, a suntan, and a reckless business approach. The sales tactics led to Ron appearing on TV's Channel 4, three years later, just a few months before Sun Harvester's demise. He once said to dad that he could only pay for the latest shipment of solar panels if his horse did well in the 3.30pm at Newmarket... not a great business partner. And when cash was tight, he would not pay his Remrod bills... which created a tough position for dad, given Ron was a 50% shareholder.

While we did well, when Sun Harvester went bust it took Remrod down with it.

My mum took it hard, and felt shame and humiliation, which was unnecessary. But my dad - trooper that he was - picked himself up, went back to his roots, and started repairing transformers. He had initiated the idea some months before, knowing that Sun Harvester was a high risk to Remrod.

He had already tried to diversify at Remrod, using the shop-floor skills for other lines. They designed and made Remrod Riders, a self-assembly go-cart for kids. It was great, but the sales and marketing let it down and it didn't sell in large volumes. The go-cart used the company's aluminium welding skills, as did further attempts to make side-cars for pushbikes (like those for motorbikes, but smaller and lighter), as well as frames which could hold netting for home golf practice nets. None of these were enough, but from this base, dad started to do bits on the side in the industry he knew: transformers.

16 PLUS

'O Level' exams were our first major academic test (that is, for those who had not sat the 11 Plus exam to get into a grammar school).

I was regarded as smart so hoped to do well, but they never really taught us exam technique, revision, etc. I liked English, but only managed a C grade. There was one question, "Do you believe in ghosts?" where they were looking for a discussion-type essay response on the merits of believing, or not, in the paranormal. Instead, I wrote a story loosely based on a Marie Celeste-type event and did not really answer the question.

I passed seven exams and missed two or three. I was surprised when I got a B for Physics, and possibly the same in Geography, and disappointed only to get Ds for Chemistry and History; the latter being a real shock. But overall, I was not hugely disappointed because straight A grades were never on the cards.

I progressed to the sixth form; a whole different world. No uniform, although we were expected to dress smartly – male teachers wore shirt and ties, and so should we. Jeans were not allowed.

We had a Sixth Form Centre where we could lounge around, socialise, make coffee etc. I did a good deal of that as my A levels would eventually show two years later. But what fun.

I was studying Economics, Sociology and Geography, with General Studies as an extra. Geography was taught by a new (and very keen) teacher Mr Dolan, along with old washed-out Mr Burton. Mr Burton oversaw external exams, and he chain-smoked. He would just leave us to take notes from the textbook, he hardly set homework ("Mr Dolan is giving you plenty"), and we hardly saw him. Maybe that was why I did so badly at A level? Mr Dolan did all he could, but he only taught half the syllabus.

We had two teachers for Sociology, one of whom was a vicar whose parish at Snods Edge, about four miles from Consett, was so small, he needed another job. They were fine teachers, but with three boys and 15 girls the distraction was too much, although I spent much of the time goading them in debate, rather than trying to woo them.

My first girlfriend was Carol Britten. It did not last long, although I would say that she pursued me. It happened that one day, we all were at the Youth Club at school, and her and her friend Susan Toon started chatting to me, and between them, manipulated the conversation so that I would take her to the party for Elaine McQueen's sister's 18th birthday, being held at Reflections 2, in the Bigg Market.

I wore a hand-me-down, three-piece brown suit from Wayne Martin that Wednesday night and felt like the bee's knees. I walked up to her house to collect her and on the way up I passed some kids playing football. "Careful of the man," one said. So, I was now a man and no longer a boy. I could get into the night club, which we duly did.

I was officially grown-up.

Night clubs were the only place we could drink after 11pm, and we could get free tickets for our friends to clubs on Wednesday nights for birthdays (a quiet night in club-land).

Scamps in Waterloo St was known as easy to get into if you were an underage because ID was rarely asked for. One night, the police came by and, although no one was arrested or spoken to, the management turned the music off and said it would not re-start until all the under-age customers had gone. Basically, it emptied the place. Scamps has now been turned into flats.

The Mayfair, and Maddison's were less regularly attended, but Tiffanys (in the Old Oxford galleries) was another regular because it also had a separate dance hall which could be cordoned-off for private parties. It also helped that Brian Hobson was the general manager and lived opposite us on Woodmans Way.

Tuxedo Junction was a posh club that we only went to occasionally. It had phones on tables to call up another table with a chat-up line but the music was so loud you could not hear a thing, so it was a complete waste of time.

"Going out on the town" became a regular feature of my sixth form years. How I managed to go clubbing on a Wednesday until 1am or later and still get to school the next day and function is beyond me. Or did I properly function?

During this time, we learned the art of talking to

girls, who had been an alien species until this point. Invariably, our chat-up lines would mean we crashed and burned, but it was all part of growing up.

Driving

I was desperate to learn to drive. Mum had a little vermillion-coloured 1000cc Mini ACU 115V, which Lisa used to get to work. After A levels, she started as a trainee nurse (a degree in nursing was a rarity) and with early and late shifts, she needed a car to get to and from the Royal Victoria Infirmary in Newcastle.

Luckily, by the time I was ready to drive, Lisa had moved into a flat in town with her friend for the added freedom it gave her… and mum's car stayed at home.

Lisa took me out on my first driving lesson, and in fact I never had any "paid for" instruction. A month after I turned 17 years old, I went for my test, which was done around Gosforth and its unfamiliar streets.

As I drove round a corner, I came to a T-junction where my road was logically going straight on, but the priority road came round a corner. The examiner had to pull on the hand brake as we flew over the white lines. I knew I had failed, but we continued with the test for another five minutes with my heart as heavy as lead.

Undeterred, just over a month later, I sat my test again. The same junction appeared and again took me by surprise. But fortunately, I managed to stop this time. I passed my test, and a whole new world opened up.

How I did not kill myself (and friends in the car) in those early months I will never know. We would screech off, and fly along country roads recklessly. Amazingly, I never had an accident. I was hit behind once while turning right, which was the other driver's fault. We got a Mini Metro as a courtesy car while ours was in for repair. One night, I decided to see if we could actually take off over a country road hillock, without realising that there was a hard left turn on landing on the other side. Amazingly, we stayed on the road, but that shock calmed me down no end. I even had to stop in a layby a few hundred metres further on to regain my composure - it was terrifying.

We had a great system for going out and about though; whoever drove never bought a round of drinks and the drivers were always on soft drinks; all my friends and I were very strict about not drinking and driving. In part responsibility, but also our licences were too precious to lose.

Mum then got rid of the Mini – I'm not sure why; perhaps Lisa was given it – but our next car was a second-hand Ford Escort 1600 Sport. It was my choice, and I fitted a spoiler on the back and polished it regularly.

Public speaking competition

When I was around 15 years old, I made the conscious decision not to be the shy retiring child who didn't say boo to a goose. Up until that point, I had kept my head down, and answered questions when asked but no more.

Now, I was determined to be more pro-active and stop being the shy, quiet kid; you could not get on in the world by being a wall-flower.

This new, out-going version of me was noticed by Mr Brunton. In our O level History class, we had been given a topic to talk about for five minutes. Everyone else paired up but, as there was an odd number, I happily agreed to do a talk on "Lord Salisbury" on my own. Everyone did a boring recitation of facts about the Corn Laws, Lord Palmerston, or the Luddites. I gave one line about Lord Salisbury, then weaved useless facts and trivia (or factoids) about random things into my presentation, such as, "Lord Salisbury was completely unaware at the time that cows could smell things up to five miles away..." The class roared with laughter. They learnt nothing about Lord Salisbury, but they had a good time.

Michael and Alistair were equally radical. Alistair sat on the ledge of the open second-floor classroom window, and threatened to jump. Michael then persuaded him down with history facts, "Don't jump, because the Corn Laws have helped you..." etc etc., adding in relevant details and historical information. It was very funny and well-delivered.

When I moved up to the sixth form, Mr Brunton asked if I would enter a schools public speaking competition. I decided I would talk about, "The Importance of Buying British"; a lifelong passion of mine, supporting those industries that support our way of life. I gathered together some powerful facts and figures, while Mr Brunton suggested that I wrote key points on six-inch cards to give me a better pace.

The evening of the competition arrived, and I was scheduled to follow a couple of girls dressed in tweeds, like old women. They "performed" as much as spoke and had a great line about how nursery rhymes were corrupt and inappropriate for children, with lines such as "Wee Willie Winky" running through town "in his night gown". They were hilarious.

I then had to stand up and deliver my serious political piece.

The judges were very complimentary about my piece - noting how hard it must have been following the girls - but they still won.

I enjoyed both standing up and speaking, while also being a little edgy and causing a stir. Sixth form assemblies were timetabled once a week and included a subject to be debated. Unfortunately, because noble subjects were typically chosen (ending poverty, ending racism) they were topics everyone usually agreed with and there was never really a counter-argument, so it was a pretty dull 20 minutes.

When our group's turn came around, I decided we should have a subject that we could spice up a bit and "The Role of Women and Equality in Society" was a perfect fit. The two girls in our group did a great job presenting the case for equality and I was nearly lynched when I put the counter-argument; I even had items thrown at me.

I stated simple facts, for example, that one of the most successful European economies in the 20th Century was Switzerland and yet they had not given women the vote until 15 years previously. Also, the division of labour in society is a well-established way to achieve efficiencies, meaning those that are best at doing something, do it. Men cannot have babies, so that is what women should specialise in. It was great fun and created much laughter, as well as nods of acknowledgement from teachers for my efforts.

Limited Intelligence

Michael Milligan was learning the bass guitar and was in a band, although I never saw them perform. It was heavy metal, very loud, and the members had long hair.

He and I decided that we ought to have a school band, so we had a few practices with the drummer from his band to see if we could come up with something. Despite having no musical capabilities, I was the singer.

It never came to anything, even though we had a teacher's backing for a lunchtime concert. But we did have a good name for a school band – Limited Intelligence.

Michael Milligan

I had known Michael Milligan from when I was 11 years old and had always hated him, because he was horrible to me. He used to jibe me because of my southern accent, by saying "in bottles". I didn't know why, until he told me it was because of a TV advert for Blood Transfusion Service, where they were asking the public where blood donations were kept, and this Cockney said, "in bottles". I tried to explain to him that I wasn't a Cockney, to no avail.

When we began studying for our O Level subjects, he was put in the seat behind me in Geography. I could not stand the thought of him verbally abusing me for the next two years; he was sharp and quick-witted, and I was not. After the first couple of jibes, I turned around and asked him to stop, explaining that I did not like it - and he did. We ended up walking home together from school, and our friendship grew.

Michael's sister, Lynda, had cerebral palsy and was in a wheelchair. He was cruel with his humour towards her but would never allow anyone to say anything negative about her. He loved her and was devoted to her.

I once saw the usually jovial Michael turn very serious and become extremely passionate during a debate on terminating pregnancies of disabled children. Lynda's life was as justified as any other.

Terry Milligan

Michael's Uncle Terry was a singer and comedian, who performed mainly at Working Men's Clubs (WMC) around the North East.

I first saw him perform as part of the nightly cabaret at Whitley Bay's Spanish City. We were with Michael's dad, entering through the backdoor, before we were shown to a table – and almost immediately, we were served a roast chicken meal. It was part of the normal entry package, although we were admitted FOC. I had already had dinner but two meals in one night is not an issue when you are 16 years old.

In the months that followed, we went to many clubs to see Terry perform. Often taken by Brenda and Mike, and once or twice by my mum and dad. Some of the biggest and best shows were invariably in some of the most deprived areas. South Gosforth WMC was a pretty poor venue and evening's entertainment, but other clubs at Percy Main, Shields, and the like, booked big backing bands and really high-quality performers.

Terry was paid £100-£120 per set and sometimes appeared at two clubs in a single night, which amounted to serious money.

He lived in Darras Hall and used to cover everything from Tony Bennet through to Mick Jagger. He never finished the entire song because he would invariably add-in a joke, or bit of entertainment. He would put a bath sponge in his mouth to look like Mick Jagger, for example, and parade up and down the stage doing a funny walk. Or he would suddenly stop mid-song, apparently to check he wasn't over-running into the bingo session, before switching into a comic set about bingo callers that then morphed into a song.

He later recorded the bingo-caller song onto vinyl. Michael and I went to the recording studios in Chester-le-Street (real Hollywood glamour) and watched the process of the recording. Featuring backing singers from London and a band, the disc was cut, and featured a B-side of Terry singing Al Jolson, far from politically correct now.

It was great to be part of this experience and see how Terry gave his all each night, using the same act but always somehow making it feel fresh as if for the first time, and to be swept up in the laughter of the audience.

We were his roadies some of the time and loved it. We tended to leave him as he was briefing the support band, but I picked-up how all his seemingly impromptu stops and starts were all scheduled. There was a different band every night, so they were somewhat naturally surprised, but knew the score from the beginning.

We eventually stopped going along as we headed off into the pubs in Whickham and Newcastle, to make our own entertainment.

Hike through the Pennines

Richard would come up to visit for a week or so every summer. One year we decided to trek and camp through the Pennines. A borrowed tent from David Marshall, a borrowed rucksack from someone else and away we went. Mum and Dad dropped us off on the edge of the moors near Hexham. With an Ordnance Survey Map we headed off towards Alston.

We crossed some beautiful remote landscapes. Richard was the navigator with the compass. He was in the CCF (Combined Cadet Force) at Loughborough Grammar School so had experience of such ventures. We crossed streams, stepped over a dead lamb, and I got blisters on my heals. The first night we had hoped to camp at a Youth Hostel as we thought (from our Youth Hostel Guide book) that this YHA offered that opportunity. It did not. We thought about heading off and finding a farmers field, when the manager of the hostel offered us a deal to stay the night. With rain in the air we accepted. There was a small group that had also arrived – all independently – who were doing a trek together from Hostel to Hostel. We had great fun chatting and joking with them that evening.

The following night we arrived in Teesdale and a man let us camp in his front garden... although more like a plot of land at the front and side of his house. We cooked on our little camp stove and had a jolly old time. The following day we headed up towards Edmundbyers and the Derwent reservoir. At this point we decided we had done enough. While we may have planned to be away longer, we had tasted the adventure but fancied comforts of home. Richard and I got on very well on the trail and it was a great opener for what would become much bigger travels a couple of years later.

Sixth Form Tour of Europe.

Every other year John Laverick and 3 other teachers – Charlie Golightly, Mike Hall, and Chris Brunton organised a 5 week tour of Europe in the school mini bus (with a back up car). John's wife Sonia (who had been a pupil at the school... no scandal there) Chris's wife and 2 young girls, and the single Charlie and Mike headed off at about midnight at the start of school holidays. We arrived in Felixtowe at dawn to get the ferry across to Zeebrugge before overnighting in Belgium somewhere. There were 7 boys and 7 girls.

David Marshall, Alistair Lawrence, Peter Brophy, David McEnery, Michael Smith (the deputy head's son. A smoker even then – year below me at school – and he died of lung / throat cancer in his late 40s), Michael Taylor, Susan Hurst, Susan Toon, Helen Cook, Helen Bridgett, Carol Britten, Diane Telfor, and Gillian Dodd.

After leaving Belgium we made it all the way to Interlaken in Switzerland. It was warm and sunny and we were surrounded by snow peaked mountains. It was fantastic. We stayed a few days and wandered around town and went on a trip. It was also the first time I had slept under the stars. Lying there someone said let us see how many shooting stars we can see. I thought it was a lost cause but then we started spotting them. It was amazing how many there were shooting through the clear night sky.

Apart from the odd trip we were left much to our own devices. A new found independence for the 17 year olds. One day we bought fireworks and set them off in the evening in an adjacent field. The person that bought the most was Michael Smith, or Mint as he was known. He seemed to have little money sense and pretty much spent up most of his cash within 2 or 3 weeks on lavish things like fireworks.

After Interlaken we headed south into Italy. First stop was Lake Garda. Each move was a well oiled exercise by now. We unloaded the tents and bags off the roof of the mini-bus, positioned them in the places to pitch them up and swiftly got them erected. We were such a well organised sight we had quite an audience as we "performed". Alastair even did a little Cossack Dance to entertain the crowd. Meal times were on a rota too, with preparation, cooking and clearing up and washing split into different groups by tent. One night we did not cook for ourselves but went to the campsite pasta evening. A huge cauldron of pasta was made. This holiday was the first time I had ever had pasta. Not on the Dormer family menu at home. I had it several times and quite liked it including parmesan sprinkled on my bolognaise. Unfortunately, one night we had some "off" pork chops. Several of us fell rather ill. I zonked out and slept on a park bench during the day but was grateful to put Spaghetti on my stomach that evening.... Until it re-appeared an hour later. The vomiting was so powerful I was pulling spaghetti strings out through my noise. I pulled muscles in my stomach really badly too. Fortunately, it cleared my system out and I felt better the next day. But I could not stand the smell of parmesan or eat spaghetti for years after.

We swam in the lake and lay around in the sun for a couple of days before heading off to Venice. Camping out of the lagoon area obviously, we headed into the city for a day. We then headed down to a beach area near Rimini where again we just lounged on the beach. The most striking memory was an Italian lad who came off a motorbike and there was quite a kafuffle. They were not required to wear helmets and he must have been in a bad way – I was not tempted to go and see.

Sienna was the next stop for the Palio. With all the surrounding villagers entering a horse and rider into a bare back single circuit of the massive main square. It was heaving and we were 30 or 40 deep into the middle. An amazing atmosphere where we stood for seemingly hours before the event. Gathering up 6 empty coke cans gave me a little raised platform to stand on and watch it all better.

We had been worried about our reservation at the Sienna campsite – in those days there was no internet and confirmed email booking. But it was fine when we arrived. Mike Hall spoke a little Italian which helped and when they asked if we were orphans he apparently milked that somewhat for a discount…

Onto Florence and all the museums, with a side trip to Pisa and the leaning Tower. In those days tourists could go up the tower, so we did. We then went on to Rome. We walked miles in Rome. Doing all the main sights from the Colosseum to the Ben Hurr Race track. We tipped David Marshall into the Trevi Fountain and the police blew whistles at us. We walked down the Spanish Steps and squeezed through the Sistine Chapel in the Vatican. It was heaving, hot, and full of tourists… and you could not enter in shorts so we had jeans on making it worse. The following day some of us decided not to go into the City but stay by the pool... but those that did saw the Pope on the balcony... typical

We only occasionally went round en-masse. We often paired off... I had paired off with Helen Cook in Interlaken as it were... or more accurately 4 or 5 of us would go around and just meet back up at the minibus at a pre-arranged time.

We then headed down to Naples, or more accurately Sorrento. We did a tour of Pompeii, and up Mount Vesuvius. The guide lit a cigarette on the rocks as we neared the top to demonstrate the volcanic activity. The guide also complained about the size (or smallness) of his tip from the teachers too. On a spare day I found a barber shop and got my hair cut. I did not take the optional extra chance to go out to Capri.

We then started wending our way homeward, with a stop for a couple of days on Lake Geneva near Lausanne, with a day spent wandering around Montreux. Next stop was Brugges before the ferry back to Felixtowe and home. The last day before the ferry we had little food in the stocks so they came up with a mash and beans and mush. It was awful. Thank goodness on the boat I could use Sterling and buy sandwiches.

A levels & University application

My university choices were pretty haphazard: Salford, Glasgow, and Stirling, for a business studies degree in one form or another.

The day of my interview at Salford was cold and wet, but it still went well, and I received an offer, both there and at a couple of other places.

Unfortunately, my A level grades were not so good.

"You get out, what you put in," never rang so true. I got a D grade in Geography, E for General Studies, O for Economics, and F for Sociology. I was going nowhere.

After much anguish, I decided to re-sit Economics and Sociology, spending an extra year at school, who were very supportive and gave me a good deal of flexibility.

My second round of university applications was no more structured than the first, although I applied to a list of polytechnics as insurance.

One of my choices this time was Essex University, and I drove myself across to their open day.

I had applied for Business Studies again, although Essex called it Policy Making & Administration. I had obviously not paid much heed to the prospectus, or my application, because as soon as I entered the presentation, the lecturer announced, "This is not a Business Studies course, in case any of you thought it was". It was all about how government (local and national) made decisions etc. I came home declaring that I was interested and, by a fluke, I managed to get in.

However, the first year at Essex was a generic cross-departmental course, and I later switched to straight Government. Or Politics. Or, as I like, to tell my children, an Essex PPE.

I was hitchhiking through Europe and had reached the shores of Lac Luzerne when my results arrived at our home through the post. I had to ring home from a local call box on August 19th, which happened to be dad's birthday. I had bagged a B in Economics and a C in Sociology. Mum was jumping with joy and dad said it was the best birthday present that he could have asked for.

A few celebratory bottles were consumed that day by the lake.

HITCHING WITH RICHARD

> Travel, because traveling teaches to resist,
> not to depend,
> to accept others, not just for who they are
> but also for what they can never be.
> To know what we are capable of,
> to feel part of a family
> beyond borders,
> beyond traditions and culture.
> Traveling teaches us to be beyond.

(Extract)
- Gio Evan, poet and songwriter.
Translated from Italian

International travel was a novelty when I was young. I had been to Benidorm for a long weekend with the family, skiing in Italy with the school, and to visit my pen friend Matthias in Germany by the age of 17. And that was it. But the school tour of Europe the summer of 1981 opened up my eyes to the joy of travel. A bug that still excites me today.

I bumped into Carol Britton's older sister Valerie one day in September after I returned from the school tour. Carol and I used to go out so I knew her sister reasonably well and she asked about the trip I had just been on. She then told me how she had returned from a couple of months hitchhiking round Europe with her boyfriend. I was captivated. We ended up sitting down on the ground by the road. We chatted for so long. It sounded like a brilliant thing to do so I drained her of information.

She had travelled through France, Spain, Italy, the Alps, Germany & Belgium. She told stories of how kind and generous some drivers were through to scary times when she was bathing in a lake in Spain when she felt a snake like creature swim round her. But practical issues too. One irrelevant, but sign of the times, was that unmarried couples could not camp together in Belgium. That had hit their funds dreadfully. Keeping the size of your rucksack small so that drivers were more likely to stop – and avoiding rucksacks that had a metal frame as they were less squashable. They had taken hiking boots, but it was a waste of space. She also recommended a book that had more tips – "The Hitchhikers Guide to Europe" by Ken Welsh.

The book was broken down by country but also some useful sections

- How to hitch
- When *not* to hitch
- How to make money go further
- How to get in and out of a strange town and what to do when you're there
- Photography hints
- International Student Identity Cards

- Embassy and Student Association addresses
- Youth Hostels
- Black Markets
- Selling and pawning items

It was not long after that I pitched the idea to Richard. He was game. I knew I could trust Richard, he would be reliable and also my mum thought he would be a solid and dependable partner. Having said that, we did come under considerable pressure to go Inter Railing rather than hitch hiking. The one month ticket was £110 (About £410 in 2024 value). We planned to go for longer and estimated we could live on that much alone. In the end we went for 44 days and the total cost including the buses and odd train was about £120. My parents were pretty good though. We used to pick up hitchhikers as a family. Two or three occasions when we were doing our monthly return to Loughborough we would pick someone up at the motorway entrance. Once we had a lad who had been to see his friends at Loughborough University and was heading back to Newcastle. First lift and it went all the way home.

Some of these chaps told me tales of hitchhiking too. One was from London and had entered a competition / race to see how far you could hitch in 24 hours. They got in a car just outside London telling the driver their mission, and he decided to cancel his plans for the day and drove them to Paris. Another from Leeds was heading to visit his brother in Cheltenham. "Why don't you get here for lunchtime and we will go to the races in the afternoon?" he suggested. Worrying how long it would take him to hitch the 170 miles he was on the roadside for 0500. The first car to stop was a Porsche, and he was going to Cheltenham. The lad woke his brother up that morning.

My monthly visits to visit Grandma in Loughborough gave Richard and me plenty of time to plan. I bought a small two-man tent which was designed for mountains as it was wedge shaped to withstand strong winds and included a sewn in ground sheet. We did not think we would need such a sturdy beast but it packed small so that was key. Little did we know. Another large item was sleeping bags – and again we chose for compactness. Richard had wanted to take a mat to sleep on, but that was forgone, and having managed on the school trip on the ground I said he would too.

A couple of small gas primus stoves, a small frying pan and Richard's army mess tins with some basic utensils covered off cooking. We took a small cookbook too, although this was never used. We also took a couple of big orange survival bags from my treks into the Lake District. These proved invaluable for just sitting on outside the tent when cooking or eating etc.

Clothing was also paired down with a handful of T-shirts and underwear, a pair of shorts, swimming trunks and a sweat shirt. We took two pairs of long trousers, but it was so hot we sent one pair back with some friends we met in the South of France. Toiletries included disposable razors that I cut half the handle off to save space. I also packed a small transistor radio, but that never made the distance and was a waste of time. We had a map that covered the whole of Europe, and with that we would navigate for the next 6+ weeks. I also had a little hard back book to keep as a diary, and this forms the basis of this chapter.

The final bits were the essentials of travel insurance, traveler's cheques (as credit cards were still not a common possession for our age group), some currency – French Francs to start - passport and a couple of return bus tickets from London to Paris. One of the key tips we had was to avoid trying the over-hitched London to Paris route. A cheap overnight bus service operated, one by Magic Bus which was notoriously bad, and another by Euroways which we chose.

Thursday 1st July

Figure 5: setting off, 1982

My Dad dropped me off at Washington Birtley Services at 0830 and my journey began. I was in no rush to get to Richard in Loughborough as he was sitting his last A level that day. My mum later admitted that my dad returned an hour later to see if I was still there with the intention of running me down to Wetherby roundabout. But within 10 minutes an articulated lorry driver who was refueling called me over and offered me a lift. It was my first time in a lorry and the view was terrific although the pace of my journey south was slow. He had picked up some massive reels of paper from the port and was taking them to Felixtowe where they would be shipped out again. "Someone will be making some money on it somewhere," he said. It was a bit of an eye opener too, as he told me of his exploits and offered me one of his pornographic magazines. He stopped for breakfast after a couple of hours at an A1 roadside café and I had a coffee while he tucked into a pretty sloppily cooked breakfast. Another lesson followed as he made a very clear hint he wanted me to buy him a cup of tea in gratitude for giving me a lift. I later relayed this to Richard and we endeavored to show our appreciation to many drivers over the coming weeks but none accepted our offer.

The remaining 3 lifts to Loughborough were less notable although I did manage to squeeze into an MG Midget with my bag on one occasion. After being dropped off at the M1 junction at about 1pm I walked the 3 miles to my Grandma's in Linford Road, had a cup of tea before walking the remaining couple of miles to Richard's house on Park Road. With hindsight I should have stuck my thumb out to hitch a lift into town, but inexperience reined at this stage. Walking miles was not uncommon at our age and was going to be normal over the coming weeks.

Friday 2nd July

We decided to take a bus from Loughborough to London to catch our overnight transport. Richard's mum had left us a filling stew for lunch and we headed off. The four-hour National Express journey included the driver getting lost in Leicester. School holidays also started that day in Leicestershire and the bus was packed. Victoria Coach station was also manic and we had to wait for two hours before we could even check in for our Paris service. The French bus driver even got lost leaving London, which many would think was an omen for a third disaster. The ferry left Dover at about Midnight and started on the road in France about 2am. It was only now that we managed to snatch three or four hours sleep so were very tired when we disembarked in Place Stalingrad.

Saturday 3 July

We found a Metro Station and Richard put his French into action getting us a couple of tickets. We were trying to be careful with money so only asked to go a few stations south and we would then walk, we decided. We got a little lost when we walked, but far be it from me to say that Richard's confidence in his sense of direction was lacking. But we passed over the river Seine and decided we ought to get another Metro as it was taking ages and we wanted to be in the south of France that day. We bought another couple of tickets. Same price. We would later discover that regardless of distance all tickets were the same price. And the best price was actually buying a Carnet – or book of six tickets.

Arriving at Périphérique (Paris ring road) entrance we just saw a line of hitch hikers. We stood with our sign "A' La Sud" for a few minutes but realized it was pointless. Tired and despondent we had a quick conflab and decided to get a train out of the city. Back on the Metro we headed to Austerlitz and surveyed the departure board with our map in hand. Orleans seemed like a reasonable distance from Paris so two tickets for 84 Francs were bought and off we went. We both fell asleep on the train and were woken by the ticket inspector. He gave me a real proper prod, as if we were feigning sleep to avoid paying... or maybe we were dead to the world. Two hours later at 4pm we arrived and walked the 5 miles to the campsite.

That evening we chatted to a couple of German lads and were shocked that it took them two and a half hours to get a lift out of Paris. This reassured us that we had made the right decision.

Sunday 4th July

We slept for 10 hours solid and did not wake until nine AM. The German lads had already left and we realized that being a Sunday it would be a slow day on the roads as there would be less commercial traffic. It was only a 15-minute walk to the road we needed but it was a two hour wait until we were picked up by an older British couple. We had a sign saying Poitier / Bordeaux but the couple were going to Limoges. Their daughter was on an exchange in the city and they were going to call by as a surprise. On arrival in Limoges they stopped at a petrol station to use a pay phone to call their daughter. The father worked for Michelin Tyres manufacturing plant in Wolverhampton and, being a French company, he had had some lessons so was quite competent. The couple headed off so we got directions to the town campsite and set off walking.

Monday 5th July

Within an hour a battered old Renault 12 picked us up. It was a mum and two kids heading off on holiday but they seemed to have half the beach in the footwells already. The upholstery was torn but they were heading to Toulouse and that was a good three hours further south. They spoke no English so communication was basic but the radio worked and we pootled along listening to Dire Straits "Sultans of Swing". A tune that kept reappearing over the next few weeks and became a bit of an anthem for us.

It was now really hot. We could not be bothered to walk out to the campsite so after polishing off a few beers bought at a little shop we headed to the nearby Youth Hostel. We had joined the YHA for such moments and it gave us a good night's sleep and a bit of comradery. A Swede and a Scotsman we met made us laugh a good deal.

Tuesday 6th

With an early start we were at a motorway entrance before nine AM and another Renault 12 stopped after about 45 minutes hitching. He was heading for Barcelona but we hopped out at Perpignon. We had decided to avoid going into Spain as the Falklands War earlier that year had shown the Spanish to be clearly on the side of their Hispanic friends in the South Atlantic. We did not want to venture into a potentially unfriendly country.

We had also come here to head out to the resort of Canet Plage, and took a bus to get the last few miles. Fortunately, we got chatting to a couple who were staying at the Mar Estang complex. Some of my school friends were here on a 2 week package. Susan Faucus, Shiela MacDonald, and Susan's sister and friend had rented a static caravan for six so we had booked ourselves in for a couple of nights. But on arrival discovered it was huge. Hundreds of caravans and tents. We wandered around looking for them for an hour or so but realised that it was fruitless. We reluctantly paid the steep price of £4 to pitch our tent.

The first pitch on the sandy ground turned out to be over an ant's nest, so we rapidly decamped and moved it to a better spot. We were feeling a little dejected by now. Very hot, only three lifts, and one of those from a British couple, and no chance of finding the girls. We headed up to the bar that evening and started mulling over our plans with a beer in hand. Then all of a sudden in walks Gillian McQueen, another school friend, with her sister, Julie Patterson and some friends. I could not believe it. And yes, Susan and Sheila were there and before long we had met up. The world looked brighter.

The following day we moved into their caravan although it was not the most comfortable couple of nights sharing a small double bed with Richard. Especially as it was steaming hot. Even the gentle breeze was hot and had no cooling effect. But we had fun in the sea and lounged on the beach

Friday 9th July

We decided to get the train out of the South of France. We wanted to head north as it was too hot. The bridge of my nose had scabbed and bled from the blistering sun. So from Perpignan we got a train via Narbonne to Nimes. There we stayed in the Youth Hostel and had some great craic with an international crowd – Swiss, German and Dutch. The Dutch spoke about six languages. What amateurs were we.

It was very hot and sweaty. We wore money belts when we were travelling with just a few Francs in our wallets or in our pockets. Our other currency, travellers' cheques and passports we kept hidden away. Unfortunately, we noticed that our sweat was damaging the passports and cheques – making the ink run on my passport. The passports of this era had thick blue outer covers, but an indented section on the front had a paper sliver where the passport office hand wrote your name at the top, and the passport number was entered at the bottom. From arriving in the South of France we started to keep the money belt contents in a plastic bag.

Saturday 10th July

We hit the road and only waited 30 minutes for our first lift that took us to Avignon. What a beautiful place that looked, but we sailed on by as the driver dropped us on the road out of town as we requested. We then had a tortuous couple of hours as the heat of the day hit us and the roads dried up. The classic Mediterranean siesta meant no one was travelling. We sheltered in a petrol station forecourt and tried to get lifts from the odd driver that pulled in. But then we walked on. The dust by the side of the road became and enduring feature of these times.

We nabbed a short lift from a farming consultant and were dropped near some shops. We took the opportunity to stock up on some provisions for the weekend. It was not long before we got another lift that took us as far as Orange where we were dropped with a line of half a dozen hitch hikers. We were dubious about getting a lift any time soon when seconds later a car pulls over for us.

He was a French-Canadian Professor and a very nervous driver but fortunately spoke English. He asked about our sleeping arrangements. "We have a tent", we explained. "Two tents?" he asked, "no just one, not enough space etc. "Do you have sleeping bags?" Yes, we replied. "One sleeping bag?"... He was obviously gay and trying to work out if we were too. Even though he told us about his villa in the South of France we did not fancy a sugar daddy. His driving was the worst I had experienced. Richard had to pull the steering wheel at one point. He went down a one way street in Montelimar (the home of nougat) the wrong way. He pulled out of a junction without looking and a car nearly hit the back end of our car. He would drive along for 10 minutes in 3rd gear with the engine roaring away, before changing up to 4th.

He then asked us if we wanted to go for a swim. Leaving our bags in his car we headed into the public pool where he paid for us to enter. Richard and I were worried that this erratic fellow would just change his mind and leave without us so we watched him go in a booth to change. We did the same, but changed in seconds and leapt back out. Hours seem to pass and we fretted he had gone, when eventually he appeared. I dived in and surfaced, eyeballed our man, then Richard dived in. We swam the length and back and he got out. "Time to go now" he said. The shortest swim I had ever had, but it was a good cooling off.

We arrived in Valence, and we decided this was the end of our day. We had hoped he would offer to buy us dinner, but instead he drove about 20km out of his way to find a campsite for us. The site was very quiet and only 15f (about £1.50) with only 2 other families camped there. As we were pushing our tent pegs in one chap came over with a mallet to help us put the pegs in. He then invited us over for a whiskey. Neither he or his wife (or two children of about 8 or 9) spoke English so it was hard work but he was lovely. He eventually put his whiskey away and produced a bottle of Ricard. I am not a fan of the aniseed flavour and wished he kept the whiskey out. He was extolling the virtues of some concrete monolith that a chap had built nearby and showing his postcards of the place. So we could bleed him of more Whiskey we "oohed" and "aahhed" lots.

We had decided to spend a second night here to do laundry and chill a bit. As a result, our friendly neighbour insisted on taking us to the concrete construction with his family. Les Palais Ideal at Hauterives (Drome) was built by the local postman over a 30 year span in the late 19th Century. We had to fake taking photos as we did not see it worthy of wasting film on what was a hodge podge construction. But our M. Petel loved it and bought us a couple of souvenirs from the shop. Back at camp he continued to be generous and lovely. They gave us some butter, a couple of beers, a tin of pilchards and a fruit pie. Did we look so down at heal and desperate or were they just lovely? M. Petel was a driver, or chauffeur, in Paris, so was not a wealthy man, but extraordinarily kind. Even if the pilchards and fruit pie were not my cup of tea. We had fun playing ball with their two children and did feel part of the local community. This is what travel is about.

Monday 12 July

The village we stayed at was a quiet one to hitch out of and despite an 18km trek to Roman where we could pick up the road to Geneva we started the hike. Thumbs out in hope of a lift. We did manage to get a few short lifts including one in a battered old Volvo where we both had to sit in the back as there was no front passenger seat. Another lift was from a young French woman on her own who taught English and was heading off on her annual holiday in Chambery. I fell asleep on this leg and woke with a start when she needed to drop us off.

When hitching we had a general direction we wanted to go rather than a specific place. A lift, an interesting town or vista, all could change or influence our plans. As Richard and I had not really had the chance to discuss route strategy after drop off we stood by the road debating what to do looking at our map, with a thumb lazily stuck out. Two seconds later a 2CV pulls over.

Hubert Marin was a school teacher and heading home to the town of Aix Les Bain. As we approached Lac du Bourget the crystal blue water and beautiful mountains all around made us decide to stay here for the night and asked to be dropped off at the local campsite. He offered us a spot to pitch on the family farm if the site was full. As Richard was getting the address another couple of back packers came out of the camp site bemoaning the fact there was no space. So, we got back in Hubert's car and headed to the outskirts of the town and Chemin du Closet.

We pitched in a garden, or patch of grass to the side of

the farmhouse. An outbuilding offered a WC, or more like a C without the W. It was like a medieval hole in the ground with a stone seat. We feasted on steak that evening in celebration of having a free pitch for the night. As we were lounging by the tent Hubert came round and asked if we wanted to join him, his brother Daniel and some friends swimming from their boat in the Lake. It was a decent size rowing boat and we had great fun diving in the warm water. This would theoretically double up as our shower or bath for the day too.

Afterwards he took us all to a café and bought us massive ice cream sundaes. We offered to pay but he insisted as he was the Captain he was in charge, and we should have whatever we wanted – price no object. I asked which one he was having and it was 30F. We were stunned, that would be our budget for all food and lodging for a day. It had cream, ice cream and fruit of every description. Gorgeous but filling. We then went to a bar where he bought us a beer. We challenged them to a game of bar football and then realised that this must be their national sport. While Richard and I would randomly whack the ball, they controlled it under one of the players. Flicked a pass and stopped the ball down the table with another. Before a lightning strike shot put the ball at the back of our goal. We had to be gracious in defeat as they had treated us rather well.

The next morning we asked Hubert if we could camp a little longer and he said we could stay as long as we wanted. We had found him in the fields working with his father and some other members of the family and we offered to help but they declined. We would have probably been more hindrance than help but we really wanted to repay their kindness.

It was here that we developed the "patented butter cooler". We actually used margarine, which was spread on our bread in the morning for breakfast through to the fat in the pan for frying our meat, making omelettes or frying eggs. Margarine would not go off like butter in the heat but it did melt and many times it was pure liquid and separating in the tub. We had progressed to keeping the tub in a sealed plastic bag after it had leaked once. If it solidified after melting and separating it was pretty unusable. But we had a tap by our tent at the Marin's and it ran cold straight from the mountains. Leaving the margarine under the tap kept it firm and margarine like.

We headed towards town and managed to get lost a few times in the suburbs. Then an old chap offered to run us down in his car. We bought provisions and slowly headed back the 5 or 6km to our tent. We decided to write some postcards home and sent them off. It is strange to think that by the time our mums received the card we would be in a totally different country. They had no idea one day or even one week to the next where we were. So that evening we thought we would phone home, but the call box swallowed our 5F and never connected us.

After dinner we were heading down towards the lake again when Hubert's friend from the night before, Jean Paul pulled over and offered us a lift. He said we could take the boat out like last night if we wanted. Thrilled with the prospect we untied it and started to row into the Lake. But the wind was picking up and storm clouds brewing. We decided to turn round but rowing against the ever-increasing wind was a real challenge. Even strong as an ox Richard was straining and I started to fear we were in real bother. Thankfully we made it back but it is one of those times that I often reflect back on that could have turned out badly wrong.

We sharply headed back to camp as the clouds formed ever more menacingly and secure the tent putting our rucksacks inside the survival bags to keep them dry. Then the heavens opened. We took shelter in the tent for the night.

Wednesday 14 July

Bastille Day, and a national holiday in France. Hubert said they would have a market stall in town today and we should call by to see them. In the main square the military and other services were parading, medals were being awarded and the national anthem sung. We wandered around a bit and bought some bread and other provisions and found the market and the Marin's selling lettuces and other green vegetables. We asked to buy a lettuce and he started to put 3 in a bag, and after a bit of confusion we realised he was giving us the lettuce. It was nearly midday and other stalls were starting to pack up so the Marin's did likewise. At least we were a help by loading their van at this time. We were offered a lift back by Hubert and as we were getting in the father appears with a couple of peaches and half dozen eggs for us.

We were just lounging by the tent when Frederick came round asking if we wanted to join them for lunch. Fred was not a member of the family but they seemed to extend their community adopting random people which now included us. The family had set out a long trestle table and chairs in the shade of a large tree in the courtyard.

They brought out bowls of mostly lettuce with a dressing and some bread. Wine was liberally poured. A light salad for lunch was lovely we thought and accepted two helpings so it would tide us over to our main meal that night. They then brought out the green veg – French beans with bacon bits. With more wine. Well ok a starter and a main is fine and double helpings were welcome here too. The third course suddenly made us realise we were not pacing ourselves well as a joint of pork was brought out. But we were not done there as a pizza or local bruschetta was brought out. With more wine of course. Fortunately, we realised it was winding down as cake and jam was brought out. But we were fit to burst. A classic small cup of French coffee followed with a demi john of local liqueur. It had grass and clover floating around in it so I have no idea what the home brew was distilled from, but it kicked a punch.

We had to collapse under the tree for a while to recover. But a challenge to play boules could not be turned down. French courtyards are almost purposefully designed to play boules with that gritty dust all about. While they tried to stack the odds in their favour by given us the old rusty boules (compared to their shiny new ones) we maintained the British pride beating them over five ends.

We then all headed down towards the lake, played a bit of frisbee before heading off on a picnic up into the hills with another brother, the original gang, and some girlfriends of Hubert and JP that suddenly appeared. As darkness fell we went back down to the lake to watch a spectacular firework display across the lake which finished with an amazing explosion of colour and noise in the finale. Full of joy and merriment we managed to squeeze six of us into Hubert's little 2CV on the way back home.

Thursday 15 July

Fred woke us at 0730 and quickly packed and had breakfast and said goodbye to the various members of the extended family as they headed off to work and market. Mrs Marin called us in and gave us cake and coffee – served in a bowl rather than mugs. Hubert then took us to a good hitching spot out of town.

Lifts followed in good succession from a swimming instructor from Annecy through to a Spanish and French couple who dropped us at the Swiss border. Most drivers would not want to cross a border with hitchhikers in case they were stopped and it delayed their journey, so we very happily exited, and crossed the border on foot without a problem. We caught a bus in, and straight out of, Geneva. We had also decided that big cities were not places we particularly want to get stuck in. Walking miles to find a good hitching spot on the road out is always a bind, so the immediate use of public transport was a given.

It was not long before we picked a very comfortable lift with a couple of lads in their boss's car, followed by a hospital worker who dropped us off at the campsite in Lausanne. It was a lovely site by the lake and we decided we would stay a couple of nights. There was a Welsh school trip pitched nearby and we met a Scottish lad who was a butcher who had a cracking sense of humour. We often searched out the British on sites. It was in part to have someone else to talk to apart from each other but I think it also gave us that connection to home in far-away strange places.

The next day we were heading into town and as we were exiting the campsite the Dutch couple from the tent by us were driving out, so kindly gave us a lift. After a bit of wandering, we stocked up on provisions. Dinner that night was to be fish fingers. It could be an issue getting frozen food as it would defrost quickly in the heat. We usually carried a stash of potatoes, and a couple of tins of peas, or green beans. On non travel days some salad would be our accompaniment – or at least some lettuce and cucumber. We always had some meat (or today fish) be it steak, pork or chicken. We shopped to a tight budget and it did mean we occasionally experimented. We bought a couple of pieces of meat from a supermarket in France which we were really unsure of. The label said "dinde", and we had no dictionary so did not know what this was. It smelt a bit fishy we thought as we started cooking it. Then we suddenly thought it might be horse. The French are known for enjoying horsemeat. We gobbled it up nonetheless. But of course, it was Turkey. Knowing languages is a great advantage.

Fellow camp mates are very sharing. The night before a couple nearby shared their beers with us, and ours with them. The next day an American from Colorado borrowed our clothes washing soap. This is probably an alien concept today but, a bar of soap that was especially for rubbing on dirty clothes so you could wash them in a tub. Greg then invited us to the bar where we had a few beers and chatted until late, which made the decision for us to stay another day.

Wet drizzly days were a bit of a pain, but we decamped to the bar area and played chess – we had taken a small set with us—and battleships in the back of our diaries. Fortunately the sun then came out and we were able to swim in Lake Geneva.

Sunday 18 July

We took another bus to get closer to the other side of town, but soon after starting our walk to a good spot a mini pulled over and gave us a lift to a prime spot. The lift of all lifts then pulled over. An open top Jeep. It was a bit of a squash with our bags but flying along through the mountains by Lac Leman on a blue-sky day with the wind in your hair was top draw fun. The driver was Swiss but spoke excellent English with an American accent. It was quite surreal and he said it was because he had American friends… but was it films & music too?

Our next lift took us to Montreux – a cool dude in an Opel with the seats way back and reclined to the point I wondered how he could drive. We then stood for ages in the blistering heat on a road with a couple of other hitchers at the spot. I then saw a car approaching and saw his UK number plate. "He's English" I called out as he passed, and through the open window he must have heard so pulled over. He did not take us far but we were dropped at a good spot with no competition for lifts.

We then had a driver who had a very heavy right foot. He must have hit 100mph, and was joking about the use of seatbelts. And took his off. A scary ride, but it got us further through the mountains… until they needed to drop us off. We were in the middle of nowhere. Our map did not even show the road we were on and it was carless.

Thankfully a Ford Granada picks us up and although he did not take us far realised our "middle of nowhere" predicament. He gave us a detailed map of this part of Switzerland and dropped us at a better spot. A gent with a couple of kids on holiday then took us to the top of the mountain pass where they were off for a walk. We were now up by the snow line and saw some very strange fellow trying to ski on a pile of snow that was no more than 25m long.

While waiting for a lift, we saw a broken down 4-seat Ferrari needing a push to get started. We obliged and were rather miffed that they did not then offer us a ride. That would have topped even the open top Jeep. Instead, a couple of Germans stopped and took us down to the town of Spiez. It was 14km to Interlaken so we started to walk. I knew the town from the previous year and it had a good campsite. After a while we were tiring and thought we may just pitch in a field when a car pulled over.

The elderly couple were lovely and said they could take us to Interlaken. We mentioned how we would camp there that night and they pulled in at the station where the old man said he would find out where the camp site was. "It is ok" I insisted "I know where Camping Jungfrau is. We can walk from here". But no. He got directions and drove us the 2km or 3km."Wait here" we were then told, while he went in to check there was space. Returning with a nod we unloaded our bags and thanked them warmly for their kindness, when the old gent gets his wallet out and starts giving us some money "for dinner". No, we assured him we were fine. But no, he replied. "She insists". The look in his eyes said it all. We realised for his sake we had to accept. We went into the campsite office to check in and when we pulled out our wallet to pay the receptionist said with a smile "Your father has already paid".

Monday 19 July

We wandered around town, lounged around in parks and dipped our feet in fountains and we wrote postcards home. We met a real mix of people here, with more Americans and Canadians than at many other stages of our journey. The Canadians were always easy to spot. It must be illegal for these North Americans to leave their country without having a maple leaf on display somewhere about them. An older couple from Florida who were heading off gave us bread, orange juice and wine they did not want to carry which was a treat too.

Next to us at the campsite was a young couple from Belfast. The news of Northern Ireland was all about Catholics killing Protestants and vice versa. I was shocked to discover the couple were one of each. How did they manage that? But of course, the reality is very different and they explained that 99% of the Northern Irish were not at war and the sectarianism was in pockets and more political than religious.

Tuesday 20 July

We walked the length of Interlaken looking for a good spot to hitch out and found nothing. A good spot is where the driver has visibility of you for a few hundred meters. They can check you out as acceptable, or at least not an axe murderer, and then an area where they can safely pull over while you get in. No one wants to block the road and infuriate other drivers, and that was the issue leaving Interlaken. There was no good spot. We eventually came across the entrance drive to a small hotel which we thought would do, but after a while I noticed a couple of Brits getting into their car. I then set about persuading them to give us a lift out of this poor hitching zone—just to the next village -- which they eventually agreed. It was a bit more of an issue than I thought as there were three of them in a midsize car. We had our rucksacks on our laps as there was no other space. But a lift is a lift. Our extra weight did make it a bit of a struggle for the little car to get up some of the hills, and I did feel a trifle guilty at these times. In the end they took us 90km to Andermatt.

The views from the Susten Pass were spectacular but the route down was a memory from the previous year where we lost the brakes on the school minibus. Not a great thing to do on mountain roads, although the teachers managed to steer us safely to a halt at the time. Little did I know this part of Switzerland would nearly see my demise for a second time.

A Belgian family took us up to the top of the next pass, and promised to take us down the other side if we had not been picked up by the time they finished their walk. I was filling in my diary while Richard hitched, and all of a sudden Richard shouted, "lift" and we grabbed our bags and ran to the car. Richard later told me how he thought the guy was in a bit of a hurry, and had overtaken someone then immediately pulled over to give us a lift, but never realised what we were getting into.

It was a Toyota Celica, and the driver spoke no English so it was up to my German to communicate and sit in the front. He flew down the mountain. Fast drivers are one thing, but this chap was reckless. He overtook on the brow of a hill. He passed others on corners with no visibility round the bend. There was a 1,000ft drop down one side and our tyres screamed as they tried to stop us heading over the edge. He also started overtaking a line of trucks when an on-coming vehicle was clear to see. Horns, brakes, smoke and we squeezed in between two trucks, narrowly avoiding a head on collision. It was not long into the journey when we realised the guy was dangerous. I tried explaining in my best German how we were not in a hurry. To no avail. I then realised that trying to talk to him also distracted him and took his eyes off the road. Instead, I turned round to Richard, and without any drama, with nothing but sincerity, I declared that I thought we were going to die. Richard's opinion was no different. I shook his hand and thanked him for being a great friend.

But we did live (obviously). Arriving in Chur he asked if we wanted the road out to continue our journey, but we were mentally exhausted from the trip and asked for the campsite. We fell out of the car, delighted to be alive. We pitched our tent and I decided to have a shower to wash off the sweat of fear. Only to discover there was a meter to but in Swiss Francs if you wanted it hot. I had no money so had the coldest shower of my life. The water came straight off the glacier I am sure and while I may have been clean, I was also blue with frost bite.

That night we were so relieved to be alive we drank too much. It was not helped by the fact a Dutch chap by us shared his beer and wine, but the consequences were not good. I managed to vomit in the grass near the toilet and shower tent and away from everyone. Richard managed to trip over a load of power cables feeding caravans. Blacking them all out in the process. He escaped undetected, but there was much muttering and complaining while they all reconnected themselves. I then woke at 0600 and could not go back to sleep. Richard was snoring away so I packed the tent up around him, made breakfast of fried potatoes and bread then woke him. First class room service as it were.

Wednesday 21 July

We walked to the other end of town and the first chap who stopped was a bit of an idiot. We wanted a lift about 14km to then pickup the road towards Italy. I used my best and politest German to get him to agree to the drop off. He had made us both sit in the back and when we approached our road he started to speed up as if he was going to fly past. We were a little worried about the game he was playing, but fortunately, he dropped us off where we wanted.

It was a quieter road so for a bit of fun I said, "I am going to get the next car to stop with first class hitching technique". Around the corner came a turbo charged Renault 4 Alpine. And he stopped.

Oh yeah. Points to Dormer.

Figure 6: Hitching through Genoa, 1982

This chap drove like the wind, but unlike the day before he did not take undue risks and we felt he was in control at all times. He said he had a Mini Cooper for the winter. "French cars rust up and are rubbish in the snow". He dropped us at Davos when a woman with a little child picked us up in her big Volvo and took us to Zernez. Her English was first class as she was a ski instructor. But she also spoke Romansh, which is the native Swiss language. The scenery on this leg was outstanding and probably the most spectacular yet.

After about an hour a chap pulls over in his open top Peugeot and he was heading into Italy the way we wanted. He stopped for lunch and we hung around with the promise he would take us further afterwards. We popped into a supermarket to buy provisions and use up the last of our Swiss Francs and re-joined him on the journey into Italy. The contrast in drivers from Switzerland to Italy was stark. We saw a truck driver get agitated with congestion and cut a corner and took up a load of kerb stones. Little Fiat 126 cars were driven as if they were Ferraris. It was lift on the way to Chur multiplied a thousand times over.

Our driver was Roland Mader and he was our 33rd lift and very steady. It was a memorable lift for driving through the mountains alongside Lake Garda in an open top car if for nothing else. We had heard a story of a chap who had stood by an Italian lake like this hitching and put his thumb out to a passing speed boat – and it stopped. Roland was also heading off on holiday and he was looking for a campsite on the lake so we stopped their too. He had no food and said he would just get a coffee from the campsite bar. We insisted he shared our dinner and evenly distributed our fish fingers and slices of cucumber – each time he gave us some back – having a smaller helping for himself.

Thursday 22 July

We woke Roland with a cup of coffee, and he kindly offered to drop us off on a road for hitching. The coffee bribe obviously worked. The road at Desenzano was on the direct route to Verona where we fancied visiting. We both studied Shakespeare's Romeo & Juliet at school and liked the idea of seeing the place. But 25minutes later a car pulls over "where are you going?" we ask. "Venice", he says. "So are we". We sailed right past Verona. Fortunately, he dropped us off right outside Camping Jolly. The same campsite I stayed at with the school trip the previous year. It was pricey though at 3,000lira per person and 2,500 for the tent. 8,500 lira was about £8 and we had been spending £2 - £3 per night at most.

After doing laundry and general chores we ate and were enjoying a bottle of wine with some Americans when some Dutch girls joined our group and shared their bottle of brandy. A very convivial evening was had by all. But we were woken by lightning flashes and thunder one after the other in quick succession at about 1am. We quickly put the inner up of the tent and our rucksacks and loose equipment into the plastic survival bags. The wind was picking up dramatically and it started to rain. More lightning, more thunder.

I scrambled in while Richard tightened the guide ropes and we hunkered down as the mother of all storms swept over us. For the next hour we were bombarded by torrential rain and continuous thunder and lightning. The lightning was so frequent it was like day time. We heard screams and crashing amid the noise and mayhem of the storm. Suddenly, my legs were floating. The sewn in ground sheet was obviously very waterproof but before long we dare not move as we could see the water level splashing up the sides and it felt like we were lying on a waterbed. The tent held and the rainwater did not breach the ground sheet edges and we started to relax a little as the storm abated, and an hour or so later we fell back to sleep.

The devastation became apparent the next morning. A tree had crashed down either side of our tent missing us by less than a foot. They were not massive trees – maybe 7m or 8m tall, but enough to have wrecked the tent. An empty bottle of wine lying by our tent on its side was as full as it could be with rainwater. We wandered around the campsite and realised we were probably the only people not to have been washed out. Even caravans seemed to have fared worse than us. There were sleeping bags and tents draped over lines trying to dry. Caravans were missing panels where a tree had fallen on them and the wind torn it apart. Out Berghaus tent was amazing and our heroine was Theresa. Inside the inner there were quality control tags in the stitching with her name on it. What a job she had done. The tent's name was now well established after her.

The sun was now shining so we headed off to get the bus to Venice. Of course, the Italians made it hard to travel by bus and would not sell you a ticket on board. You had to find a tobacconist's or similar, to buy a bus ticket. This took us half an hour, but eventually we arrived and spent the day wandering around the canals, crossing the Rialto bridge and sitting in the thick of tourist-ville also known as St Mark's Square.

Saturday 24 July

With plans to head to Yugoslavia, our sleeping until 9am meant we had to pack and be away as quickly as possible to make the most of the day. A little Renault pulled over to another couple of hitchhikers and then after a conversation pulled away. I did not want a live one to get away so waved him down. He was not going to Trieste as we had planned but it was away from this spot so in we hopped and a while later arrived in Udine. We walked across town realising that we would soon be crossing over the border at Gorzia so spent the last few hundred Lira on some water melon from a barrow in the street.

The next driver spoke none of our languages, and with no front passenger seat it meant even sign language was a tough call. But the next driver had some French and drove like the wind towards the border. Until police stopped him brandishing machine guns in the process. He leapt out and produced his documents and on seeing us the police insisted we got out and they searched our rucksacks. We were soon on our way, and our driver admitted he was let off with a warning as he showed them his ID as an officer in the army.

We walked across the border into Yugoslavia and the guards checked our passports for a long time. They also wanted to see how much money we had. We first thought they wanted a bribe, but showing our Travellers cheques in our money belt assured them we had enough to live on and we were soon able to pack everything away and pass into the country.

Traffic was scarce. Obvious really, considering it was a poor communist country where consumer goods such as cars were real luxuries. All of a sudden a tiny Fiat 126 skidded to a halt and in we jumped. Just getting us and our bags in the little car. He only took us about 15km and then we waited for about an hour with little prospect of a lift. A bus came along and we decided to take it and seeing its final destination of Postojna we thought that seemed like a good enough place. The fare was pennies and we had the two front seats so could enjoy the journey. We stopped in a town on the way and thought it was our destination but the conductor gestured for us to wait. We saw him and the driver go and get a coffee and have a 5 minute break before returning and pulling round the corner. We saw the crowd waiting for the bus and realised why they needed a coffee first.

It was mayhem as hundreds of people tried to get on board. There were old ladies being pushed out of the way, soldiers squeezing on and crying in the process, businessmen, children, and people fighting for the last place. There was shouting and screaming, and no organised queuing. We felt really uncomfortable in our ringside seats, and guilty that we had these seats when so many seemed so much more desperate for a place. As the door was eventually shut it was against so many being left behind. The bus pulled away and the conductor gave us an apologetic look. It must have been the last bus that night.

The campsite was a 5km trek out of town but an Italian family in a camper van stopped when we were about half way and gave us a lift the final bit. We pitched among the trees on very gravelly ground which is not great when the only cushioning you have is a very thin sleeping bag. A bit like sleeping on a bed of nails. Very quickly night set it. It was dark when we were cooking and dinner was sat at an adjacent picnic table with a candle between us. A romantic meal a deux.

Sunday 25th July

We struck lucky on the walk back to town with a lift from a couple of Germans, and once we found a spot out of town had another older couple of Germans give us a lift. They were heading to the coastal town Rijeka so decided that would be our destination too. It was a good site near the sea and it was not long before we had cooled off in the water.

A trip to stock up on food highlighted the difference between communist Yugoslavia and the west where we had just arrived from. The shelves were not well stacked despite being a tourist location. Over the next few days we had times when all they had in the meat section was chicken, then the next day nothing but steak. Bread was fine and basic vegetables, but choice was severely lacking.

We did our usual wander around the campsite and found a group of three British families who were all RAF personnel based in Germany. They were really friendly and invited us to join them for a few beers and wine. We referenced them as the BFGs—British Forces Germany. They were a lovely bunch of people and asked us what we missed the most on our travels. Toast I declared. Not something you can make when camping and I love it. Just as we were ready to say our goodnight, they stopped us leaving. And out came a couple of rounds of toast. As they were in caravans they had the capability to make such luxuries.

The following morning we had a rude awakening when the Hungarian "tank" next to us would not start and the constant cranking and spluttering was impossible for even us to sleep through. It was a dull day but the coastline was beautiful and we had a good long walk. By the late afternoon it had brightened up and the BFGs invited us round to share their BBQ which was lovely of them and a very enjoyable evening was had.

They BFGs had a 16 year old called Neil and a few much younger kids. Neil was keen to tag along with us and we were happy to have him along. With a couple of Dad's, the next day we climbed a hill overlooking our site. The start of the route had loads of brambles and bushes and we were scratched and bloody for the first section. The swim in the sea on our return was not pleasant as the salt water bit into our cuts. The climb cleared and became rocky as we ascended opening up fantastic views down the coast line. The two hours climbing in the heat was worth it, despite the fearful drops over the edge.

We went off with Neil in the afternoon and found a great spot to dive into a sheltered pool off the rocks. Slowly but surely, we edged higher up the rocks and dived in. We were relatively low when a couple of crackerjack young English lad appeared above us on the rocks and after a few expletive-ridden comments on how good it looked, just dived in from about 10m up. No checking if the water was deep enough, no caution, just in they went. Nutters.

We again ate with the BFGs and I tried my first ever garlic bread. It was amazing and I loved it. Such exotic food was not served in the Dormer household. My father insisted to his end it was an horrendous concoction and garlic was the work of the devil, or foreigners, or probably both.

All bottles in Yugoslavia had a deposit on them – precious commodity that you recycle. Richard and I therefore made sure we picked up any we saw lying around and took them back to the shop to supplement our funds, and it proved to be a good little bit of pocket money and funded the odd beer. Particularly good this night as there was a band on at the bar that we went along to enjoy for an hour or so.

Our shorts had not been washed for nearly 4 weeks by now. The BFG mums had become our surrogate mums, so when they suggested we washed them, we felt we had no choice. Having complied they then took us out on a trip to the island of Krk where we snorkelled and swam in the sea. They treated us to lunch and had a great day. They also rented a couple of kyaks so we could go out with Neil into the sea. If nothing else I think they were pleased we were giving him some more fun than the younger children could.

Our last full day was one of the couple's 15th wedding anniversary so after we had had spent a day in the sea and having fun they invited us round for some bubbly to celebrate. They had been a great group and gave us a lovely time while we chilled and enjoyed the sun. But the following day we had decided to start heading back north.

Friday 30 July

Figure 7: using the BFG BBQ with Richard in Yugoslavia, 1982

Up bright and early and after a farewell coffee with the BFGs, caught the bus to Optija and started walking, but got a lift to the main junction where we started our hitch at about 11am. By 12.30 we were pretty despondent. The road was busy and a good hitching spot but every car was full to the gunnels with tourists, families, and luggage. We had hoped to get out of Yugoslavia that night, with a target destination of Vienna or maybe Salzburg. We doubted this would happen.

Then a German car pulled over with a couple of young chaps in. "where are you going" I asked. "Germany" they said. "So are we" Was our reply. What transpired was our longest ever single lift. A total of 731km, through three countries over 11 hours. At one point when they stopped for fuel we thought we were by Salzburg and said we would stay here and got out, but about 50yards from the car we had an epiphany. It was 7.40pm on a Friday, we had no Austrian Shillings and no food. The German lads were going right past my old pen friend Matthias Schwartz's house on their way to Stuttgart. So why did we not just go there? We ran back to the car and asked if we could continue our journey with them.

The chaps were a little alternative. They played punk rock at full volume plus, smoked high tar cigarettes, and as we cruised along the passenger had his feet stuck out of the window. They took a junction badly on one occasion and the police saw it and pulled them over for a few questions. Our passports were checked as well of course, but we were all soon allowed on our way. A while later they were zipping along and we went past a police speed trap. An officer stood there and signalled us to stop but our driver just carried on. We were aghast. We were fugitives on the run, but no one chased after.

Richard and I got to the point of bursting for a pee at one point but did not want to ask them to stop working on the principle they would need to go too as we had been in the car with them a few hours by this stage. Eventually they did pull over on a busy A road and just stood on the side of the carriageway and peed. Very Continental. So when in Rome.... They also ran very low on fuel and trying to get to cheaper petrol in Germany turned the engine off and freewheeled down long stretches of downhill motorway. It did not quite work and they eventually had to stop to buy a couple of litres when the gauge went below red.

Once hitting Germany they pulled over, re-fuelled, bought us some beer and shared some chocolate. It was the only food we had eaten since breakfast. I borrowed 1DM and called Matthias's house and desperately trying my German Matthias's younger brother Roman just told me to speak English. A relief. But more so that we were welcome to stay and could arrive at any time. It was 12.30am when we were dropped off. Our lift kindly agreed to take us the 25km up from the motorway to Herbrechtingen and once in the town I remembered where to go. It was great seeing Matthias, Roman and his sister Sabine again.

Saturday 31 July

Breakfast that next morning was the first food in 27 hours and tasted gorgeous. But not as lovely as the warm shower that we luxuriated in. We wandered around town and showed Richard the hot spots from my visit 2 years earlier. Matthias then showed us the slides from my visit with a full projector and screen bringing back lots of good memories. Matthias's parents then arrived home after their mini break away at their place in the mountains and they were delighted to see us.

That evening we went out for dinner with Matthias where we ate cuttlefish and salad which was my first time and quite enjoyed it. We then went on clubbing in Heidenheim with one of Matthias' friends in a very hot and multi floored disco. It was all very wild and crazy and we did not get home until 2am.

Although a late start on the Sunday we made the most of the day. Of course, it started with lots of hand shaking and "Guten Morgens" with his dad Rudi. The Germans love to shake hands. We then had a full day from going cycling down the river valley, calling in to see his 79 year old Grandma who still owned and ran a pub in town through to a few hours swimming at a local outdoor pool including trying somersaults off the 3m diving board.

The previous evening they had let Richard and I both phone home. That evening my mum took the opportunity of calling me back, but she managed to dial the wrong number and apparently had quite a time with another German she reached by mistake. With my mum having no German and only limited English on the number she called she must have caused them much angst until she realised it was not the Schwarz family she had phoned.

Heading back to Heidenheim with the whole family we had a fantastic Wiener Schnitzel in a castle restaurant. They really did treat us well, so the next day when the banks were open we changed £30 in Deutsch Marks and after buying a few provisions for our onward journey bought Rudi a bottle of wine and Frau S a pot plant to say thank you. That evening we had a BBQ in the garden and Rudi produced a bottle of homemade Elderberry wine my dad had made and bottled in June 1980 and had given to Matthias after he stayed with us. It was really fruity but not a bad glass of wine.

That evening we went to a local pub too, and met 3 English builders – all from the north east, well one from Southampton and two from Billingham. They told us how they could get much better paid work here than in the UK particularly as their work rate, or speed of work, was much better than the locals making them very popular. The following year there was a comedy series made for ITV called "Auf Wiedersehen, Pet" basically around this migration of builders to Germany. It launched the career of several actors such as Tim Healy, Timothy Spall, and Kevin Whatley. But we saw it in real life before it made the small screen.

Tuesday 3 August

Rudi kindly offered to run us down to Ulm as they had some shopping to do there so Matthias came too. We had a good wander around town and climbed the cathedral tower which was allegedly the tallest in the world with a spire 530 feet high, and 768 steps. Saying our goodbyes to them all we headed out to a Youth Hostel as there was no campsite nearby. On the way out we bought food and a 2 litre bottle of wine. Outside the shop the carrier bag handle with the wine in snapped. The bottle smashed and our precious wine went all over the pavement. I looked at Richard, and he at me. Without debate or discussion, we both said. "Better buy another bottle then".

We thought we could camp at the YHA but we were told no, and at 12DM a night we were rather miffed. At this point we were shown a field by the hostel and told we could pitch there. Another couple of lads followed suit and we were rather pleased with ourselves. A free night, but we got to use the showers and kitchen of the hostel. One of the lads who pitched by us was an arrogant know it all so I spent a good deal of time arguing with him on politics and economics.

Wednesday 4 August

Finding the right road out of town could sometimes be a challenge when walking. Signposts tend to be for cars so are spread at a distance, they follow one way systems, avoid the central areas or are only on the outskirts. So, we regularly asked locals with our map in hand. Ulm seemed to have a collection of complete and utter numbskulls as time after time we were sent in random or wrong directions. Eventually we found the road we needed and before I could slip my arm out of my rucksack a car was pulling over for us.

We heard Germany was a hitchhiker's paradise and it turned out that way. 120km later we climbed out. No sooner had we said our goodbyes and the little VW pulled away, when another car pulled over to give us a lift. This old gent was in a big Audi but was not going very far he said, but a lift was a lift. His English was very good, and we complimented him, asking if he had been to England. "No, I wanted to go once but you would not let me in". We were somewhat surprised. "It was 1941 and I was driving a tank" he replied. Our driver was heading back to work after lunch and soon we arrived at his destination. He was the clerk to a castle museum. He opened up and then allowed us to go around Schloss Langenstein for free and gave us a couple of postcards as we left.

We walked back to the main road and again were soon picked up by a very old Peugeot. It had been restored but just plodded along. He was heading to Freiburg but on the way we stopped at a tourist beauty spot so we had a wander around with him. He bought us a couple of Coca Colas which was kind but on arrival in Freiburg instead of dropping us at a campsite he took us into the centre of town. We then had to walk back out of town, asking directions at an English pub on the way. One thing I would have thought about a publican in an English pub would be his ability to speak English. But not here. We did not have far to go and we were not even trying to thumb a lift when a car pulls over and asks "YHA?". "No, campsite" we say. "Get in" he says, and takes us just a few hundred metres to the site. Hitchhiker's paradise for sure.

Not long after we had finished eating it started to rain. When you have a small 2 man tent it is really only good for sleeping in, so we headed off to a pub nearby, only to discover it is closed. But we decided to sit under its canopy. Soon after another camper joined us. Kees (pronounced Case like suitcase) joined us and we then collectively agreed to find another pub. A couple of beers later and the rain eased so we headed back having had a great time with our fluent English-speaking Dutchman.

We liked the site and decided to stay another day before heading off towards France. We changed a whole £5 at a bank to keep us afloat for the day and did chores, stocked up on provisions and wandered around town which was lovely. That afternoon some new arrivals on the site made the evening a riot. They were three Irish lads from Dublin who were funny and full on. Some other young campers joined our merry gathering and before we knew it bottles of Irish Whiskey were produced, Pernod, vodka and more to supplement our wine. The Irish lads were passionate IRA supporters and thought the bombing campaign was justifiable, the BBC coverage was biased, and all manner of objectionable things. But the strange thing was how charming and polite they were all about it. I could not dislike them, and we just agreed to disagree. The noise and drinking eventually resulted in us being asked to move away from the camping area by a polite old English chap. He said he could see we were having a lovely time and did not want to spoil our time but he was trying to get to sleep. We moved to the edge of the site.

Friday 6 August

The joy of hitching in Germany continued as we had multiple lifts even if only a short distance to get us to a better spot. We even had a Dunlop van—our first commercial vehicle, give us a lift. We were soon at the border crossing by Mulhouse and we walked across the Rhein into France. As we were heading out of Mulhouse centre a young chap pulls over and says he will take us to a better spot. In the process he asks if we have had lunch. Again, the generosity of drivers kicked in and he diverted to the hospital where he had a part time job, and sneaked us into the staff canteen and bought us a subsidised lunch for about £0.50 each. Now we were in France he also insisted we had a coffee afterwards, before dropping us off at the best road for Belfort. A couple of lifts later a chap picks us up with a big barking dog in the back… Quite unnerving. After dropping us off he turned the car around and went back the way we came from. Strange or kind? Who knows?

It had started to rain and we were pleased when we actually managed to get another car to stop. This chap then told us we were going in the completely wrong direction. He was going to Colmar. We were pretty convinced we had come from that direction. A signpost a few miles later proved us right and him wrong. It was a real blow as it meant we had to get out in the rain. Fortunately, a driver in the inevitable 2CV pulled over and took us all the way to the campsite in Belfort.

Saturday 7 August

The first lift was going to Chaumont, 173km away, which was quite a contrast to all the short lifts over the last few days. Our next lift wanted us to get in quickly. It was a 2CV of course and instead of putting our bags in the boot, we just sat squashed with them on our laps in the back. After about 5 minutes they suddenly pulled off the road and swung into a lane behind some trees. Richard and I looked at each other in fear. We thought we were about to be robbed it was the strangest behaviour as they both leapt out the car in this secluded spot.

It transpired that they just wanted to put our bags in the boot. They could not do this where they picked us up as we were stood outside an army camp. They were conscripts and were not meant to be leaving for the weekend, but it had been Pierre's 23rd birthday the day before and they wanted to get out and celebrate. We were then invited to Jean Pierre's parent's apartment in Montgeron, Paris for the night, as the parents were away and had space. They bought food and cooked us a special Algerian dish called Cous Cous, which took them until 10pm to finish making. One of JP's local friends had joined us but there was still enough food for a dozen more. They even passed shot glasses of Calvados around as this was meant to create more space in our bellies.

We were fat and happy, but our AWOL soldiers wanted to party on and took us into the city to a nightclub. It was hot and small but we danced the night away to a mixture of everything from the Rolling Stones to Disco. We danced until nearly 5am when we headed home. In the process our driver Francois decided to give us a mini tour of the City passing the Eiffel Tower, Place de Concorde and in the fun of the evening an attempt to fish tail around the Arc de Triomphe.

We woke at 1pm, and sorted our bits and pieces out and helped clear up the debris from our meal the night before. As the boys had to go back to camp that day we could not stay another night, and while they suggested we could pitch in nearby woods Richard delved into his book for an emergency Paris contact his mum had given him. An old school friend's daughter had married a Frenchman and lived only 10 minutes away. We tried calling but there was no answer, and we were working out a plan B when we tried again at 6.45. Fortunately they answered.

Relieved, we rendezvoused at a nearby car park and stayed at Andre, Pamela's and their two young children's home for the night. Pamela seemed delighted to have some Brits to talk to. They were somewhat surprised we were happy to just roll out our sleeping bags on the lounge floor. But this was a luxury for us. Foam backed carpet was like a mattress of goose feathers compared with the hard dusty ground with ant's nests we had experienced.

The following morning Andre took us to the RER station on his way to work and bought us a couple of tickets. Andre was quite sheepish about his job. A vivisectionist is not something everyone agrees with I suppose. He also had a battered old Renault 4. His city car he called it, compared to the pristine family car he had picked us up in the night before. Parisian drivers are known to be quite aggressive, and will merrily shunt cars to get in or out of a parking spot.

Once in the city centre we searched out the travel office to reserve our seats on our overnight bus back to London on the Tuesday night. We then headed out to Paris's campsite on the Bois de Boulogne. It was known to often be full early afternoon, hence why we did not go the day before. The Bois was also famous for all manner of low life so wanted to be in the secure campsite.

Once pitched we headed into the city to do the sights. Arc de Triomphe first followed by the Eiffel Tower. We splashed out and paid to walk up to the first observation level of the Tower. It was cheaper to walk than take the lift, but also there was no queue. Exhausted from the climb once down we went to lie on some lovely grass to chill for a bit, until a policeman started blowing his whistle and waving us off the lawn.

The evening at the camp was full of different nationalities from Dutch, Brits, American to an Australian who had been travelling for over 2 years. One of the group had a guitar and it was not long before we were all singing along as he played.

Tuesday 10 August

We had a leisurely start knowing we had our overnight bus journey coming up. Heading into Paris we decided we would treat ourselves to a Burger King on the Champs Elysees where we feasted on a large burger and frites. The Sacre Coeur gave us a great view over the city but we thought there were too many tourists so headed off to a park. On the way we passed a McDonalds so decided it was time again for a Big Mac. On the way out we started chatting with another couple of back packers and together we headed off to a nearby park with a bottle of wine.

The two girls had had a disastrous trip down the Loire Valley where they had planned to visit lots of Chateaus. But did not. Tandy explained how she was destined in life to have nothing but disasters and failures. Not to die, just suffer. She explained how she had this spiritual insight into these things. She then proceeded to read my palm and tell me my fortune. She predicted I would live until I was 75, been comfortably off, if not a millionaire, be married twice and would have 2 children. She got so much right.

Tandy and Gillian were at Glasgow University together but Tandy was from County Durham. "Whereabouts" I asked?

"Just outside Durham", she said.

"Where?" I pursued.

"You will not know it" she insisted.

"Try me".

"Beamish".

"By the museum, or by the Shepherd and Shepherdess pub?" I replied. That floored her. For all her clairvoyant skills she had not read that I was from the area too.

We later met up a few times once back home. She claimed her parents were mad, and her name Tandy came from the side of a tin of cat food. She was once given a twig stuck in a pot of soil as a birthday present and was told it was a bonsai tree, in winter. Her father was a lecturer at Durham University, and when I called round, he was having his dinner at the end of a kitchen table with tins of paint the other end as if they were in the middle of redecorating. When I asked about the decoration work, the mum and dad both looked a bit startled as if they noticed the painting stuff for the first time.

We headed off and caught our overnight bus at about 9pm. Amazingly it was the same driver that had brought us over 6 weeks before. The toilet stop at Amiens gave us the chance to spend the last few Francs on a coffee, and as we were sipping away who turns up but Tandy and Gillian. They were on another bus service but had the same stop.

The ferry left for Dover at about 1am and we arrived in London about 7.30. Richard got a bus back to Loughborough and I went out to see a girlfriend in Swindon.

Thursday 12 August

Mandy's dad was a navigator on RAF Hercules and he arrived back this morning in full flying kit after an overnight leg from Ascension Islands. But he agreed to drop me off on a road for my hitch back north. I had a series of lifts including one from a vicar that landed me in Loughborough in the early afternoon where I visited my Grandma, but went on to stay with Richard.

Friday 13th August

The homeward leg was a breeze, although a Land Rover driver misunderstood where I was going and failed to drop me off for the M18 across to the A1. But he was a decent chap and cut across from the M1 later on to drop me off on the A1.

Reflection

We had a fantastic experience, with a few scares but mostly laughter. We encountered great generosity and a friendship among fellow travellers that I will never forget. We may have passed great mountains and historical sights but the people are what we enjoyed the most and remember the most. Without doubt Richard was the best travelling companion I could have asked for. We complemented each other, supported each other, and enjoyed our time together. The BFGs asked if we argued, and said we never did. But they then pointed out how we spent half the time contradicting or correcting each other. "The second lift yesterday was a 2CV" "No it was a Renault and it dropped us off by the River" "No he took us into town"… things like that. We agreed with each other in the end and never fell out. The only time we had a disagreement was when I insisted on putting water in the frying pan after cooking to help the cleaning after. Richard said it would make no difference. Once he refused stubbornly to put water in. He was then given the job of washing up and had to put it back on the camping gas and heat water up in it to remove the congealed fats. We put water in after serving dinner from there on.

It was brave of our parents to let us go and I admire them for cutting the apron strings and setting us free. We had no mobile phones, no credit cards, and no way they could contact us. Looking at the photos of the time we looked so young. Maybe that is why so many drivers and families took us under their wing.

In total we had 60 lifts

Covered 5,730 km, 3,870km were hitched

And were away for over forty days

We spent about £140 each apart from the overnight bus and travel insurance. It worked out about £3.50 per day each for travel, accommodation food and wine. My dad said it was cheaper than having me at home and would pay for me to go next year.

So we did.

UNIVERSITY

My first day at Essex University was a Monday. Dad took the day off and, together with mum, drove me down on the Sunday.

Cousin Linda and her husband Mark had a two-bed flat in Saffron Waldron, so I stayed there, while mum and dad stayed in a small hotel in town before heading over to Colchester.

My allotted accommodation was Room 13, Flat 5, Bertrand Russell Tower, on the fifth floor. There were seven rooms either side of a central lounge area and kitchen/ diner; 14 rooms in total. There was a WC and shower on each side, with a loo in the central area. Nothing fancy, but all we needed and entirely self-catering.

After dropping my stuff off, we had a wander around and picked up some provisions from the university shop on campus.

Shortly after mum rustled up a couple of sandwiches for lunch in my room, there was a knock on the door from a chap inviting me for a cup of tea with the other residents. So mum and dad headed off, leaving me to start my life on my own.

There were three Davids on our floor: David Grant,

David Thame, and David Ward. To avoid any confusion, we decided to call the latter two Davids by their middle names – Harry and Bill.

Apart from myself, the other students were: Paul Pickup from Petersfield; Chris, who was a little older who watched black and white movies on a portable TV every afternoon; Gary, who was a keen footballer from Aylesbury; Richard, who had scars from open heart surgery on his chest; Phil, from Hackney (who had a car) but was from a single parent family and was studying laser technology, a seemingly "young" black lad from London; a Hong Kong Chinese chap called Beedee, studying computing; and a 40-something Nigerian chap doing engineering. The overseas (very studious) students must have struggled with the drinking and Tom Foolery of us younger ones and, at times, I did feel a little sorry for them.

We also had a third-year student, Andrew Herrington, who managed to bag a room on campus on the basis of a back injury. He was also captain of the cricket team, and was soon joined by his girlfriend Jo (a second year) who moved in too.

One night, we had a water fight with empty washing-up bottles and water pistols. One of the engineers pulled the light fuses so it was pitch-black in the corridors and we crept around ambushing each other, with all the ensuing mayhem. It was great fun. But probably late, certainly after the bar had closed at 11pm... Not great for those students who were rather more diligent than ourselves.

But Beedee and another Chinese student got their own back when we had a dusting of snow that winter. They woke us up on a Sunday morning at some ungodly hour (probably 8am) squealing and yelping as they experienced snow for the first time.

There were a good number of Hong Kong Chinese students. They were all doing computing or related subjects, all worked like Trojans, and never went to the bar or student parties. They tended to congregate together, eat together, and work together. They secured an amazing number of First Class Honours degrees come graduation.

Only one, Edmund Ho, was different. He ate fish fingers, mixed with us, and studied law. He lived in Flat 13 as did other friends I made; Adrian Finch and Michael McDade.

There was another Chinese lad here very briefly, in room 13, floor 13, but superstition made him move rooms. A creepy, black-haired lad from Letchworth then moved in and was unfazed. Apart from also wearing black all the time, he had extremely right-wing views and, all told, was very odd.

One very good thing about having Chinese students in our flat was that I started to appreciate Chinese food. I once bought a ready-mix packet of sauce and the Chinese student could not believe how much I paid and offered to make me one for free next time. They were a good bunch.

Beedee moved out after a few weeks to be with his friends. Not great for their mastery of the English language, but they cooked together, and studied together as a gang.

We had another Chinese male student, called Su, who

was actually from Macao. A boy named Su, just like the Johnny Cash song, we thought. But that reference fell on unknowing, Far Eastern ears, so the joke was lost. Su stayed the course with us, and did not really socialize with the Hong Kong crowd.

The Nigerian student was married with kids, although they had not joined him in the UK. He had an electrical, or electronics business, in Nigeria and had come to Essex to expand his knowledge. He never cooked but always went to the cafeteria on campus for his meals. I went myself a couple of times, but was not overly impressed by the food and could not imagine going there for every meal.

Unfortunately, in October, when the clocks went back over the weekend, no one thought to mention it to him. He only realised on the Monday when he arrived an hour early for his lectures.

During the Christmas break, there was a coup d'etat in Nigeria and he either couldn't get out of the country or felt it was better to stay at home. Our cleaners were instructed to pack up his belongings in boxes so that they could be shipped back to him.

The first term of the first year is always the toughest for students. Everyone invariably falls ill, having brought with them a mix of bugs and infections from all over the country, if not world, which we spread through lack of immunity and congregating together in small areas. We also spent hours in our rooms with our windows shut, particularly as winter approaches, so we feel miserable. We also get homesick. I suddenly did and decided one winter's day to go home for the weekend. It was the pick-me-up that I needed, and I went back to university full of vigor. As the years passed, the time periods between my trips home got longer and longer...

But some found it very hard. David Ward, who we all called Bill, had a complete breakdown. The trigger was unknown. He had spent the afternoon drinking cider in the bar as it was on special offer and reminded him of home (he was from Wiltshire). When he came back to the flat later that afternoon, he was not just drunk but obviously not right, and was muttering and rambling. We got him to lie down on his bed before trying student Samaritans line, but they said they could do nothing unless he approached them.

Later that evening, he vomited all over me. We cleaned it up and took it in turns to stay with him all night, before calling his parents the next day. They came up, but by the time he arrived he had been admitted to hospital. His mum was so upset that he was on a mental ward, "with all the loonies; he is not a looney."

David returned to the flat and his studies a few weeks later, and graduated with everyone else. It was just a blip in his life, but it was my first encounter with mental health and our complete lack of understanding of it among the general public.

The First Aid kit contained nothing that could have helped him.

University Politics

I had always thought that I was a good old Labour/left-of-centre type of chap.

Dad, and I had his influence and views embedded

in me. But on arrival at university, and expressing my opinions, I was firmly pigeon-holed into the Conservative and right-of-centre camp. I aligned with the "hard work brings rewards", "enterprise is a good thing", and "Britain is a great nation", schools of thought.

The left at Essex were further left than I had ever experienced. There was the usual Labour Party, but also the Socialist Workers Party, the Communist Party, and one group that was so far left, they were banned from campus. They did not just want regime change, they wanted an immediate violent overthrow of the Government and its institutions. I declined to join them and ended up joining the Conservatives.

As a student of politics, I became increasingly caught up in the mix and ended up before my year was out putting up posters and campaigning for our representatives to enter political student office such as Student Union President, the Conservative candidate being the future MP, Speaker of the House of Commons, John Bercow. We had to put up posters after the bar shut and as out of reach as possible as the Left just tore them down if they could reach them.

The Left appreciated and welcomed free speech and freedom for all to express their views, unless they disagreed with them.

There were a couple of occasions when a Conservative politician or Government Minister was invited to speak. They did not always get the chance, as the Left would demonstrate, or nearly riot to stop them getting to the lecture theatre. Cecil Parkinson once made it, although he was hit by a couple of eggs on the way through, and the university made the national newspapers in the process. It was fiery and exciting all-round.

The Left had sit-ins, demos and caused as much mayhem as possible. During the miners' strike, the docks at Wivenhoe were used to bring in coal. The Left joined the picket lines with miners from "the North". I am not sure the well-meaning, politically correct, nice, middle-class left students who put the miners up at the university quite knew what they were taking in. The big, burly miners were not well versed in middle-class ways and a few of the girls were rather appalled.

One occasion, we had a guest speaker from The Campaign for Peace through Security. It was the nemesis of the Campaign for Nuclear Disarmament (CND), which was massive at the time. Our guest explained how they had pennies in funding, tiny resources and virtually no membership compared to CND but made their impact by working smarter.

Once, knowing CND planned a London rally that would finish in Trafalgar Square, the CPTS decided to take action. CPTS knew this would gridlock London and dominate the headlines. The rules meant that they needed a permit from the Local Authority, and this could only be granted a maximum six months before the planned event. So, the CPTS arranged to meet an official at midnight to get the permit for themselves, even though no CPTS rally was planned. It denied CND the venue it wanted.

So, CND had to book somewhere else, opting for Hyde Park which was great for CPTS, as they could then get a good aerial shot of the crowd and employ a specialist to count the rally attendees. They could professionally refute claims of 250,000 attendees and show there were only 55,000. They also flew a light plane overhead on the day with a banner fluttering behind saying, "Congratulations from Moscow", or something like that. The news that night had a two-minute segment, more than half was dominated by the CPTS actions. Work smarter not harder.

By my third year, I had become Vice Chair. The university had started to calm down by then, and extremism was less obvious. I never stood for any Student Union office but did enjoy my time.

Societies

Fresher's Week was when new undergraduates joined loads of societies and clubs, but never went.

I joined badminton, squash, and sailing; the latter I did briefly attend. The university had a sailing pavilion in Brightlingsea. We had a collection of Laser sailing boats and a motor launch. I went out on a couple Sundays but did not bother buying a wetsuit so stopped going when winter arrived. It was also a bind to get to without a car – especially at a weekend, when buses were less frequent. And I was busy with other things. Our flat put a five-a-side football team together and we played in a league. I was making up the numbers but had fun.

By my third year I had binned all societies except the Conservatives and a new society that a couple of us put together. The Lingard Society (named after a 19th century priest and historian who allegedly liked wining and dining) was formed so we could escape the cold, wet, bleak and dismal concrete blocks of the university campus. We had hopes of inviting famous speakers to address our dining club from famous actors to acclaimed authors, but our list came to naught. We did have Capt. John Rumble, Director General of the Royal Over Seas League speak at a dinner... but only because we had the black-tie affair at his place of work: The Royal Over Seas League in St James'. We managed to get that dinner announced in The Times Appointments and Events Section, which rather impressed him. No cost, we just took a punt of writing in.

Another time, we asked an Essex history lecturer, Hugh Brogan. He was a sort of Noel Coward character in every sense. He was a great sport and we travelled to London with him on the train. We were a little early for dinner, so as we passed the Ritz, he said, "shall we have a little pre-prandial?" And in we went. Black-tie wearing guests have no trouble getting a table at the Ritz and Hugh ordered a bottle of champagne: his treat, as he had just received an advance payment on his new book "History of America," that was being published by Penguin.

John Bercow

John Bercow was a gifted orator. He could stand up in front of the baying crowds of opponents and command the room, unphased by the violence in their voices. He had a clarity of expression that I admired, and he was clearly destined for political office.

He had a part-time job working for an MP, which was easy for him to get to because we were only an hour from London.

Figure 8: With Speaker, John Bercow, and Emily Dormer in 2015

IAN DORMER CBE

I once visited him in the House of Commons, and he showed us around and we had lunch off Parliament Hall, where I found myself sitting at a table opposite Peter Shore, a Labour front bench MP. It was quite a time, and I realized that I enjoyed being around the power of the country.

John was the year ahead of me at university, so by my third year he had graduated (with a First) and moved to London, although he did pop up to see me a couple of times.

I had had a girlfriend in my first year for a few weeks, Jane Robinson, who he then went out with during my second year while I was in America. Later, when he was an MP, she had tea with him in the House of Commons. John and I were never close chums, but we had tea, drinks, and dinner on occasions over the next few decades. He even became Chancellor of Essex University.

One of my most memorable moments was in 2015, when my daughter, Emily, was a Youth Parliament Member for Newcastle-upon-Tyne and was attending the annual sitting in the House of Commons Chamber.

John was a great supporter of youth politics and chaired the event, and it was broadcast live on BBC Parliament TV.

Emily knew I was an old chum of John's and - fearing she might approach him with this point and catch him off-guard and out of context - I dropped him a line to warn him that Emily was going to be in the Chamber.

All day I watched proceedings. The day was set with three motions in the morning and three in the afternoon, where a couple of nominated speeches started each debate and then John called for contributions from the floor. He did it cleverly, inasmuch as you had to stand if you wanted to speak (as is tradition in the House), but you could only speak once, so numbers in the Chamber dropped as the day went on. He also only called on them to stand by geography – i.e. "all those from Scotland", "all those from the North" etc. – and in rotation. We watched Emily leaping up and down waving at every opportunity a northern speaker was invited.

By the last debate, we thought her chances were up. Then John called on the North again, pointing at Emily saying, "You, yes you. You have been jumping up and down all day you must be exhausted." Emily stood up, gave her name and where she was from, and spoke well and with a passion on a subject she had not even thought about: the age pay gap.

When she had finished, John said, "Ladies and Gentlemen, I did not know this was Emily Dormer. I am now going to embarrass her in front of you all. I know your Dad. We were at university together. He is a very clever bloke". The camera panned on to the embarrassed Emily. The Twitter feed announced the Speaker's statement, "I know your Dad!"

Over the next year or so Emily met John several times, including at an IoD Dinner, a school conference, and she also spoke again at the Youth Parliament, but this time from the dispatch box. He never embarrassed her again – perhaps not surprisingly, given that I had seen his hesitation the first time.

Georgetown

During my first year, a lecturer mentioned there was an opportunity to spend our second year of studies abroad, potentially at an America university. Essex campus can be pretty grey and soulless in winter, so the prospect appealed to me. I suspect one of our lecturers was equally keen to bag a trip to the US.

I took some brochures, and was particularly taken by Georgetown University, in Washington DC. The scheme would be an exchange, so I would pay Essex accommodation costs, but no tuition costs, and the year in the US would count to my Essex degree. I jumped at the chance.

All I had to do to gain entry was pass my first-year exams, which I did (although only just in one subject). In the end, three students ended up securing places at GU. As well as me, there was Greg Sweeting from Weston Super Mare and Rubina Mirza from London.

Lisa's wedding

Lisa had been seeing a man called Eric Harrison on and off for some time.

In all honesty, our parents did not consider him an

ideal candidate. He was 13 years older and previously married with a daughter from that marriage, he smoked, he was a maverick, he did not keep regular office hours because he was in the restaurant and hospitality business, plus he did not wear a suit and tie to work. I could go on.

But the 23-year old Lisa was smitten and when Eric asked her to marry him, mum and dad accepted her decision.

They were only engaged a few months, managing in that time to find a wedding venue at the Swallow Hotel in Newcastle, while The Methodist Church in Whickham agreed to marry Eric (as a divorcee) and Lisa.

The only snag was that I was heading off to Georgetown University in August. Lisa said she would pay for me to fly back for the weekend as she wanted me there, but in the end, I missed the first induction week at Georgetown but flew out the day after the wedding to be there in the time for classes when they started.

The wedding day all went to plan, although there was an unspoken fear that Eric would do something to cause mayhem. He had already thrown a few curve balls in, including inviting his motor mechanic to the reception the week before on the basis that, "We can just pull a chair up at the end." Then we discovered he had not ordered a morning suit like the rest of the wedding party. We had wanted to make sure we were renting the same outfit as Eric, only to discover he was going in full highland dress, including kilt and sporran. The day of her wedding, Lisa refused to leave home until she knew he was at the church. We had borrowed walkie talkies to confirm this to her.

Life with Eric was never going to be boring.

USA Bound

Before I left for Georgetown I had to go to a US Embassy or Consulate to collect a J1 Visa, which covered both study and authorised work - the latter being the special bit because it would allow me the chance to work on Capitol Hill.

Edinburgh was the easiest and closest consulate for me, so I had my visa issued there. I was waiting at reception when a back office official called out my name. Oh dear. What is wrong?

"Are you Ian Dormer?"
"Yes.
"Are you going to Georgetown University?"
"Yes."
"Are you staying at the International Student House?"
"Yes."

I was starting to get very concerned...

"You will have a great time," he said, "I spent four years at Georgetown. Have a safe trip".

The day after the wedding, I was up early to catch the train to London and onwards to Heathrow. Amazingly, Lisa came to wave me off, which was lovely, and off I went, suitcase in hand.

The chaos at Heathrow – or, at least, the huge numbers of people - was overwhelming. The queue for the Virgin Atlantic check-in was massive. There were delays and I was stressed.

Direct flights to DC were very expensive, so my plan was to fly to Newark and then catch a connecting flight to

DC. But, because of the ticketing system, I could not get a through-ticket.

I could have gone to Baltimore, but I then faced the problem of getting to DC.

Checking-in so late at Heathrow meant that I had a seat near the back of the 747 in the middle. Next to me were a couple of very confident American chaps who had been on holiday to London. Listening to them chatting with the flight attendant, I felt very nervous and intimidated.

On arrival at Newark, there was a long crush to get off, which, compounded by the queues at immigration meant that I was sweating more than the hot humid day required; wearing an English wool jacket did not help.

I got to the People Express budget airline terminal to find there was just one flight remaining and a queue of people on standby. So, no chance for me and I was told to come back at 0700 the next day. My name was on the list, but they didn't take payment, which made me concerned.

I had made a friend at Essex, Julie Zeidner, who lived in DC and was a student at George Washington University. She had offered to collect me from DC airport that evening, but of course that was now off, so I called to let her know and promised to ring back the next day.

I then faced the problem of where to stay that night. A board with hotels and freephone numbers underneath solved that problem. I chose a motel that looked cheap; it was. I took a taxi and paid for my room in reception through a Perspex screen.

It was a classic US motel where the doors to the

rooms opened out onto the car park. New Jersey, airport hinterland, cheap motel. Sleazy?? Sure. I slept badly that night.

I got back to the airport the following morning to find my name was on the passenger list for the first flight, and on I went. At that stage, I still had not paid for my ticket and I began to wonder if I was going to have to pay at all. The flight attendants came round selling coffee; I bought one as I had not had breakfast, and still, it seemed, that I was flying for free. But not for much longer; shortly afterwards they came round to collect payment. What a system.

By then, I had paid cash for the motel, taxis, and flight, and I suddenly realized I was getting short; I should have paid by card. The lessons you learn in life.

I took a taxi to Georgetown from the airport to the ICC. With my wool jacket and suitcase with no wheels, I was puffing a bit until a kindly fellow student offered to give me a hand; without doubt, he was a born-again Christian in the Jimmy Carter mould, and I was very grateful.

Arriving at the ICC, I went straight to the admin office to register my arrival. Lisa Gappa was delighted to see me (I was the last of her students to arrive) and she gave me a sack truck so I could (finally) wheel my case to my accommodation, which was a couple of blocks away on 35th and Prospect. She also provided me with a list of instructions about getting ID-card, a room key, and a map.

Lisa Gappa was a great support that year. She organized activities for foreign students and orientation. She encouraged Greg and I to go to lots of events and offered us dinner at her flat. We went to everything from polka dancing, to a BBQ at Rock Creek Falls, all with the international crowd.

One major event was a ball at the US Naval Academy in Annapolis, which was designed to give all the predominantly male naval officer trainees the opportunity to dance with some girls. We wore suits, but they were all in dress uniform. On arrival, a sailor would take the arm of a girl to escort her in.

It was a great event and a privilege to see the place. Greg and I were "picked up" in a platonic sense by the only two women naval students. They were charming and certainly not blind to the contrived nature of the evening.

It was good fun and educational for us, but it was dry. US law was 21 years + for alcohol, and students were invariably younger. DC had a grandfather clause so 18-year olds could still drink beer and wine, but unfortunately Annapolis was in Maryland.

Lisa's apartment was on the outskirts of DC (again, in Maryland). Greg and I had dinner with her and flatmate, Jill Derderian; I kept in touch with them for many years after my return home and when mum and dad visited, Lisa and Jill invited us all up for dinner.

Crime was a feature of DC and the surrounding area. Lisa didn't live in a bad area, but even she was robbed at gunpoint while pulling into their underground car park. She was a small woman, but she had a huge Cadillac. As she lowered her window to enter the entry code, a gun appeared along with the demand to, "give us your purse" (handbag). She did so but, in the process, she grabbed her house keys; a risk, but she got away with it.

International Student House, aka Xavier Hall

American students invariably share a room. My roommate was James Matthison, which sounds very Scottish, but (even if his grandfather had been from Scotland) James was Venezuelan. His grasp of English was limited to begin with but by the end of his stay, he was fluent.

Sharing a room for a year, requires tolerance and understanding and, thankfully, James and I got on really well.

I had paid in advance for bed linen without realising that this did not include blankets or a pillow. Fortunately, Rubina's parents were still on campus, and bought some for me.

I sorted out a bank account at Riggs bank, a phone line in our room (which was amazing) and soon settled in.

Even though it only dated back to the 18th Century, Georgetown University had an old Oxbridge feel to it, which was a great contrast to Essex. It was also very Metropolitan and, at night, you could hear the police sirens and helicopters buzzing around.

My room overlooked a back service alley but one night, looking out of another window on to Prospect, we saw limousines pulling up to a very grand townhouse opposite. As the guests dressed in black tie entered the building, they each left a big chap outside on the steps, eyeing the movements on the street. Within an hour, there were three or four of these bodyguards; who lived there? We never found out.

Just along from this townhouse was a famous staircase, leading down to the Potomac River (and Dixie Liquor where we bought the odd case of beer or two). These steps featured in the movie The Exorcist, as did a bedroom window on the same alley, from where the possessed girl "threw" the priest to his death. The windows to the stairs were actually very far apart, but the film was a talking point and scared all the newbies on campus.

The communal areas of Xavier were down in the basement. They included a small kitchen and seating areas, and even a small TV room. Cockroaches were a real menace in the kitchen. Every so often someone would fumigate it, but you still had to either keep food in the fridge or in a tightly sealed container. If you went in at night when place was in darkness and turned the lights on, you could try bashing and killing the 'roaches with a wooden spoon. There were always dozens; some a good size.

If I decided not cook, I could get a burger at Wisemiller's Deli, which was opposite the entrance on 36th. Their burgers were made to order and they asked what toppings you wanted. This is where I discovered American pronunciation.

"Lettuce, onion and tomato please?"

"Lettuce, onion and what?"

Of course, they pronounce it, "Tom-MAY-Toe", not "Tom-MAR-Toe".

It took me longer than you would imagine to work this out, but we got there.

Washington DC

The first semester I decided not to get a job and, instead, to make the most of the times when I was not studying by exploring the city.

The Smithsonian absorbed a good deal of time with its unique features, from the IMAX cinema, to the displays of Apollo rocketry. The Air & Space Museum was where I not only saw my second bit of moon rock, or tiny pebble, but actually touched it.

The Archives featured "The Declaration of Independence", and then there was the American History Museum, which housed every First Lady's dress.

I also saw the original of my favourite work of art: "A Young Girl Reading", by Jean Honore Fragonard.

And I stood in awe outside the White House to the Capitol. Great iconic places that I had seen on the news, and was now seeing in person.

When my parents visited the following Easter, I had a good idea of where we could go. Some places required a Capitol Hill sponsor to get tickets, which was usually through your own Congressman, but I could also approach members of staff who I knew.

So, we did a tour of the White House that was guided by Secret Service Agents. While we could not go into The Oval Office, it was still a great privilege to have such open access, knowing that we could not get similar tours of 10 Downing Street or Buckingham Palace.

Dad was also pleased to point out to the Secret Service

Agents that it was the British who set the White House on fire during a battle in 1814, and this led to the Americans painting it white.

A tour of the FBI building was also special, particularly as we saw the guns confiscated during the St Valentine's Day Massacre, and the gun that shot President Reagan. At the end of the tour, we also had a shooting demonstration (through a glass screen) from an agent. He took questions afterwards, and was asked about issues ranging from whether non-metallic or plastic guns posed a risk to security, through to whether he had ever shot anyone. To the last question, he promptly and succinctly said no, and then moved on.

DC has a great Metro system, although ironically, we had to walk across the Key Bridge to Arlington, Virginia, for our nearest station. I rarely took buses until my second semester, and I had worked out the system of dropping the correct money through a hole onto a plate in a glass bowl, which the driver could see. They checked the fare was right and released it into the tub below, clearing it for the next passenger, without any human contact with the cash.

Homeless people were everywhere in DC and some could appear quite intimidating at times, particularly in winter when they had big beards and 15 layers of clothes. I never had any bother, but it was a sight that was unfamiliar in the UK at the time.

Thanksgiving

Thanksgiving in the US is bigger than Christmas because theirs is truly a multifaith society.

On the last Thursday in November, the whole nation

is seemingly moving in some direction or other to see family and friends. Most students at GU headed home. Fortunately, Colleen Coyle (a girl who had been at Essex, and who I had briefly met) came by to find me ahead of the festival and asked if I would like to visit her family in New York. Yes please! Better still, she had a brother who had a share in a ski lodge in Killington, Vermont, and if I wanted to, we could travel up there the following Saturday, and spend the day skiing.

Her other brother, who was at Medical School in DC, joined us for the drive up on the day before (Wednesday). Her mother and younger sister lived in the family house in Queens. That evening, Colleen and I met up with some of her friends in a bar in Queens and they plied me with numerous Long Island Ice Teas. The following day, we helped prepare for the big turkey lunch. The ski lodge-owning brother lived in Boston and worked in sales. He, too, had invited a friend and partner from Wisconsin so, with her mother's partner plus all of us, it was quite a crowd, but great fun.

The following day, Boston brother gave the Wisconsin couple and me a tour of Manhattan. He was a great tour guide, and I saw a huge amount that day, from riding on The Staten Island Ferry for a view of The Statue of Liberty, right through to a stroll through Times Square. We even had a Chinese lunch in Chinatown, helped by the fact that the girl from Wisconsin had lived in China and spoke fluent Mandarin. As the day drew to a close, we hopped in the car and drove up to Killington, ready for skiing on Saturday.

Colleen chose not to come skiing, but the medic brother had invited up a friend called Sandy Liddy, from Boston, and I spent the day skiing with Sandy. It was a great day and only about half-way through did I start to think about whether my medical insurance covered me for this activity. Fortunately, I never tested it.

As we had slept on the floor of the ski lodge the previous night, medic-brother said we would go to Sandy's flat for the Saturday night, which would be more comfortable. Sandy was a nurse in Boston but, more interestingly, I later discovered that she was the daughter of a very famous figure - G. Gordon Liddy; the only person to be jailed for his part in the Watergate scandal that eventually toppled President Richard Nixon. I subsequently read both Liddy's and Nixon's autobiographies. G. Gordon was certainly committed to the Republican cause and loyal and faithful all the way through. He later became a successful radio talk show host.

Colleen was an amazing character. She was paying her own way through university by waitressing from 7–12 midnight-ish on Thursday, Friday, and Saturday, and working two afternoons in Ted Kennedy's office on the Hill, answering correspondence.

As a waitress, she could make $100 a night in tips. America was a tipping society, and I could see that people tipped more, the better the service they received. It was a great incentive to deliver the goods and it explained the very high level of service given pretty much everywhere.

The Kennedy job was for Colleen's CV. He came to GU to speak one day; he was controversial due to the Chappaquiddick Incident, where his passenger, Mary Jo Kopechne, drowned after the car he was driving went into a pond and he fled the scene. He was also famous as a brother to JFK and Robert Kennedy. Because both brothers had been assassinated, a bodyguard stood on stage while Ted spoke.

I asked Colleen if he had just the one bodyguard. No, she said, he has 27 bodyguards at the event, but only one was on show.

Tysons

Tysons Corner is a famous development just outside DC with a shopping mall, offices etc.

I had dinner with (the eponymous) Mrs Tyson and her daughter at her home with a born-again Christian chap whose room was a few doors along from me in Xavier. His dad knew Mrs Tyson (he was an old school-friend) and he had been invited to dinner with a friend. I said I'd be happy to join him, both for the free meal and chance to get out and about.

Mr Tyson had been a major property developer but had died a few years earlier. His wife had come from the Mid-West but, thanks to his success, now lived on Embassy Row in DC.

I took a decent bottle of wine – a Pouilly Fuisse - and I am pleased to say that Mrs Tyson was suitably impressed. She had a phenomenal apartment in what was an older building. The walls were adorned with paintings. As I was admiring them, she told me how, when her husband had worked in the Caribbean, he had taken payment in artwork (probably a tax dodge). That pretty much confirmed that we were looking at both some masterpieces and collectables on the walls.

She cooked us a lovely meal, with my lasting memory

being the French green beans being a little al dente. She did admit that she never ate in, and this was the first meal she had made in months.

AIESEC

I tried to throw myself into as many extra-curricular activities as I could, appreciating that I was only in the US for a year.

One of these was through an organization called AIESEC. (*AIESEC* (pronounced: eye-sek) was originally a French acronym for *Association internationale des étudiants en sciences économiques et commerciales* (English: International Association of Students in Economics and Business). The full name is no longer officially used, as members can now be graduate and undergraduate from any university background). The organisation helped match students with work experience placements, on an exchange basis. They were running a trip to a conference in Philadelphia, staying at a Hilton and, as it was subsidised, the cost was just $40 for a weekend away including food. I was not bothered about the exchange, but wanted to see Philly, so I signed up.

There were plenty of activities to get involved with over the weekend – tasks and challenges, as well as learning about working abroad – but I bailed out of some to see the city.

I saw The Liberty Bell and even met-up with a cousin (or niece) of Lisa Gappa.

I later utilized the services of AIESEC for Rosh Engineering as we were trying to expand into the Netherlands. I even ended up chairing the AIESEC

Newcastle chapter as an employer.

We had several Dutch students join us for between two months and 12 months over several years. They were paid a small salary, but for me as an employer, the key advantage of using AIESEC was that the local chapter picked the students up at the airport, found them accommodation and gave them orientation etc., which took a lot of pressure off us.

Halloween

Although Georgetown was a Catholic university – in as much it was founded and run by the Jesuits – I discovered that it had a strange tradition on Halloween. At midnight, all the students went to the graveyard on campus and howled like wolves.

It may also seem strange that the university had a graveyard, but this was because it was founded around the Church.

Basketball

While US college football is famous, Georgetown did not have a team of note in this decidedly blue-collar sport. Instead, it had a top-drawer basketball team.

The head coach was allegedly paid $1 million a year. The top players (all African American) - Patrick Ewing being one – were all on scholarships that gave them the best education to boot.

The university had a somewhat unusual policy which was that if the players did not average a C in their studies, then they would have to withdraw from playing until their grades improved.

On graduating, they went off to sign contracts for the

biggest teams and earned massive salaries. They were superstars.

I remember seeing Patrick Ewing sitting on the steps of Copley with a chum one day, just chilling. Some girls ahead of me became very giggly and said "hello" as they passed. He politely smiled and said "hello" back. The girls went off in a dither, while Patrick's chum made fun of him, saying, "Ooohh, Patrick Ewing just said hello to me". For all his stardom, he seemed like a really decent fellow.

Just before Christmas, we had the chance to watch them play. They did not play on campus, but in a big stadium outside the city which could seat around 40,000 spectators and games were televised. This was no regular student sport on a Saturday afternoon, and it was amazing to think that I had walked past these giants on campus the previous week as they were going into class, just like me.

I flew back home on World Airways that Christmas. It started in LA, and stopped off in Dallas, Baltimore, London, and then Frankfurt. Fortunately, I only flew from Baltimore to London, but as I boarded and tried to put my bag up into the overhead locker, there was a cowboy hat. I wanted to move it to get my bag in, but the Texan owner, who was sitting next to me, took umbridge. My bag had to be placed under the seat in front of me for the entire overnight flight. Not pleasant, and not a very pleasant Texan.

<u>Prof Bill MacDonald</u>

Bill was a criminologist but taught me statistical analysis.

He was very friendly and amiable and invited a handful of us up to his home in Virginia to watch the Super Bowl with his family. He and wife Irene came to pick us up and we had a great meal and watched a little football, but generally we had an all-American experience. Outside, there was a freezing cold blizzard so it was great to be tucked-up in a warm and friendly environment.

I kept in touch with them for years and his only daughter, Lisa, came to visit Newcastle a couple of times while she was doing a master's degree in London before she headed-off to work on Wall Street.

On visits to DC, we always went to see Bill and Irene, and when I visited GU some years later, I dined with him in the professor's dining room.

The US Election & Inauguration

The 1984 election year saw Ronald Reagan re-elected as president. Studying politics in DC at this time was great as we felt very much in the mix.

Professor Lengle managed to get us invited into the audience of a live TV show that was analysing the candidate debate. Our classmates dressed in chinos and blazers and ties. Greg and I were a bit scaggy in shirts and jeans. The US students also complained when they were asked to take off any badges or pins that showed their political allegiance, which they had by the dozen pinned all over their lapels. Not at all the style of a Brit.

We were told that on the discussion table there were two of the top collegiate debaters from the Ivy League. When we had the chance to ask questions, the audience approached them as if they were surrogates for the

Presidential candidates, and they had to be reminded they were there to discuss the substance of the debate. Debates like this were alien to us because no British Prime Minister at that time would have put themselves up like that. It all went on until 1am... rather late for me.

A friend who had a part-time job on the Hill managed to get me tickets to watch the inauguration from the Mall.

It was sectioned-off into different areas and I was scheduled to be some way back from the Capitol building where the ceremony was taking place. But the weather had been rather cold and snowy and on Inauguration Day, the temperature dropped to -4°F (-20°C), the coldest on record. Sadly, the event was cancelled, and my chance to see a unique bit of history was crushed. But it was so cold that the Potomac River froze over; you could drop a brick 56 metres from the Key Bridge and it just bounced on the ice.

The ceremony eventually took place a few days later, in an indoor sports stadium with just a small group of spectators.

I was doing a course at GU which required us to write-up a project from our work experience in the Capital. One girl had worked at the White House, or more accurately, the Old Executive Building (OEB) next to the White House. Her job was not as glamourous as it might have seemed; she had to reply to letters to the President. She had standard replies which she cut and pasted, and they were not very varied. Often the letters they received asked, "would the President open our fete, school, new offices?" etc. These were all a "no".

A "yes" would only arise through a connection such as a Senator, or major donor, and typically came through different channels. But she did manage to get us an invitation to a press briefing on the conflicts and issues in South America. Pumped-up that the President might be there, we headed off and found ourselves in a rather boring, technical briefing in the OEB. But still, it was an experience.

Meanwhile, I had managed to secure a placement/internship at a political consultancy, Global USA near Du Pont Circle. They were looking for someone to do 12 hours a week – unpaid but covering expenses. In fact, the expenses were very good; more than the cost of my bus fare and lunch.

Based in a converted house, my immediate boss was Joanna – a real Tennessee Southerner, as was her boss. The most senior directors were Bill Conklin and Bill Timmons (although he was never at the office). Bill T was famous as a friend and supporter of President Richard Nixon.

One day, as a treat Joanna managed to arrange for us to have lunch in the Senate Dining Room on Capitol Hill. No senator was with us, and I am not sure how they managed to swing this exclusive opportunity, but it was a special occasion.

As part of my work at the consultancy, I was asked to do some research on the deregulated airline industry in the US. This was for one of their clients, All Nippon Cargo. I found a great book in the university library and my first report bullet-pointed the key issues. It was so well received that Mr Conklin asked for a meeting. I developed the report over the following weeks, and it eventually formed the basis of my final-year dissertation at Essex, which was looking at the political obstacles to deregulation of the airline industry, drawing on my experiences in the USA.

It is hard to imagine now but, in the 1980s, governments would decide which airline could fly where and when. It was pretty much a cartel for nationally owned flag-carriers, which made flying expensive and exclusive. One or two routes were slowly opening (London to New York), but the rest were not.

Deregulation crept in over the next decade, giving opportunities for the likes of Easyjet and Ryanair to fly all over Europe, at rock-bottom prices. While some may wonder how, or why, you can fly from Doncaster to Poznan in Poland for £30 return (as I did in 2018; less than the cost of parking my car), it was not even a pipedream back in the 1980s.

Kevin Montgomery

I attended a political philosophy class with Father Schall one evening. It was primarily for post-graduate students, but it gave me some core teaching which I needed.

One PhD student in the class sounded English… but not really. I approached him after and discovered he was from Texas but had been raised in India and Sri Lanka because his father worked for the State Department. He had been surrounded by English teachers and students, and he had picked up the accent.

Kevin Montgomery was charming; we ended up socialising a fair amount, and we have kept in touch ever since.

He came to my 21st birthday brunch and impressed my parents because he was the only one wearing a tie.

Our paths crossed professionally over the years too. While working as a journalist at Flight International Magazine, I was due to fly over to the States to do an interview at the aviation company Evergreen (more later). Pretty much the week before I flew, I had a letter from Kevin saying he had just got a job working for a company called Evergreen in Oregon, but he would still be based in DC. He spent weeks at a time travelling the world, negotiating everything from traffic rights for their cargo operations, through to agreeing lease deals on the aircraft they owned, which ranged from 747s to 737s.

We had dinner in London once; he had been away from home for about a month, yet he looked immaculate. Hair trimmed, nails manicured, shirts crisp and pressed.

We also arranged to meet for dinner at the Paris Air Show, one year. I was in some two-star hotel, while Kevin was staying in the George V. I headed over to meet him at reception, only to find that he was most embarrassed because one of their non-executive directors, a chap called Bob Hoover, and his wife had also invited themselves along. Not a problem, I said, and we had a lovely dinner with them both. We chatted about everything from theatre to music; ironically, aviation was never really covered.

The next day, as all the Flight journalists assembled at our base at the air show for breakfast, I was asked what I had done the night before, and mentioned how I had been out with Kevin, Bob Hoover, and his wife. All their jaws dropped. Bob Hoover? One of the greatest aviators of all time? The man who should have been the first to fly faster than the speed of sound, except that he had buzzed the control-tower the day before and had been grounded. I was not a truly aviation person...

Kevin is the most charming and disarming person that I have ever met. He was generous without being showy. He had more tales to entertain and amaze than anyone else I have known, and yet you always felt like you were the centre of attention.

Many years later he came to visit us in Newcastle, and I asked if his dad was Ambassador to Sri Lanka or had another role. Kevin then admitted that, because his dad had been retired many years, he could tell me. He had been Operations Director for the CIA for the Indian subcontinent.

Kevin's providence, his role with Evergreen, and his later role with Polar Air Cargo travelling the world led us to ask him whether he was also CIA. A bit like James Bond and Universal Exports. "If I am, I would deny it, as I could not tell you. If I am not, and denied it, you would not believe me," he said. One day I will know.

Kevin had lots of wonderful stories, from how he was mistaken for Prince Edward – which got him a table at a very posh restaurant, where they called him Your Highness, through to meeting famous people.

His travels meant that he met President Gorbachev while in Russia, and on another trip to the Far East a very famous US actor. He had been at a drinks reception and was chatting with this fellow who seemed familiar. He asked if they had met before? Was it at the GE reception, the week before? Or at the Avionics Conference, the previous month? "No," says the fellow. "My name is James Coburn, and I am an actor."

Another time, he was staying at the Okura Hotel in Tokyo and saw a confused westerner in the lobby, so offered his help. The chap asked where they served breakfast. The Okura is a big labyrinthian hotel, so Kevin showed him the way. That evening he bumped into the fellow again, who asked Kevin how his day had been, and what he did for a living. Kevin asked him the same question. "I am a musician," the chap said. Kevin then waxed lyrical about what a tough business it was and hoped he was doing alright etc. On parting, he asked his name. "Sting," he replied. Kevin was not one for popular culture, so only realised who he was the following day when he read an article about Sting's Save the Rainforest campaign.

But, for me, the best anecdote was when he came to Newcastle. Lisa and Glenn had also come round for dinner, and we were chatting about travel etc.

I had read Nelson Mandela's autobiography after a trip to South Africa and was about to ask if Kevin had, when he volunteered what a lovely chap he was.

"Have you met Nelson Mandela?" we asked.

"Only a couple of times," he replied.

"When?"

"Once, when I sat next to him at a White House dinner."

That sentence alone summed Kevin up: a White House

dinner and Mandela.

So, Lisa then asked him who had been the most inspiring person he had ever met, caveating it with the expectation that it could have been a teacher, or an uncle? Without hesitation, Kevin said that was easy: Mother Teresa of Calcutta. We all howled. A living Saint, no less.

His family had worked with her when they lived in India.

Elizabeth Feeley

Late one evening, a girl knocked on Milton's door, which was just along the corridor from mine.

He was not in, and she was dropping something off. I said she could leave it with me, which she agreed to, and wrote him a note. We got chatting and I then offered to walk her home, as it was dark. She lived with her sister Kate, a few blocks away in a basement flat on N Street.

Elizabeth and I fell for each other and spent a great deal of time together over the next six months.

When mum and dad visited DC that Easter, her family invited us all to their home in Tenafly, New Jersey, just a stone's throw into Manhattan. Her dad worked for the telecoms company AT&T, and her mum was in admin at the Julliard School of Music & Theatre. She also had a brother, John, who was a helicopter pilot in the US Marines.

Through Elizabeth, I met Lindsay Lloyd.

Lindsay Lloyd III

Lindsay seemed like a very quiet and considered chap, but he had great intellect and, in particular, considerable political knowledge. But the most wonderful thing about him, was his generosity in spirit and kind. He would come round to N Street and have a bag of goodies to share: food, drink, cigarettes.

A show was taking place at the university in an old auditorium called The Cherry Tree Massacre, after the famous story of George Washington's childhood. The show was an acapella/barbershop singing competition, featuring singers from a number of universities including Yale and Harvard. It was sold out, but somehow Lindsay got us tickets. It was a fantastic evening and another unique experience.

Although I did not know Lindsay that well, when I was coming to the end of my year at GU and was planning my travels on the West Coast, he insisted that I visit him and his family in San Diego. They were wonderfully hospitable, and he took me on a trip into the Mojave Desert – wow, that was like an oven, and so hot it was painful to breathe – and on a trip into Mexico. San Diego is just a short drive from the Mexican border, but he chose to leave his car States-side and we walked across the border before getting a taxi into Tijuana.

We wandered around for a bit, and I picked up some souvenirs. I bought Lisa's Eric a packet of cigarettes, which proudly stated on the pack that they were horse-shit cigarettes, not donkey-shit or mule-shit. I think they were Marlboro, or similar, but it was funny.

We had dinner in a restaurant whose inside had been made to look like we were outside, with roofs of neighbouring buildings, laundry drying on a balcony, and a star-spangled night sky. I also foolishly drank the water that was poured; which unfortunately meant

I then discovered that you could have pretty bad gut rot from just water.

We then headed back to the border, and I realised a rather catastrophic error. When we had walked across from the US to Mexico, no one batted an eyelid. But immigration was a good deal tighter on our return, and I had not brought my passport. Lindsay flashed his driving licence and did the talking. I kept my mouth shut, because my accent would have given away the fact that I was obviously a foreigner. Fortunately, being white Anglo-Saxons, we were waved through, but it was a nervy few minutes, as well as my first experience crossing a border without the correct paperwork. The next, some 10 years later, was a bit more of a trial.

Lindsay was a great correspondent. Not everyone I met kept in touch – bearing in mind that you had to write letters and post them at this time – so it was more of an effort. He even came to visit me in the UK the following year, so that I could reciprocate the hospitality.

He worked variously on Capitol Hill for many years, for Congressman Duncan Hunter, on non-partisan Committees, and even on Jack Kemp's Presidential Nomination bid.

We saw Lindsay a good deal more when he moved to Bratislava after the Velvet Revolution. He worked for the International Republican Institute, advising Slovak (and neighbouring countries') parties on how to campaign and organise themselves. I knew he spoke Spanish, and had learned Slovak, as well as some Hungarian and Polish while in Slovakia. But he really threw me when we went to visit him one summer. Bratislava is close to Austria, so we popped up to

Vienna for the day. Having found a restaurant for lunch, I suggested that I handle the conversation as I had studied German at school and he had not. But as I struggled to find my words, Lindsay popped in with a couple of fluent sentences and sorted us out. "I didn't think you had learned German?" I asked. "I just picked up some bits during my trips up here," was his overly modest reply.

Bratislava had a seriously communist mindset. We heard Lindsay do a talk to some Christian Volunteer workers one morning, briefing them of the politics before they headed off into the country. He received quite a backlash from them when he advised that they would discover many people in Slovakia did not regard communism as necessarily a bad thing; American democracy was "the one true way", to these well-meaning visitors. But Lindsay was right; under communism there was no crime (unless you were against the state, of course) and everyone had a job. The elderly found the new ways very tough.

However, under communism, the disabled were hidden away and the quality of food was poor. It was still not good when Lindsay first arrived and, to begin with, he would fly to Newcastle every couple of months to visit us and, "get his hair cut," we used to joke. But it was pretty grim.

Lindsay was there to show them the ways of western democracies, such as knocking on someone's door to ask them to vote for you. This was quite a culture shift given that for previous generations, if someone had had an unexpected knock on the door, it was the State Police about to take them off to the Gulag. He had a very big and, at times, I am sure a challenging job, but I don't think there could be anyone better for the task.

After a few years, he went back to DC and worked in IRI's office, staying there until the Democratic leaning and Capitol politics wore him down, so he departed for Texas to work at the George W. Bush Foreign Policy Think Tank. It is funny to think I know someone who had had a one-on-one dinner with a former President and his wife. Lindsay had also met president Richard Nixon some years before, and had his photo with him.

Mitch Cohen

Through Milton, I also met Mitch Cohen. Again, he was very kind and offered me a bed if I ever visited San Francisco.

His family were terrific and lived up by Twin Peaks, which was only a short hop on the Muni tram system to San Francisco Downtown.

Mitch was a first-class tour guide and I fell in love with the city. Alcatraz was just an abandoned prison in those days, accessible via boat - not the visitor experience it is today. Meanwhile, his sister took us to Muir Woods, and on our return we had Chinese food in the largest Chinese community outside of Asia.

I went to see them again on my way back from my travels to southern California and Arizona, and even helped them move house.

I was able to reciprocate their hospitality when Mitch came to the UK, and I showed him around and entertained him. We kept in touch and visited each other often, on both sides of the Atlantic.

Mitch became a lawyer and his wife, Sue, worked in banking. When Emily and Mark were young, we went over on Halloween, and they had the true American "Trick or Treat" experience with the Cohen kids.

Ian Corey

I also stayed with another Xavier Hall resident while I was in San Diego – Ian Corey.

Ian's mother was French; she had met his father when he was in the US army and stationed in Europe. His elderly French grandfather was also staying with them at the time, and Ian and I took him sea fishing in the Pacific. We caught barracuda as big as golf bags. They were scary but too small to keep, so had to be put back. We then had lunch at the Hotel Coronado, which was famous as the location for the Marylin Munro, Tony Curtis, and Jack Lemon film, *Some Like it Hot*.

Out West

My travels out West continued with a flight to Phoenix, Arizona, where I hired a small car and drove up to Flagstaff. It was phenomenally hot; so much so that I burnt my hand on my seat belt buckle which had been in the sun.

I stayed overnight in a motel and then drove up to the Grand Canyon for the day, driving through spectacular scenery that gave me picture-book memories; the cacti, the rugged rock formations. This was the joy of travel. However, I found The Grand Canyon underwhelming. Maybe it had been so built-up as a great wonder of the world that it just disappointed? Or maybe it was just too big to grasp the vastness?

I had seen posters for a rodeo in Flagstaff that night, so

headed back and put that experience into the mix too.

There were lots of people in cowboy hats, as well as plenty of hooping and hollering. The big bull riding was the last event and not something I would ever want to try.

I had been chatting with a family next to me at the arena and, as I parked my car at the motel, they pulled up next to me. They had followed me back and wanted to invite me out to dinner. I had already had a pizza, but what the heck, out I went with them for a steak dinner. They had a young son, so after dinner, we dropped off mum and child, while the dad and I went out for some beers, stopping at a country and western bar with all the relevant toe tapping and gingham.

Summer in NJ & NY

Arriving back on the East Coast, I stayed with Liz for several weeks. We spent time with her grandparents in their cabin in upstate New York and took in the sights and sounds of this beautiful part of the country – including a cattle auction one evening, with a fast-talking auctioneer, who was impossible to decipher.

We also spent time with her cousins on Long Island where they lived. I learned to waterski during this trip, which was great fun, but a good deal harder than I thought it would be.

On July 4, we went down to watch the fireworks in Manhattan from the New Jersey-side, which was a magnificent sight. The Feeleys were Catholic, and did a good deal of charitable work. I helped sort some clothes and donations out once. I was amazed at some of the new clothes, including several pairs of jeans in different sizes. They had come from Tatum O'Neil - or a similar actress of the time. Her mum was also active in the church and the actress was regularly sent free clothes, which she just donated. We also went to a convent in New York one evening as Mother Teresa was visiting, but her schedule meant we did not get to meet her.

Our relationship then started to slide. No particular reason, but it was decided that I would head home. TWA had recently had an aircraft hijacked so I bought a standby ticket, thinking this was the cheapest, and most likely to be available at short notice. It was full, but I got a seat at the back by a US marine heading to Berlin for Embassy protection duties. His first time abroad and he had partied all night before, so he slept all the way to London.

I had not told my parents that I was coming back, I just showed up at home. Partly as there was no time to send a letter, partly as I wanted to surprise them. I was glad to be home, but sad that things had come to an end with Liz; I had been pretty smitten.

She messed with my head a bit that following year.

Unbeknown to me, she had won a place at the Webber Douglas Academy of Dramatic Art in London, and one day she suddenly turned up at my flat at Essex University. She then left, and when I subsequently went to London to try and catch-up with her, I realized she was living with one of her brother's friends, who was a merchant banker. It was not platonic.

Final Year

I felt invigorated going back to Essex after a fun-filled year in America.

I had convinced the university that I needed campus accommodation, because as I had been across the Atlantic in my second year I had not able to sort alternatives.

Tawney Tower 10, and a corner room, was my home for my final year. We even had an American in the flat – Efthimious Kalavrouziotis (or Tim) – on exchange from Fordham. Stephen Benzikie was also there, and he headed-up the Liberal Democrats on campus. After graduating, Stephen started training as an accountant, but then worked in a city brokerage before becoming the City reporter for the Daily Mail.

We also had Zafar, a computer studies student who was our age but dreadfully stiff. I'm sure he thought we were all a bit wild and reckless. So, we had to take the opportunity to wind him up a bit. One day, we quietly taped sheets of paper across his door frame leaving a space between the inward opening of the door that we filled will shredded paper and the like. It was the sort of thing we would do to anyone. When he opened the door, it would all fall in and he would have to tear his way out. We did it late at night and I suspect he did not emerge until the following morning when we were asleep. We never heard what happened because he never mentioned it, so really it was not much in the way of fun.

Another time, when we were heading off to London for a Lingard Club dinner in black tie, someone convinced him that we were flying to Paris for dinner that evening. He believed us. We cemented the deception when we saw a copy of Paris Match on sale at a news agents on Trafalgar Square, so we bought it and left it lying around the next morning for him to see. Some years later, Zafar phoned me up after seeing me featured in an Essex alumni publication and we had a good old chat. He was a computer consultant working from home and he seemed to have fond memories of our time in the flat together, so we did no lasting damage.

In the first year, I had to do some core subjects – politics, philosophy, economics, and sociology, but by the third year, students had a pretty free rein. I had binned the 'policy-making and administration' option during my second year, so was now doing a degree in government. Or politics, as some would say; or PPE, as others would try and suggest… like Oxford.

I had a European element, international relations, American politics… you get the drift.

I also had to write a dissertation. As I mentioned earlier, because of my American experience, my dissertation was on the deregulation of the airline market in Europe, drawing on the experience of the United States. My supervisor, John Owens, was newly appointed, so we learned the process together. Greg Sweeting's dad worked for Dutch Aircraft manufacturer Fokker, and he very kindly sent me a whole parcel of documents; too many, in some respects.

I managed to convince the department that I could use their computer to write it up. PCs were a rare and precious commodity, but having returned from the US, I persuaded them that I was now used to using such things. They even gave me a key to the office, so that I could work on it, on the PC, over the weekend.

I also tried to get some corresponding work experience

in Westminster. My work at the political consultants in DC led to them connecting me with Sir Peter Emery MP. He had done some work with them, but seemingly had not been paid by the client. The connection was made in part so that I could let Sir Peter know that Global USA had tried to get him recompense. Sir Peter was not interested in having me; he only had post-grad students. Instead, he passed me on to Lord Bethell who was a staunch campaigner for "Freedom of The Skies". The elderly gent was a well-respected historical writer, and a deregulation champion.

I met His Lordship at his very smart home in London; the sort of townhouse that you would expect a Lord to live in.

We sat in his drawing room with his PA, but the conclusion was not really what I hoped. He was pushing me to get answers from government bodies which I thought he would find it easier than me to do. We corresponded a couple of times, but it all came to very little in the end.

I'm sure that underneath all this ambition, I was simply hoping for a pass to the Palace of Westminster so that I could swan around with 'the great and the good'.

But my dissertation did win me a fan with one of the markers of my work – Tony Barker. Tony coined the phrase 'Quango', after the concept of non-government bodies was highlighted by the Carnegie Institute.

Tony thought I had a journalistic style and connected me with Vic Smart, an aviation journalist at The Observer newspaper. I met Vic for a drink in London, and he then passed me onto a specialist airline publication, Airline Business, which was edited by Kevin Page. In turn, Kevin passed me on to David Mason, editor of sister publication Flight International. But that is another chapter.

I also applied for several other jobs. I really fancied British Airways, but got nowhere. I also applied to several firms of accountants for their training schemes. This was in part peer pressure, as I knew of a few doing it and they reflected a very professional and successful image. Mum also liked the thought of this respectable job.

I did get one offer (and several rejections) from a small(ish) firm in central London. I accepted the offer when I got it, only to bin it when I received the offer from Flight. The prospect of more studying and exams was a 'no', and probably a wise call at the time.

I also had an offer to sell advertising space for a magazine group. Everyone seemed to smoke, which put me off somewhat, and the reality of it was that these were high turnover jobs which I could get in the future, if needed. But I wanted to be in London because that was where all the action would be. With three job offers, times were booming for young graduates in 1986.

I was very pleased to graduate with a 2:1. There had been some discussion apparently about the grade transfer from GU, but all was good in the end. I was told my grade by a lecturer who was having a pint in the Student Union bar. No posting out (although that was probably done), no pinning up on a board, no great announcements.

The Union bar was not my regular hangout; I preferred

the Top Bar, which was run by the university, not by students and was a bit classier. Beer in the Top Bar was £0.52 a pint, compared to £0.51 a pint in the Union bar, so you paid a premium too. They also put a sandwich bar in there, which I frequented for dinner if I was in a hurry, or late getting essays done for departmental deadlines.

Looking back the workload was not heavy, although near the end of the course I did end up with a handful of essays to do and just three days to do them. Ridiculous really, but I started lunchtime on Friday and worked through the night. I slept for a couple of hours on Saturday night and about four hours on Sunday, and I got them all in on time. Every day they were late meant deducted marks. Incredibly, the one I did last, when I was most tired and most rushed, got the best grade.

I was no academic star, I but did what was needed and scored a couple of Firsts in my on-going assessments. Around 40% of the degree mark came from continued assessment.

One First was for 'Competition Theory in Economics', where I quoted Schumpeter; I have lived on this for years. I had been given the theory and example by my A Level economics teacher who went to Oxford; it also impressed Essex.

Another First was for a 'Critique of Conservatism'. I did the same on Marxism which I thought was a better essay all round and was given a poor 2:2.... No one criticised Marx at Essex.

Elizabeth Hughes

Chris DePhillips was one of my flatmates. He was an

American on a similar exchange to the one I had done the year before.

He is still the only person I have ever met who was born on the same day as me; March 30, 1964.

We used to banter a lot so, one day, as I was sitting at my desk actually doing some work, I saw Chris heading back at his room and, of course, shouted some abuse. At which point, a girl popped her head round the corner. She had been playing squash with Chris and had come back for a coffee.

Chris introduced us, because Elizabeth was from Sunderland; she was in her second year reading English and knew Chris from the Catholic Chaplaincy. We chatted more over coffee and agreed to meet for a drink during the Christmas break. From that point, we became an item.

Rev Michael Butler

As so many of my friends were Roman Catholic, it was perhaps inevitable that I would end up knowing the university Catholic chaplain, Michael Butler.

He was a very open-minded and inclusive fellow with a small parish in Brightlingsea which gave him time to officiate at the university. I even had dinner at his home with a couple of the chaps.

I kept in touch with him after graduation, and he came to stay in the North East (with a young trainee Polish priest) some years later. Needless to say, when Elizabeth and I got married in a Catholic service, I had no issue with Michael officiating. So many of our guests said he had delivered a wonderful service, even though the majority of them were not Catholic. He explained everything he was doing and made it very personal; little things like why the bride takes her veil away before the vows, "so the groom knows he is getting the right wife," through to the symbolism of the wedding ring, "it is like love, there is no beginning or end to a ring."

LEATHERHEAD & WALLINGTON

Starting work didn't change the fact that I still had to live in shared accommodation. I moved into a large suburban house with a garden and four residents, owned by Sarah Allan. Sarah had worked hard to get as much compensation as possible for the noise from the M25 motorway which was a couple of hundred yards away. She had a bric-a-brac store in Kingston, which (on its own) would not have generated enough income to cover the house and living expenses.

Other fellow residents included: Angus Grey, who worked for the Surrey Professional Golf Association, so worked very little in winter but 14- to 16-hour days in summer; Andrew Long, an IT chap who had been doing a PhD but just started with a firm nearby; Helen, a new pharmacist at Boots in Leatherhead.

There were changes in people during my time, including Shani who ended up marrying Andrew some years later. We had a good time and got on well, although every other weekend I went to Essex to be with Elizabeth, and she came down the alternate weekend.

After about a year, I got a car; a burgundy Ford Escort. It was actually a Rosh Engineering company car, as a treat from dad. It was second-hand, but it gave me a great deal more flexibility for getting out and about, seeing the area, and going up to Colchester etc. Parking in the streets around Flight's office was always a challenge, but there were no "residents only" permits. My journey took me past the Derby racecourse in Epsom, and there were many occasions when I was held-up by some beautiful steeds heading out to train. However, Derby day completely gridlocked all the roads, meaning that my normal 20-minute journey took more than two hours.

Leatherhead had the Sybil Thorndike Theatre and we went to a few productions there. The most memorable was the one-woman Willy Russell play, Shirley Valentine, and I saw it with ITV's Man About the House actress Paula Wilcox. She was spellbinding, and it was the closest I have ever been to giving a standing ovation in a UK theatre.

At the Harry Secombe Theatre in Sutton, we saw modern fast and funny productions such as Bouncers. We also took the opportunity to go to West End productions, from ballet through to regular theatre, to see some great stars on stage. One highlight was seeing Rex Harrison and Edward Fox in The Admirable Crichton.

During that first year, my grandmother died in a nursing home in Derby. She had moved there because it was run by the Railway Pension Fund – Derby being a big railway town – and she was increasingly suffering with dementia.

I visited her a couple of times, and her passing was a

blessing in the end. Mum gave about £5,000 each to Lisa and me from her estate, which I doubt amounted to more than £30k in total. This gave me enough money to think about buying a flat of my own.

Property prices at this time were going through the roof – particularly in London and the South East. I wanted to be closer to the office and found a flat in Wallington, just over two miles away: 46 Willow Court, off the Woodcote Road. I paid £30k for a one bedroom, one bathroom, first-floor flat, with a small balcony, overlooking a very busy road. I was probably earning about £10k pa, so it was top of my borrowing limit.

On the day of completion, I had planned to go to work in the morning after which Richard was going to meet me in a van, so that we could head north and collect various bits of furniture which mum and dad had put together for me, from a bed to a sofa.

Richard had a job interview with Technical Blinds first thing which he passed, leading to life-long career in the industry as a blind and lighting control expert.

I could not understand why I had had such a bad night's sleep the night before the move. Was it the excitement? No. A storm, or hurricane, had swept across the South of England, completely paralysing this part of the country. October 16, 1987 may have been the day that I bought my first home, but it became famous because of BBC weatherman, Michael Fish's dismissal of how bad the storm would be.

A massive tree had blown over and lay across the end of our drive in Leatherhead, completely blocking my exit. The trunk must have been more than three feet in diameter. I climbed over and found a couple of chaps walking down the street with chainsaws; I gave them £20 to cut us out. I eventually got to work, and Richard arrived with the van.

Amazingly, the flat purchase also went through so we headed north, battered by strong winds in our Luton Van.

Richard came over to the flat on several occasions, to help me build some bookshelves. He had the tools and the wherewithal, and I supplied the food and drink. The latter was a bit of an issue at times; the wonkier shelves in the flat were assembled after we had downed a couple of bottles of red.

Now that I was all established as a homeowner, I decided to propose to Elizabeth. We went up to London one sunny Sunday and, while sat on a bench in St James Park, I popped the question. She said yes.

Unfortunately, her father had never been keen on Elizabeth having a relationship, let alone getting married. I have no idea why he was so against his eldest daughter getting hitched, but he was, and this never changed throughout our time together. He was an intelligent man; an English lecturer, and even Head of Department at Sunderland University, but he did not come to the wedding.

We were married by Rev Michael Butler on September 17, 1988, at St James the Less Church in Colchester. My mum and dad paid for it all, including the reception at the Mill Hotel, while Elizabeth's maternal grandparents, who lived near Ealing, West London, bought her dress. Her brother walked her down the aisle and, while her mum came, she did not want to sit on top table.

Richard was my best man, and I was overwhelmed by the fact that both Lindsay Lloyd and Ian Corey flew in from the USA to be with us for the weekend. Ian had a bit of a tricky journey too, having spent the night before on a bench at Liverpool Street Station having missed the last train up.

As if storms were to mark this part of my life, our planned honeymoon to Jamaica did not happen. A few days before our big day a hurricane flattened the island. Fortunately, the travel agent managed to change our booking to two weeks in Barbados. It was a great place, and we had a lovely time in the warmth of the Caribbean.

Living in the South-East meant that we could make the most of being close to Europe, so one year we travelled to France for New Year's Eve.

In Elizabeth's last year at university, she was asked to babysit in Paris. Between school and university, she had been an au pair for a British family in Paris. He was the deputy MD at Reuters, and the couple were off to the Caribbean on a conference for a few days. I popped over to join her for the weekend, and for some reason decided to go via train, hovercraft, and train. It took me all day, and was not that much cheaper than flying, but these big hovercrafts no longer operate, so I am glad that I had the chance to experience the crossing.

Elizabeth went to work for London Electricity, based in Bexleyheath. The easiest way to get there was driving across London; otherwise, it would have been a 90-minute train journey, each way. This meant that she dropped me off at Flight at 7am before heading to work. She then picked me up at around 6pm.

Such a schedule, combined with the high cost of living, meant that the offer of taking over Rosh Engineering was a great opportunity for me. The business was steady, and we could have a house not a flat, and it would be a better environment to raise a family.

I sold the flat for about £45k and, once again with Richard's help, on July 14, 1989, we headed north.

Unfortunately, I had not completed on our new home: 32, The Copse, Burnopfield, so we had to move in with my mum and dad for a few weeks - which also happened to be the head office of Rosh Engineering.

FLIGHT INTERNATIONAL 1986 – 1989

I was invited to an interview at Flight International's offices in Sutton, Surrey, after graduation.

I took a bus from Newcastle to London as it was cheaper than the train (although Flight ended up paying me back!) and then took a train out to near Guildford to stay with the family of university friend, Lydia Jasinski, who lived nearby.

Business Press International published more than 200 titles, including Flight International; it was later taken over and became Reed International. Its magazines ranged from Bird Cage and Aviary monthly, and Power and Dam Construction News, through to Computer Weekly. Every specialist industry and hobby was taken care of and Flight International was one of the top journals. Founded in 1909, it was the oldest aviation magazine in the world with a team of about 35 in both publishing and journalist roles.

David Mason, the editor, interviewed me and seemed to spend more time grumbling than quizzing me, at one point advising, "if you are prepared to work for peanuts, you will be fine". In fact, the starting salary was excellent: £7,500, while most graduates I knew were starting on an average of £6,000.

I had no idea whether I had done enough after the interview. I obviously still had several options open to me, so I pushed David for a decision. I called him first on Monday ("I will let you know on Friday") and then again on Friday (to be told, "I am making the decision on Monday.")

I am not sure whether me calling him that following Monday bullied him into taking me on, or whether he had any clue as to a start date, but tenacity is a vital attribute for a journalist. David was a lovely man, but his heart was not really in running the magazine. He was a great writer, but poor manager. He left a year or so into my time and was replaced by Allan Winn, an editor for another title in the group and a little more focussed on the job.

On my first day at Flight, I put on my suit and tie, and off I went. I continued to wear a suit and tie for the duration of my employment, while others were mostly, at best, just jacket and tie. But mum had taught me to dress professionally for work, so I did. While it caused a stir in some circles in the office at first ("We will never know when you are going for another job interview") it became my normal attire and accepted.

The Team

I reported into the Air Transport Desk Editor, David Learmount. He was a former RAF Hercules pilot who had had to retire from flying because he developed epilepsy. He even had an attack one morning at his desk. At first, I did not know what was happening. I was chatting to him, when he just sat staring into space, holding his typewriter on the sides, and shaking very slightly. Flight photographer, Janice Long, had come in and was about to tap him on the back playfully, when I stopped her. We did not know what to do, so asked assistant editor Tom Hamill who had been at Flight for ever. Just stay with him he said. David popped out of it, quite suddenly, as if nothing had happened.

My relationship with David was not always great but having some 'Smart Alec' graduate arrive in his suit, with an unsatiable drive and determination, must have been annoying.

David had three kids – two daughters and one son – and was sending the son (not the girls) to private school. It must have been a stretch, though, as he was always doing freelance work on the side. If you were invited to do TV, you got an expert fee then too: £100, plus expenses. If there was ever an air crash or issue, David would be invited on. Flight did not mind as it raised the magazine's profile, and David needed the money.

Once, ITV invited me up to do a bit for the 6pm news on BA's takeover of British Caledonian because David was on holiday, and I had answered his phone. When I got there, I think the producer saw this child and decided against it. The reason given was that the crew who had been scheduled to film me, had had to go off to cover a fish bone stuck in the Queen Mother's throat; I still received my £100 though.

I did do something for BBC Radio 4 (although that was not paid) but my piece in the International Herald

Tribune, during the Paris Airshow, was paid. This was just before I left the magazine.

Seeing David suppress me somewhat, the editor used a re-organisation to change my line manager to Graham Warwick. Although the seating was the same, it eased the tension, and David and I then got on fine.

Graham took my enthusiasm and made me fly, metaphorically. He was technical editor, before becoming news editor. He was encouraging and supportive, even though I was not a good writer when I started. I had no problem phoning people and getting the story but lacked the natural writer's skill. Part of my development plan included training and their in-house courses were good. By the time I left I was a half-decent writer, but some writers could do so much more.

Lee Paddon

Lee Paddon was another new starter in my first year at Flight. He was on the technical desk, and I made sure he was invited down to the canteen at lunch. The following week he was not there. People were often gone for days at a time on assignment, but it was odd that it happened in the second week.

He came back a week later, and was obviously losing his hair, having been off to have chemotherapy. Lee was four years older than me (so, 26 years old) and had first had cancer at 16 years old.

He later left Flight to become a tax inspector, but we kept in touch. His cancer returned repeatedly over the next 25 years until he died, aged 54 years old. But Lee was the most positive and cheery fellow that I have ever met. When I was down, he lifted me up. And I had, comparatively, no reason to be down.

He was a rebel too. He had previously worked on a computer games magazine, and he put all sorts onto my computer (against the rules), including an F16 aviation fighter game, which he thought was legitimate as we worked in aviation. I must confess that slow afternoons did not produce much copy for the pages of the magazine.

At the Christmas Party, he got me more drunk than I had ever been before or since. He also had a wit and charm and an intellect broader than his physics degree suggested. He could quote Wordsworth and was a gifted writer. He once had a feature to write on baggage handling. He must have somehow annoyed the editor (again) to get that one, but Lee made it his own. "Breakfast in London, Lunch in Paris, Baggage in Amsterdam. Such are how aviation stories are told," he started. I was hooked in the first paragraph.

Robin Blech

There were a few great characters at Flight, and no greater than Robin Blech. He was the general aviation editor, so covered private flying and corporate jets, i.e. little aeroplanes. He was a pilot, and could also test-fly aircraft.

He was full of stories about his youthful flying career. He had flown to remote Eskimo settlements, making deliveries of people and produce to places where the main road through the settlement also served as the landing strip. We laughed as he described with great theatrical joy how the process was to fly down the length of the high street so they would create a clear passage before landing. He then had to shoo away kids from his tailplane, as they hung on to stop him taking off.

He also had scary stories, such as when he was flying a King Air from the USA to the UK on a delivery flight against a strong head wind. A King Air twin prop (twin propeller) needs to take a very northerly route via Greenland as it has a small range. Then they lost an engine and he had to decide whether to push ahead, turn round, or ditch and try and survive in the artic waters in a life raft. Scary stuff.

Pete Middleton

Deputy editor, Peter Middleton, was a great chap who worked his socks off. This was partly due to David Mason's lack of daily engagement, and partly due to his own professionalism. But the combined effect was a nervous breakdown.

The following re-organisation and shortage of staff gave me a leg-up in the final year of my tenure because Graham became news editor/deputy editor and I filled a deputy news editor role, that in reality was as much as the full news editor position. But I was only given an additional £200 for my extra graft, which was close to a 10- or 11 hour-day at the time.

Peter also had a history that had rocked flight a few years earlier. He was in a small aircraft, with a pilot and the then Flight photographer taking pictures in another. The two aeroplanes collided in mid-air, and both the photographer and pilot of the other aeroplane were killed.

Colin Paine

The art editor, Colin Paine, arranged the stories on each page and married them up with the correct pictures.

He used a manual system, with scissors and glue. He was assisted by a young woman whose husband was the Father of the Chapel – the fancy name used for the trade union rep in the print world. His name was Charlie Dickens; you could not make it up.

Colin was a great artist, and the walls of his flat were hung with rich array of his paintings.

When I was at Rosh, I commissioned Colin to paint a Christmas card for the company – including power transformer and sponsor equipment – which over the next 20+ years became a real talking point in our industry. I also bought a beautiful oil painting from him of a Spitfire in a massive blue sky and wispy cloud scene, which was inspired by a poem. He loved aircraft, and Flight was his dream job.

He had a share in a glider at an airfield near Stansted and, one weekend, we went up to meet him. I then had a practice flight with the club instructor. An air tow, then circling the field a few times before coming in to land. It was so serene and quiet gliding over the Essex countryside.

After I left, Flight had a reorganisation and Colin was made redundant. They just wanted fresh blood and no number of attempts by Colin to re-design the look of the title would have kept him in post. It was a real body blow because he loved the job and the industry. He odd-jobbed around and did more painting, with some of his works displayed at the Royal Aeronautical Society summer exhibition.

Alan Postlethwaite was on the General Aviation desk too. He was married to a very glamourous Russian, but it turned out she simply wanted to leave communist Russia, and he was her ticket, which upset him come that fateful day.

Mike Gaines ran the Defence desk and smoked like a chimney. A grumpy old goat, he died in his 50s.

Technology

We used big old typewriters to put our stories together, with two sheets of paper and carbon paper in between, so that we kept one copy, while another was sent to the sub-editors and then typeset for the layout. We also had secretaries to re-type any heavily edited text and do general admin. David Mason always thought it odd that we needed them, but many of us were not properly trained journalists so we did not have typing and shorthand skills. When John Bailey joined our desk to replace Julia Hayley who had gone to Reuters, we got a trained journalist, but that was rare.

I had started to use a PC in the USA and at Essex, so was surprised that they did not do the same at Flight. The Union would not allow it, I was told. I had joined the NUJ to be part of the team, but I had greater need of a computer. The company was happy to supply one, but the Union thought we should have a pay rise as it would make us more productive. To my mind, it would make my life easier so there was no logical need for a pay rise. I resigned my membership of the NUJ and got a PC. Others then saw how easy my life was. Slowly but surely, one by one, the others started to ask for a PC and resigned from the NUJ. Ian Gould held out until last.

The NUJ was de-recognised shortly after, as so few staff were still members.

Many years later (around 2015), I was on a national BBC Sunday morning political TV debate – *The Big Question* with Nicky Campbell - as a lead panellist. I was pitted against the traditional Labour MP for Blyth Valley, Ronnie Campbell, debating the intransigence of trade unions against modernisation, which was prompted by a railway union issue at the time. I strongly praised those unionists who work with business leaders and their employees to instigate change. But I used the Flight International experience as evidence of bad unionism and how, in the end, they lose out. The Twitter trolling that I received was quite remarkable, pretty much labelling me as a Victorian Mill owner wanting to crush the proletariat.

Assignments

While the pay may have seemed poor for a middle-aged person, the lifestyle at Flight was top drawer. Any press conferences in London were invariably held at posh locations with lovely lunches, including Browns Hotel, The Connaught etc.

The British Aerospace Christmas Drinks in The Strand offices were a lavish, free-flowing affair, with gifts of leather wallets and bottles of drink as guests left.

Central London was only a 20 to 30-minute train ride, so we were up in town regularly.

One year, Air New Zealand invited me to Centre Court Wimbledon. It was great watching Martina Navratilova play, but I was racked with guilt as it was not particularly productive work given that the magazine's pages had to be filled each week. I had lunch, with the compulsory strawberries and cream, and then headed back to the office.

Working for Flight had a kudos that resonated throughout the airline industry. It was one of the most respected publications and, as a journal of record, we had access and attention that lesser magazines did not. When I say 'journal of record', this came from years of accuracy and thoroughness.

We published an annual record of that year's crashes and major incidents involving commercial aircraft. At the time, some in the Communist Bloc were extremely hard to find out about and record, but we did.

Meanwhile, new aircraft announcements included very detailed cut-away drawings of the inside of the aircraft, all done in cooperation with the manufacturers and their original drawings. Our technical art team would take weeks doing them.

Our reputation meant that, when we went to a press conference or reception, we had access to the CEO or chairman. During my time, the head of Rolls-Royce was Sir Francis Tombs, and he would greet me by name. At British Airways, Lord King, or Sir Colin Marshall, would come over and have a word. Sir Michael Bishop, of British Midland, was another who came and had a chat. If you want an ego boost, these interactions delivered.

But the international travel was the real bonus. My first was a trip to Amman, Jordan for the launch of the new branding of Royal Jordanian Airlines. They invited journalists from airline publications and travel magazines and, one Sunday, flew us out business class (although, in those days, business class was no better than Traveller Plus is today. We got a bit more legroom and better food, but no sleeper seats).

That night, we all went to a banquet which was held in an aircraft hangar, sitting under a newly painted 747. There were hundreds of invited guests, including the King of Jordan. I was by the entrance as he came in, and he said hello to me; a little fellow, but absolutely charming. The following day, we attended the press conferences and had a chance to do some sightseeing before heading home.

Most news stories were initiated by press releases that arrived in the post or, latterly, by fax. Sometimes a PR officer would call us, and sometimes we would hear of something major on the news.

The news cycle for a weekly specialist journal was a little slower, and most of the book was done by Friday, with two pages left for current news on the Monday. We went to press in the afternoon, and it was shipped and on desks by Tuesday or Wednesday. We later changed to printing on Fridays, because it was felt that any "news" from the previous week was getting old.

Every week started slowly, with non-time sensitive pieces, or features. The features were two-, three- or four-pages long, and mostly featured our international travel.

I had done a couple of short news stories on aircraft sales to express parcel companies before picking up a short feature opportunity on XP Express Parcels based out of Schipol. I flew business class, with their PR officer, from Heathrow to Amsterdam. I was amazed how a meal service, with wine etc, could be delivered in this 40-minute hop, all seemingly unrushed.

I interviewed the owner at his offices, then we were driven south to their hub at Maastricht so we could see the overnight operations. On the way, we stopped for dinner at a chateau and had the most exquisite nouveau cuisine meal. It was a late night, and we flew back the following morning on an old Vickers Viscount - the Viscount being the first turbo-prop airliner in the world.

The Vickers Viscount was also operated by another airline, and I heard through a contact that it was going bust. They also flew Shorts 360s and served places like Jersey in the Channel Islands. (My mole, incidentally, worked for a firm of accountants working in liquidations and corporate restructuring. Over the following months, he and I had a great many chats, giving me the heads-up on various corporate problems and issues; the failure of the AVR Super2 was another example. He probably used me as much as I used him, but it was a fascinating time and exciting for the young journalist in me).

So, I phoned the managing director of the airline and quizzed him as to whether he had used his credit card to pay for fuel for the aircraft etc., which he denied. He then suggested that I fly to Jersey for the weekend and see just how good their service was. "Take your Mrs..., or someone else's Mrs, on me," he said. I explained that I could not accept tickets for personal use. "They're in the post now," he said.

I had a chat with the editor, and he agreed that I could go Friday night and come back Monday, provided that I tried to speak to people when there. So, Elizabeth and I flew out and, embarrassingly, she was given a bouquet of flowers on arrival; the airline was really laying on the charm offensive. Although it was winter, we had a good weekend pootling about in a little hire car.

On the Monday, I had a chat with various people at the airport, other airline owners (Aurigny), and the airport managers, as well as chatting to the pilot after we landed. Nothing substantive was unearthed, although some months later the airline did go under.

My first front cover was a feature on Aer Lingus. Not a masterpiece, but a work-a-day job. Having a handle, or headline-making thrust, was what we all wanted. But mostly it was mundane information-sharing about an airline operator – why they chose a particular engine type, or aircraft type, why they had expanded into new markets etc.

The headline caused the most debate; Aer Lingus wanted what were known as 'fifth freedom' rights where they could fly from Dublin to, say, London and pick-up passengers for onward transport to, say, Berlin. This was not allowed at the time. My headline was to be *Freedom Fighter*, but with Irish Republican tensions of the time, "Fifth" was added.

A "jolly" to the Airbus manufacturing plant in Toulouse was one of those lavish occasions which yielded very few column inches for the time I was away but was the perk of the job. The Canadian airline, Wardair, was taking delivery of some A310s and we went for the handover.

I met Mr Ward and his daughter, had a tour of the

factory and enjoyed a great gala dinner. The craziest part was the table-centre decorations had candles in. As the night progressed, the candles burnt down, and the surrounding dried arrangements burst into flames. I grabbed a water jug and chucked it over the fire, making a mess but stopping us burning to death. The decorations on adjacent tables followed suit, and it wasn't long before the staff were running out and removing them all.

We then had a fashion show... I'm not sure quite why, but it may have been to showcase the new crew uniform; either way, it was a very professional catwalk spectacle.

One of the Airbus PR chaps was David Velupillai who had formerly been a Flight reporter like me and landed the Airbus job with just 'O' level French. I fancied his job and some years later at the "100-Year Flight Reunion" party, I chatted to him again. He was still at Airbus but marketing their airliners as executive jets. To be able to use a big passenger aircraft as a private jet marked this audience out as quite an exclusive clientele...

These trips invariably involved the same aviation journalists, so it was a jolly party trip on most occasions. Aviation Week reporter, Guy Norris, was about my age and we got on like a house on fire. He knew the ropes better than me so made sure I made the most of the opportunities that came our way. He and I were supposed to be competitors, but it never felt like that. At my first Paris Air Show he asked where I was having lunch one day, and I said I was not sure. He recommended the GE pavilion for a great lunch. When I said I had not been invited, he replied, "You are now" and managed to blag me in on his coat tails - and indeed it was a very good three-course lunch.

A new airline, Highland Express, was flying a Luton – Prestwick – Newark NJ – Prestwick – Stansted route with a 747-100. I flew over on July 4, and stayed in New York, heading down to the riverside to watch the fireworks. One of the investors was Sir Ian MacGregor who was famously Chairman of British Steel and British Coal during a turbulent time for these industries. He was on the flight back the following day, so I got to meet and interview him.

Highland Express did not survive long and went bust within a year; aviation is an industry that is tough to make a margin. There is a saying: how do you make a small fortune in the aviation business? Start with a large one.

I covered one story which involved spending the day bobbing around London airports with aviation Minister Michael Spicer, looking at potential executive jet hubs. We went from Farnborough to Biggin Hill in a twin turbo, took a helicopter over the City to Luton, and then flew out of Northolt in an RAF transport. The latter was interesting because all the seats faced backwards, which is the safest way to travel. Commercial airlines only have seats facing forwards because of alleged customer preference. The RAF's customers are not allowed preferences, they just want troops safely delivered. Some VC10s with backward-facing seats were produced for BOAC in the 1960s. Seats facing the rear offered more protection in an accident, but they were unpopular with travellers and eventually sold to the RAF.

On another trip, I flew in around the UK in a stretch King Air (a twin-engine, turbo-prop aeroplane) with potential buyers. I did not cover the small aeroplane sector very often, but this was fun. We flew up to Edinburgh, then down to Barrow-in-Furness. Its shipyard builds submarines, and the facility has its own airstrip and air crew who fly staff in and out. It is stuck out on a limb and that day there was a brutal side wind. We went in at 90 degrees to the runway; I could see down the runway out of my side window. At the last moment, the pilot flipped the aeroplane straight to land, which was quite hairy, but even more so when the corporate pilots asked if they could have a go. A bit like me when I was a kid, and a chum got a new bike.

We flew a further circuit around south-west Cumbria. However, this King Air was a few metres longer than our new pilot was used to so, when he put the wheels on the tarmac, he did so with such a mighty crash that I thought the undercarriage was going to pop-up through the wings. His laughing amazement was explained by the fact that the stretch meant the wheels were further back thannormal.

On the flight down to Bristol, I sat up in the right-hand seat with the pilot and enjoyed the wonderful clear views across Shropshire, while learning a bit more about the controls. This was interrupted by the calm voice of an air traffic controller over the radio, querying our altitude. I am not entirely sure why, but a pilot sets his altitude from a datum point at sea level, or where the airfield is. With our ups and downs, our pilot had forgotten to adjust it and while he was broadcasting on his transponder at one height, air traffic could see we were at another. A simple thing, but one that could have spelt disaster if not for the controller's vigilance.

Just before Christmas one year, David, John Bailey, and I, were offered a visit to the control tower at Heathrow and the National Air Traffic Services (NATS) centre a few miles up the road at West Drayton (it has since moved). I have never met a group of people who are so calm, considered, and measured, despite what at times must be frantic activity. We would be chatting with controllers when, in mid-sentence, he would cut off and talk to a pilot, and then return to our conversation as if nothing had interrupted him.

We watched a Virgin 747 beat down the full length of the runway and seemingly strain into the sky. That has a full load, he told us, and there must be lots of presents in the hold.

At NATS, the corridor was split in two; one side was darker and staffed by RAF personnel, the other side was civilian, which was the side we went to. There was a similar calm pervading across the room and used one of the most basic techniques for handling aircraft. As the aeroplanes came onto the radar from the Atlantic, a strip of paper went into a holder the size of a six-inch ruler and an overhead camera projected this to give visibility and allow a handover to another controller as it entered into his air space, either as it passed through, or as it made its final approach into Heathrow.

We also learned about how much separation was required between aircraft on landing and take-off, because of the turbulence created by big aircraft. The turbulence following a 747 could crash a smaller, 20-seater aircraft if insufficient separation had not been provided. Hence why bigger airports, like Heathrow with its limited runway space, prefer only to handle large aircraft, otherwise air traffic in and out of the airport would be severely limited.

We also chatted about the forthcoming digitalisation of the service, while sitting around a spare screen looking at aircraft coming and going from our airspace. I learned how aircraft "squawk", which gives their information to the ATC. The North Atlantic is not covered by radar, so once leaving UK airspace, they are popped into a corridor, or a tube, which they must not leave – although they have a few thousand-feet latitude up and down as well as left and right to avoid storms etc. This avoids head-on collisions, while the spacing keeps them apart.

The squawk transmission also had a panic mode if an aircraft (civilian or military) was going down. All stations and towers could pick this up and reference back to a special room in West Drayton where the computer triangulated it from the reports so the ditching site could be quickly identified. It was incredibly quick, with locations being pinpointed down to a few metres just a fraction of a second after the squawk. Two staff then did a demo – and almost immediately these locations had to be "stood down" as they reported in.

The controllers here spent most of their time just waiting for a disaster... which is fortunately rare.

Jump Seats

Pilots were a prime audience of Flight, although they

joked they read the back pages first because it was where jobs were advertised.

Whenever I was flying, I would ask the cabin crew if they would give my business card to the Captain and see if I could visit the cockpit to have a chat. In the days before 9/11, this was readily allowed. On several occasions, I was allowed to sit on the jump seat behind the Captain for take-off or landing. The first time was on a return from Paris one Sunday. We had clear blue skies and, with the headset on, I could hear all the conversation between pilots and ATC. As we were on our approach the Captain said to the First Officer (who was in control that day), "Gate 15? Isn't that this end of the runway? Tell you what, put it down at the front end and, if we hit the brakes firmly, we can take that first right and save a long taxi. It will mean we get home quicker."

London's City Airport had quite a short runway and a very steep angle of approach because of noise abatement regulations.

I was invited to City airport for the very first landing and take-off – there were two airlines permitted at first, Brymon Airways, and British Midland division, London City Airways. They both had DeHavilland Dash 7s, which could manage the steep descent. When I later sat in the cockpit for the landing it felt like I was straining at my harness and, had I not been strapped in, would have fallen through the windscreen and yet the angle was only something like five degrees, compared to the usual three degrees.

The most exhilarating landing I experienced was on a Cathay Pacific 747 into Hong Kong's Kai Tak Airport. I had gone up during the flight for a chat and the

Captain invited me back for the landing. He apologised in advance that he would be unlikely to be able to chat much during landing, "as it gets a bit busy at this airport". It was at night and, as we approached, all you could see were lights from buildings. No runway lights or runway. He did come on at one point and just said, "that is the checkerboard". Ahead on a hillside were red and white squares, all lit up. Tower blocks and hills on an approach to a runway is hairy. We then made a sharp 90-degree right turn - an amazing feat for such a big aircraft - and right in front of us was the runway. Or, more accurately, right beneath us. A few seconds later, we had wheels touching down. Wow.

I went to interview the Engineering Director at Cathay, and he had just ordered some new 747s with an uprated Rolls-Royce RB211 (L). It had much more thrust and, although this was more than the 747 routinely needed, it meant they could take-off heading out to sea with a five-knot tail wind, which was much preferred, and I could see why. The move to the new airport on Lantau made life easier for them.

North Carolina

We were regularly sent event invitations, which would be offered around. As David had a family (and was renovating his house), he often gave evening receptions a miss unless really top drawer – such as the Opera one night. I did a good many of them, because I wanted to take every opportunity offered to me, often on my own, until my last year.

I attended a BBQ hosted by a regional Australian Airline and held on the roof of a building.

I took Elizabeth along to one big reception, which was hosted by Piedmont Airlines at the American Embassy, attended by 200+ people. After drinks and a buffet, we were entertained by George Hamilton IV, a very famous country and western singer of the time. We were also asked to drop a business card into a box for a prize draw. Elizabeth had no card, but they gave her a slip of paper so she would not miss out - and her name was pulled out of the hat. Two free tickets to Fayetteville, all-expenses paid, taking in everything from golf to an airbase tour. I was worried that it might seem as if I had accepted a gift, which was not allowed, but because I was just tagging along (and took it as holiday), we managed to sort it out. We also negotiated a couple of flights, courtesy of Piedmont, to fly up to DC to see Lindsay for the weekend.

We flew into Charlotte, and then on to Fayetteville, which is famous for its massive military base, Fort Bragg, 50 McDonalds restaurants... and not much else.

The Tourist Bureau hosts were great, but I think they were a little disappointed because Flight was a trade journal, and not a tourism publication.

The golf was interesting, notably for the warnings of alligators in the water hazards. The Club professional was the top-rated Raymond Floyd, so a quality course. Although not the Deep South, it had a southern charm, people spoke with the distinctive accent, we had grits for breakfast, and it had a fascinating Civil War history.

It was also good to catch-up with Lindsay in DC, but we had a scare on our Sunday afternoon flight back to North Carolina. A major storm on the Saturday had meant that many passengers had to be moved to Sunday flights, and as our tickets were free staff-grade, we had no priority. The flight stopped en route and we were told that we could be bumped off on the second leg, which would mean we missed our UK connection. It was stressful but, fortunately, we made it all the way.

Lockerbie

Pan Am Flight 103 was a regularly scheduled Pan Am transatlantic flight from Frankfurt to Detroit, via London and New York City. On December 21, 1988, terrorists planted a bomb in luggage and it came down in the Scottish borders near Lockerbie.

The Flight team was having our Christmas dinner at a Sutton restaurant when we heard the news, and David called the BBC for an update. It was tragic in so many fronts and - although at the time no one knew the cause and even technical failure was considered - it changed commercial flying. It also pretty well spelt the end of Pan Am and, a year or so later, it went bust.

I flew Pan Am back from Seattle the following summer in economy but was able to lie down across the four centre seats, because they were empty. The oxygen masks in the row in front came down during the bumpy take-off, and were sellotaped back up, which said it all.

Pan Am had leased some aircraft from Evergreen (Kevin Montgomery's company) and, he said that the backlog of maintenance that they had had to do, on their return, was shocking.

Arizona, Oregon & Seattle

One of my early big trips began with Evergreen and its aircraft "graveyard", or storage place, in the Arizona desert. In reality, there was a good deal more to the company than that and a trip was organised from Tucson to their HQ in in McMinnville, Oregon. It was suggested that I then paid a visit to the Boeing offices in Seattle.

I asked if I could fly to America a couple of days early, and stop-off in DC, which the boss agreed to. It meant that I had the July 4th weekend with Lindsay. The two of us spent the big day on the Capital lawn, listening to a concert and eating and drinking... although the latter was in brown paper-bagged bottles (or cola bottles topped up with rum) because drinking alcohol in public is illegal in the US.

The airfield that was used to store aircraft in Tucson was quite a sight, with dozens of redundant aeroplanes scattered across the landscape in the dry heat of the site.

I then flew on an Alaskan Airlines flight (with their distinctive portrait of an Eskimo man on the tailplane) to Oregon to have dinner at their HQ with the team and the owner, Delford Smith.

I spent the following day flying around in helicopters over the Oregon forest. The business had started as a forestry spraying operation before branching out, and the scenery was spectacular.

We flew over miles of forest, occasionally cut through by a road before climbing into the hills and passing over the spot where the Jack Nicholson movie *The Shining* was filmed. We then changed to a Bell Helicopter and flew down to Portland before being driven back up to McMinnville.

I Interviewed Del the following day. He was quite a character – an orphan who started with one helicopter before building an aviation empire. They leased aircraft – sort of white-label operations – to other airlines, ran cargo operations, owned airport ground handling companies, even a local bank.

At the end of the interview, Del asked what I was up to. I said that I was on the 1pm from Portland to Seattle, where I was meeting Boeing. At which point, he turned to my host, Carol Jernigan, and said, "Carol, cancel his flight and take him up in the Learjet. Get permission to land at Boeing field and arrange for him to be collected there."

Want to feel like a million dollars? I know a man who can do that.

Figure 9: Learjet from McMinnville to Seatle 1988

Thirty minutes later, we boarded the Learjet (complete with bowl of fruit on the table between us) and went shooting down the company's own runway to head north.

We flew over Mount St Helens – a volcano that had in 1980 unleashed the deadliest and most economically destructive volcanic event in US history. As we passed over it, the pilot tipped the aircraft on its side so I could get a better picture. That never happens on your average Easyjet flight.

The two Boeing factories in Seattle are based an hour

apart. One had the 747 and 767 production line and the other, the 757 and 737. These were huge facilities; so much so, that they used golf carts to carry staff and visitors around. Strangely, the overwhelming impression was that no one was on the production line. Not that it wasn't a busy place, while every so often, there were chaps doing wiring, but it was not the hectic cacophony of a car production line.

I was focused on the 757: "The Late Great Hot Cake," as I called it, for the simple reason that for many years, they had hardly sold any at all, and then suddenly it boomed. It had been used on short, fat holiday routes and was now extending into longer haul operations (such as Florida-UK), although not in its original design concept.

Ditch testing on the Isle of Wight

I took over the chair at Flight from Alyson Chambers, who then worked at a regional airline magazine. When Alyson left the journal later that year, I was interviewed for her job as editor of this quarterly publication, but it was not for me.

She and I flew together on short hop from Farnborough to the Isle of Wight on a tiny Britten-Norman Islander aircraft, seemingly held together with tissue paper, string, and a single row of seats.

The pilot's pre-flight safety briefing was simple, "if anything goes wrong, get out that door." After which, he turned back around in his seat, and started engines for a journey that felt like 'real' flying; bouncing in the wind, just a few hundred feet off the ground (or so it seemed).

We flew to a factory that not only built hovercrafts it

also had a big, long, water tank which simulated aircraft ditching into the sea. They built scale models that were perfectly weighted to emulate the real thing. They could also create waves and simulate crosswinds, before letting the model land in the water.

The boffins believed it was more accurate than computer-modelling, and some real-life ditching proved that their tests were spot on. Sometimes, they had to make design-change suggestions to help a ditching aircraft perform better. "Have you ever had a suggestion turned down?" I asked. The engineers sheepishly looked at each other. "Only once," they replied. To a journalist, this is red-hot stuff and I probed more... who, what, when? They then swore me to secrecy, but as they are now probably dead and the aircraft is no longer in service, I will spill the beans here now.

Concorde, it was discovered, acted "like the yellow submarine," on ditching, and went straight to the seabed. For some aircraft, they could suggest ways to land or ditch in order to stay afloat. However, the only solution they discovered that worked for Concorde was to fit some canards (small winglets) at the front of the aircraft's fuselage. These kept the nose above water on landing, allowing time for passenger evacuation. However, the additional weight this created meant losing four revenue-generating seat rows; an unacceptable option for an aircraft that was never financially viable. The suggestion was ignored, but fortunately Concorde never ditched in the sea.

Medical Men of Verona

Helicopter ambulances were pretty much unheard of

in the UK in the 1980s, so the UK distributer of Aerospatiale flew us to the factory in Marseille to see them being built, before we headed over to a Verona hospital in Italy to see one in service.

At the French factory, I met a young American woman who had gone to Georgetown University and, amazingly, knew Mitch Cohen. What a small world.

I had wanted to visit Verona when I was hitchhiking with Richard but the lift we got went straight past, and so did we. On this trip, I managed to see the rather uninspiring balcony that allegedly Juliet stood on in Shakespeare's tale.

Our hosts in Verona had the swashbuckling charm of Italian helicopter pilots. They took us to lunch, parking the car in the middle of a wide bit of road with the hazard lights on (as if broken down), before going to eat in the restaurant.

After that, we then took a helicopter trip over the city, with the pilot demonstrating how it could land on uneven surfaces next to the river, before sweeping the Roman Auditorium. Our visit stirred the interest of a local Italian TV company, and I was interviewed for their evening news.

Not much happens in Verona.

Paris & Farnborough Air Shows

While I was invited (and occasionally went to) smaller regional airshows in the UK, such as Duxford in Cambridgeshire, or Southend in Essex, these were for the public and simply entertainment. It was always good to be entertained even if no copy came out of it although, occasionally, contacts were developed or enhanced.

The big trade air shows were alternate years and held in Paris and Farnborough. Major manufacturers and industry suppliers had exhibits, from hydraulic hose suppliers, through to Boeing Aircraft. There were representatives from commercial, military, and general aviation. Exhibitors also included anti-aircraft gun makers (which seemed a bit ironic at the time).

These big trade shows were a good opportunity for exhibitors to make news announcements, from multi-aircraft sales to engine launches. It also gave the Flight team a chance to network extensively and schmooze advertisers. It was hard work, lasting from dawn until late at night, involving lots of eating, drinking, and of course writing.

We used to assemble in the Flight Chalet at 08:00hrs for coffee and breakfast, to share out the different press conferences and plans for the day. If you had any free time, you went out and found news yourself. It was rare to have the opportunity to look up and see which aircraft were actually flying that day.

Paris (at Le Bourget) had substantial "chalets" for hosting food and drink, whereas at Farnborough they were more like temporary marquees.

Brazilian aircraft manufacturer Embraer once gave me a great lunch at Paris. I was building up for a trip to South America with my contact there, but in the end I moved to Newcastle before this came off. But he gave me a T-shirt and a bag of coffee beans, which was a change from the usual freebies that ranged from model aircraft to pens and umbrellas.

The Far East

On March 29, I flew Cathay Pacific Business Class to Hong Kong on my first trip to the Far East. I arrived the next morning and, while waiting for my connection

to Taipei, Taiwan, I realised it was my 25th birthday. I mentioned this to the chap I was sitting next to, who I had sat next to on the flight out from the UK and who was also heading to Taipei. Off he went and came back with a beer. It was probably 0900 and a beer was the last thing I wanted but I felt obliged to drink it.

I was staying at The Grand Hotel, Taipei; a huge, pagoda-like, building overlooking the city, which was the host venue for an aviation conference.

Our first-night banquet was a lavish affair of a dozen courses. There were very few westerners there and a Brit beside me, from Rolls-Royce, asked for a knife and fork; I offered to show him how to use chop sticks, but

he refused. He didn't eat until the 6th course, when his cutlery finally arrived; I could not believe he was such a plonker.

The conference the following day taught me a great lesson. The audience was predominantly local manufacturing businesses seeking opportunities to work with the big western aerospace companies. But the representatives from the western businesses simply stood up and told them what they made, and how good they were.

A couple of chaps from GE sitting next to me cottoned on to the others' mistakes. They left the hall, returning two hours later to do their pitch. This consisted of slides and drawings of the components that they needed and for which they were seeking subcontractors or partners, and they stated, "If you can make this, to that standard etc, please come and talk to us." A practical and direct approach that was much more useful for everyone.

The defence desk had set up an interview for me with a military chap, as there was a rumour that they were building a fighter with US assistance. Technically, democratic Taiwan and communist China were still at war, so many countries were more concerned with having friendly relations (and political/economic ties) with China, than recognising Taiwan.

It was the strangest interview I'd ever conducted as he would not confirm anything from the list of questions I asked, simply repeating, "No comment".

This meant that, in my article, I simply stated that X refused to confirm that the engine was based on the GE203, and X refused to comment on the alleged top speed of the aircraft at Mach 2.

Before he left, he gave me a photograph of the said fighter aircraft.

After the conference, I went to see the Evergreen Shipping Line, which was setting up an airline. They had hoped to call it Evergreen Airways, but the US company of the same name - whom I had previously visited - vetoed that, so it became Eva Air. It was backed by the shipping conglomerate's money, so they took me on a tour of one of their freighters, and then around a container manufacturing plant. The noise as they rivetted and drilled the metal containers was deafening, yet the workers simply had tissue stuffed in their ears and no proper safety equipment.

That evening, the Evergreen team took me into the back streets of Taipei to Snake Alley. The alley was full of small shops and outlets with a rich variety of produce, but the highlight were the stalls which ritually butchered the snakes. One had an Orangutang swinging from posts above, while a man with a necklace microphone whipped a snake out of a case and goaded it with a stick so that it raised up and hissed. The crowd stepped back apace before the man grabbed the snake by the tail, swung it round and the bashed its head against the counter. A knife was produced, and it was filleted. Cheers went up. The noise, the smell, and the atmosphere were something else - and I was the only Westerner in sight.

We then went into the back of a shop and ate a traditional Chinese meal on Wedgewood China, of all things. I also had my first - and last - oyster.

My hosts then said that we were going on to a piano bar, although the reality was less that of *Casablanca*, and more that of a night club.

There were about six of us in our party. Various senior executives from Evergreen and Suzy Su, the PR officer. We had a private booth with glass doors looking into the central area, and we were served by a couple of hostesses who arrived with a bottle of whisky; obviously a real treat. By now, I was exhausted and ready for bed, but they insisted that I stay as they had ordered me a birthday cake. Eventually, the cake arrived, I ate some and then asked if they could call a cab.

"Which girl would you like to take back?" a senior VP asked.

I thought that I had misheard, but Suzy Su confirmed that Mr Vice President would like me to have one of the hostesses for the night. I was in shock; firstly, I was married, secondly, it must be illegal, and thirdly, no way. It took me by surprise, not least because the hostesses were respectfully dressed.

The team then panicked that they had offended me, so I was ushered off with Suzy Su, who tried to get reassurance that the incident was not going to damage the article which I was going to write about them. No, I assured her, I was simply tired, and happily married, etc., etc..

The following night, I met up with the same group of executives at a hillside spa and restaurant for a meal in a private dining room. This time, our driver joined the table as we all sat an cushions and stools around a low table.

Suzy, the driver, and I arrived first and although they were talking in Mandarin, it was obvious that they were talking about me. Suzy then turned to me and said in English, "You know he laugh at you?" "Why?" I asked. "He think it strange you not go with girl last night." Explaining that I was married simply caused them to laugh more. After the meal and some musical entertainment, they asked if I would like a massage. Given my experience the night before, I suddenly decided I was very tired and would like a taxi called.

"It is ok," they said, "we have a blind man for you tonight," and in walked a man with a white stick. I immediately understood what people mean when they say their stomach fell through the floor and felt faint.

"Go into the bedroom over there, and he will look after you," they said.

A thought flashed through my brain, "Oh my God, they think I am gay because I did not take a woman last night." But for some reason, I went into the bedroom.

The blind man spoke no English and simply tugged on my shirt to get me to take it off, which I did. He then tugged on my trousers. "No," I said sharply, ensuring that there would be no mistaking my meaning. I then lay down, and his strong hands started the massage. It was incredible, and my sake-filled, fuzzy brain, slowly cleared. At one point, he had me sitting up and held my head in his hands. He rocked it gently to the left and back three times, then CRACK. It was such a violent action that I thought he had broken my neck. He hadn't, but then he started rocking my heading to the right – and this time, I knew what was to come.

On my last day, Suzy showed me around the capital.

We started with breakfast at one of her favourite places, but it put me off street food for life. As a guest, I didn't feel I could say no, even as we sat on plastic stools watching a man break eggs into a grubby, steel oil-drum top. He whirled around with a variety of items that I could not name, all the while leaning over it with a lit cigarette in his mouth… I knew it could all go wrong, and it did, as my subsequent time on the toilet testified.

Suzy then took me to a Buddhist Temple, and as a Buddhist herself, was able to show me how to look into the Buddha's eyes and, with hands on forehead, pivot incense burning sticks in homage. There was also some chanting, but that was beyond me.

We then had a traditional tea ceremony where a small pot was constantly topped up with boiling water, while its long tea leaves plumped up with the water. The ritual and respect for this activity was beautiful; I loved how the Chinese made such an occasion of such a simple matter as having a cup of tea.

We also went on to walk through Chiang Kai-Shek Memorial Park. Chiang Kai-Shek had led the Taiwanese against the Mao revolution in Mainland China and established a non-communist state on Taiwan. While we were there a couple of teenage girls approached Suzy. "They want to have their photograph taken with you," she explained. Obviously, that was not a problem. Then all of a sudden, all their friends rushed over, and I had my picture taken with about 10 or 15 giggling Taiwanese.

I was intrigued as to why they wanted the photo. "They think you film star," Suzy explained. But not any particular film star; just a reflection of my good looks and demeanour. "Does this happen to you a lot in London?" she asked.

The story is particularly resonant in our family because my father had a similar tale. As a young man he lived in London. One weekend, he came back to Wolverton and had a drink with his brother Ken at the Engineer's Arms.

Dad bought the first round and then his brother Ken went to the bar, at which point the landlady asked who my dad was, asking if he was a film star - same drill, no one in particular, just good looks and demeanour.

Mind you, I think Taipei has more of a resonance than a

pub near Milton Keynes...

Hong Kong

Elizabeth had flown out to Hong Kong a day or two before me, where we had booked into the Holiday Inn Golden Mile on Kowloon side.

By the time I arrived, she had worked out the lay of the land. We took buses around the island, and a trip on a junk out of Aberdeen and generally soaked up the atmosphere.

I interviewed the Engineering Director at Cathay, and also an executive of regional airline, Dragon Airlines, but had enough time to see some sights. One night, we had dinner with Flight's stringer, Bob, in Hong Kong (a stringer is not an employee but is retained and paid by the stories they file). I regularly liaised with Bob about what he should write-up, what we did not already have etc. He was a cracking fellow, and we had a great dinner at Jimmy's kitchen, followed by too many whiskies in a hotel bar nearby. He explained how he could up-sticks and be out of Hong Kong in 24 hours with all his possessions the moment the communists took back control of the province.

On our last day, we headed out to Lantau Island. We were looking to visit a monastery but, having apparently got off the bus in the middle of nowhere and wandered for ages without a sight or sound, we started to worry about getting back in time. Today, Lantau is well connected with a bridge, trains, housing, the new airport and even Disney. But at the time, it was a real, rural contrast to the hustle and bustle of Kowloon.

I checked-in for the midnight departure back to the

UK, only to be told that they were overbooked, so I would be on standby as I was flying on a staff ticket. Elizabeth was fine having paid for hers. But the check-in attendant was great, and upgraded me to First Class because it increased my chances of flying that night. It was only when the flight closed at 11.30pm that I knew I was going home and swanned my way upstairs on the 747. Again, nothing more than bigger seats – more like lounge armchairs that reclined a long way. The food was fantastic though. The flight attendant kept referring to me by name but had to check what it was too often for it to sound natural. I did pop back to see Elizabeth in economy and took her up to see the captain when we were over Outer Mongolia.

I knew that, once we landed, I was going to hand-in my notice. We were returning to the North-East where I was going to take over Rosh Engineering.

I waited until my expenses had cleared as I had slipped-in meals with Elizabeth, and Flight did not know that she had joined me. The editor, Alan Winn, was on the point of trying to talk me out of leaving when I stopped him; the reason I was leaving was not one that he could improve on, which he understood.

I worked my three-month notice fully expecting that I would be stuck with nothing more than the most boring tasks, but Flight were great.

I got to fly on Concorde up to Manchester Airport, to attend the official opening of a terminal by Princess Diana. It only justified a few column inches, but it was a great jolly.

Concorde certainly packed a punch on take-off as it

sped down the runway, but it was much smaller than I imagined; just four seats across, so it did not feel like a long-haul airliner. We did not go supersonic, though.

On the flight to Manchester was Sir Colin Marshall (CEO) and a junior transport minister, who I did not know. However, in the press conference in Manchester he seriously impressed me with his mastery of his brief. He was challenged by some Yorkshire journalists about a Sheffield by-pass, handled it with detailed knowledge and understanding. Michael Portillo later became famous both in politics and in the media. Years later, I shared the platform with him at various corporate events.

I was also surprised to be part of the team which went to the Paris Air Show, which took place just a few weeks before my departure. I had thought that I would be left holding the fort in Sutton, but they said they wanted good, experienced journalists who would deliver on the ground.

I left feeling very positive about my time in the print media. They had taught me how to write, interview, and work hard. I also had had some great experiences, and I realised that I loved travelling to new places and meeting new people.

DOMESTIC LIFE
1989 – 1996

Elizabeth and I settled into the rhythm of working together well. To begin with, Elizabeth also worked at Rosh before she got a job at Northumberland County Council in administration.

We joined Durham Squash Club and played in the leagues. Michael Milligan had started teaching in South Shields after a spell as a toilet-roll salesman for Bowater Scott, followed by a spell in the Army. Unfortunately, the military wrecked his knees so he had to leave.

He was often round at ours, chilling, and when he started to go out with another teacher, Pip, we often socialised together. Pip and Elizabeth became good chums, although Michael and Pip's relationship did not last.

When Pip moved to Spain to teach in an English School for a couple of years, we went to visit her and got to see the coastline as well as the sights of Barcelona.

We went hill-walking in The Lakes, travelled around the UK meeting friends and had plenty of friends come and stay with us, too. One New Year's Eve, we travelled to Allendale with Pip to watch a Middle Ages tradition where local men carry old whisky barrels filled with burning tar on their heads. It was quite a spectacle, but the reasons for this fire ceremony are not clear.

One of Elizabeth's friends had joined a convent as a postulant or trainee nun, and we went to visit her. It is a strange commitment. From the outside it seems to be all holy and serene. But she was so excited about our visit because she was allowed to have multiple cups of coffee with us, where normally she would be rationed. To make money, they sewed ecclesiastical gowns - mostly for Anglicans. It seemed like a proper little sweatshop, and not the cathedral of faith and praying that I had imagined.

When Lydia Jasinski married her husband Edward, we went to their wedding which was held in a marquee in the family's garden in Surrey. It was a cracking day, plus we shared our table with a couple called Andrew and Fionnuala, as well as twins Geraldine and Teresa Agin. Collectively, they helped make the day so much fun that we have kept in touch ever since. They were always willing to head north to visit, so I ensured we caught up with them whenever we were in London.

Andrew and Fionnuala have moved a few times, and we have kept up with them in Edinburgh, Dorset, and then Bath.

Other visitors included Mitch Cohen, who came to visit us from the States, Lindsay Lloyd, Rev Michael Butler, and a couple we met on honeymoon, Judy and Rick, who lived in Boston. We then returned the favour, visiting Mitch in San Francisco, and Judy and Rick in Springfield, Massachusetts.

Elizabeth loved theatre so we went to lots of productions in Newcastle from the Royal Shakespeare Company (RSC) through to musicals and dramas, including one starring the great American actor Jack Lemmon. Although some may consider me a bit of a traditionalist, the RSC productions of Midsummer Night's Dream where the fairies wore hob nail boots, and The Merchant of Venice, set in the 1930s, were brilliant.

My sister Lisa had moved to Gosforth some years earlier and it very much seemed to be the place to live, so we started to look for a place.

We had bought The Copse for about £60k and ended up selling it for only a little more. The property market was flat, so I worked on the principle that it was a good time to buy.

With savings from the profits, a small inheritance of Elizabeth's, and a bigger mortgage, we managed to buy *3, The Drive* for the bargain price of around £120k.

It was a bargain because of the condition that it was in. It needed a completely new kitchen – there was no oven, just a hob and a microwave – while wires dangled where lights should have been fitted.

We took our time, and did much work ourselves, and slowly made our house a home. Although there was only a postage stamp of a garden at the front and a yard at the back, it had seven bedrooms, a couple of bathrooms, high ceilings and lots of character.

Unfortunately, a good many features had been taken out, including the original fireplaces. Over time, we replaced them.

Built in about 1910, it had the tradition of the main drawing room on the first floor which we made into a bedroom. The drawing room downstairs had no TV, but we made a den/sitting room on the first floor and this became a cosy TV room, filled with bookshelves, so that my books covered every wall.

Adam & Michael Harrison

Lisa's sons (and my nephews), Adam and Michael, were cracking little chaps, born in 1986 and 1989 respectively.

Eric had a Burger King restaurant, so he worked on Saturdays, which is why we often used to see them.

Adam's nappy was the first one I'd ever changed. I had been looking after him while Lisa went out, and he would not stop crying, so I assumed it was a dirty nappy. It was not, he just missed his mum.

As I've mentioned before, Eric had been married once before and had a daughter, although he did not see her regularly.

In the summer of 1985, I was at Lisa's having a coffee and saw a newsflash on the TV teletext service that there had been a plane crash at Manchester Airport earlier that morning. A few minutes later, the phone rang. I picked it up. It was Eric's brother asking for Lisa, which was odd. He was phoning with tragic news that Eric's ex-wife and daughter had been on the flight; the daughter had died, while the mother survived.

Lisa then had to convince Eric to come home from work, without telling him why; he was not keen, but Lisa did not want to tell him over the phone. I stayed with her until he pulled up. I cannot imagine how tough that day was.

Eric was a terrific father to Adam and Michael, although a dreadful worry to Lisa. He would take them off camping, building fires in the woods and would let them set off fireworks. Even when young, he bought them quad bikes.

Everything a boy wants and a mother fears.

The End

No relationship is without its ups and downs, but I never expected my marriage to Elizabeth to come to an end. I thought there might be something wrong, given her behaviour, but did not think it was anything too serious. She had wanted to go out with friends from the office after work on Fridays - and not just for a quick drink.

I occasionally went to Mass with her on Sundays, but not every week, and there were times when she seemed to get back later than usual from church.

And then she told me that she wanted to leave.

I asked her to go to counselling with me, which she agreed to, and we went the following week. However, I realised then that it was a done deal as far as she was concerned, and that that chapter of my life had closed, so I had to move on. This was easier said than done as I struggled to understand what had happened and why. Had I been working too hard? Had I been away on business too much? Had I not been attentive enough?

Whatever the reason, one thing I vowed not to do was criticise or smear her name or let anyone else do that. It would not heal the hurt and it did not undo the love that

I once felt.

While she denied that there was anyone else, within a couple of weeks I knew the truth. About 14 months later, we both attended Phillipa and Paul's wedding and she was nine months pregnant.

By then we were divorced, having done the whole process ourselves and made it as straight forward and amicable as possible. We could not see the point of letting the lawyers profit from it all. It also meant that moving on was so much easier.

JULIA NEWTON, AKA MRS D, 1996 – PRESENT

When you know, you know, and Julia and I became joined at the hip. She said she liked me because I did what I said I would do. If I said I would call, I called. If I suggested going out, I booked it. I have no idea why everyone is not like that, but I suppose not everyone is reliable.

We went away for trips, many of which combined business (for me) with leisure time for us both; travelling over the weekend made working time far more efficient.

One May Bank Holiday, I suggested going to Scotland. The first night we were in Perth, the second in Inverness, and Sunday night in Thurso, although the last stop-off was less than glamorous; even in May, the hotel had an electric blanket on our bed. But the real test on that trip for Julia was joining me on site at Dounreay Nuclear Power Station where I was measuring some transformers.

We then decided to book a proper holiday to Minorca in

the last week of June. By then we had known each other less than four months, but I was happy, and wanted to spend the rest of my life with her.

I bought a ring before we left and hid it away. We had a lovely evening meal at a local restaurant and romantically discussed the future in general terms. I secretly got the ring out when we got back to our room. Julia tried to talk about something else, so I had to carefully manoeuvre the conversation back to the future while we sat on the balcony enjoying a post-prandial glass of wine. I then proposed and had a weeping "yes," as the reply. It was June 25th 1996.

Phone calls home followed, and plans for the wedding started at great speed, partly because in November, Julia was going back into clinical medicine as a registrar and would have little choice of when she could have holidays. Plus, with on-call rotas, our world would be very different. Up until then, she had been doing a PhD and only did a little clinical work around her time in the lab, enabling her to have a normal 9-to-5 existence. But as she started writing up her doctorate - which looked at the thinning of the gastric mucous layer with age, and the effects of helicobacter pylori on the stomach - the normal life of a junior doctor was in sight. But we also wanted to get on with it, so why wait?

I was a divorcee, limiting the possibilities of a church wedding, so we decided to book the Newcastle Civic Centre. Finding places for the wedding and reception before the end of October that complied with all the rules meant we had a limited choice for both. We also wanted to get married in Newcastle because that was where most of our friends were based.

The rules of the time were that the room used for the wedding ceremony could not be also used for celebrations involving eating and drinking for two hours after the wedding (or some such bureaucracy).

We settled on The Copthorne on Newcastle's Quayside for the reception.

October 26th was a beautiful sunny autumn day. I arrived early at the Civic Centre, which was no surprise, I suppose. Peter Blakeman was also early, and hurried me, my best man Michael Milligan, Richard, Lindsay, Oz, and Harry, to the nearby pub – where he bought a couple of bottles of fizz and we toasted the day ahead. The service at the Civic Centre was far more personal and warmer than we expected.

Michael, despite all his years performing comedy in clubs, said he was more nervous about his speech than any event he had done, but he still did a great job.

The evening included the Ray Chester Big Band. A full Glenn Miller-style orchestra who we had previously booked for a 65th party for dad. They were terrific so it was great to have them again. The sound was amazing and heart-warming, although maybe it is because it was one of the few LPs that mum and dad had when I was growing up?

The following day we flew off to Cancun, Mexico, via Chicago. We routed that way because our return included a medical conference that Julia needed to attend. Unfortunately, our bags did not make the connection. Julia was a bit stressed by that but all we needed to buy were T-shirts and swimming costumes and we were fine until the bags arrived.

We then headed back to a crisp and cold Chicago for the American Association for the Study of Liver Disease (AASLD) Annual Conference. It is a major event, attended by some 6,000+ delegates and it became an annual event for us over the years. Julia had booked our room at the Renaissance on West Wacker Drive well before our honeymoon was planned and as we checked-in they noted that there was only one name on the reservation. We explained that we had just got married and were on the way back from our honeymoon etc. In typical, top-drawer, American service standards, the receptionist then said, "well if that is the case we ought to upgrade you to a suite."

A few years later, when Mark was a baby, we returned to the Conference when it was once again held in Chicago. We had to stay at the Renaissance with its positive memories, and as we checked-in, we were asked if we had been to Chicago before. We explained how the first time was on our honeymoon and how we had left our babies at home etc. for this trip. "Well, in that case we need to upgrade you," the check-in clerk said. This time they gave us, not a mini-suite, but a full-blown apartment. Dining room seating eight people, kitchen, living room, a bed as big as Illinois, and views through a picture window right into the heart of the city.

Medical Conferences

Medical conferences were responsible for a good deal of travel throughout our marriage. Julia was never keen to go on her own, while I was always happy for an excuse to travel places and see the world. As she climbed the career ladder, she would only attend the bits that she was involved in and had a need to attend.

We did a few in Europe, but mostly when the children were small. One conference in Paris, which spanned an August Bank Holiday weekend, was lovely. I spent my time looking after 10-month-old Emily while Julia was diligently attending educational sessions.

Lunch was a cold tin of baked beans, which I gave her straight out of the tin. We wandered around the city together with Emily in her buggy and found a small park/play area for toddlers. Emily could move around holding on to things but, up until then, could not walk. That day, she commandeered a kid's walker but, unfortunately, the other child started to cry. The mother came over and took it back from Emily. Before she had come back with another device Emily had toddled off on her own. Her first steps.

We also travelled to Vicenza, Rotterdam, Amsterdam, Freiberg, and Geneva. They often spanned a weekend, so trips were easy. Geneva was even easier because it coincided with one of our early summer trips to our chalet.

The key purpose of Julia having her paper presented in Geneva was so that she could cite it academically in other papers. She had planned to attend the whole day, but Emily, Mark and I were no more than 10 minutes down the road when Julia came running after us, saying that she would rather be with us than at the conference. A great day was had by the whole family, exploring Geneva for the first time.

Mark was only three or four years old on this trip and kept asking us if he could go on one of those things with sharp wheels. We could not work out what he meant; sharp wheels? Then he pointed at a tram as it went past. Of course, it had sharp wheels and made that metallic screech as it went round corners. It was such a relief to work out what he wanted. So often the older sibling understands more than the parents but, this time, even Emily was baffled. From that moment on, all Geneva trams have had sharp wheels to me.

The only stress of the Geneva trip was leaving all our passports and ID in the chalet in France. The Swiss – French border is hardly manned, or at least you get waved through. We were in a French hire car, so looked like locals, but it did not remove our concerns. These were heightened as we thought we had passed through on our way back without issue, only to be pulled over by a special customs and border check three miles further on. The officer put their head in the window, saw the two young children in the back, and waved us on. Phew. Close call. They were obviously looking for someone else.

The biggest conferences were in America. We mainly did geriatric or liver conferences in Washington, Boston, New Orleans, San Francisco and Atlanta.

Julia was pregnant with Emily when we were in New Orleans, so we did not properly do the jazz clubs and bars. In Atlanta, I had some time on my own and took the opportunity to tour the CNN studios. I was nearly a member of the audience on one show but I had promised to get back to meet Julia.

On the New Orleans and Atlanta trip, we added-on a few days in Florida. We met up with Donna Lee Roden, an old Georgetown friend in Sarasota, and had the disturbing experience of her boyfriend of the time wanting to join hands and say grace over a Little Chef burger lunch. Definitely not British.

But best of all were the few days we spent experiencing Disney for the first time. This started a lifelong love of the Disney parks. At the time, we could not see what would appeal to children. Then we had children, and we wondered when they introduced all these wonderful things for kids. Such is the magic of Disney. Everyone is catered for.

We managed one great holiday outside of medical conferences too. Unfortunately, this two-week trip to Kenya, which started in Nairobi, had a less than pleasant start.

I have always felt confident walking around foreign cities but here it was different. We were approached by some locals who wanted us to take a safari with them. No thank you, we said, we have one booked already going tomorrow. "You will be taking an Indian safari. Why aren't you taking an African safari?" they replied. No, we said, we are taking an African safari. The verbal exchange was both challenging and aggressive.

We were then approached by a handful of pre-teen lads. We briefly chatted with them, then one yanked off my watch and they all ran. Fortunately, it was an old cheap plastic digital watch, but it was the first and only time I have ever experienced this in my travels.

In our first week we travelled between the Samburu, Masai Mara, Lake Naivasha and Tree Tops in a large Land Rover with one other couple and our guide, Lawrence.

The food and accommodation in the bush was good,

and I was amazed that I could still have HP Sauce with my cooked breakfast in the morning. But the overwhelming emotion was awe at the wildlife.

Trundling along a dirt track, we came round a corner and faced a herd of elephants, which took our breath away. Brown from the dust and dirt, they meandered past us if we did not exist, while the baby elephants trotting alongside these majestic beasts made our hearts melt. It was the same with lions and even zebras. The TV wildlife documentaries suddenly came to life in front of us.

I would never regard myself as an animal lover. I will not rush to pet a dog or a cat at someone's home and I will always donate to a human charity before any animal charity. But I would never deliberately harm an animal either. I am not a fan of zoos in this regard, particularly for bigger animals, despite what I am sure is often laudable conservation work. Seeing these animals in their natural setting is something worth fighting for, and that is how it should be.

We took a balloon flight early one morning and because it was October we were able to see thousands of migrating wildebeest, which was spectacular from above. And from that altitude, we were even able to spot a lion stalking the herd.

Other animals we saw included hippos, baboons, giraffe, cheetah, and even a leopard (in the far distance), as well as all the animals that were preyed upon by the major predators. Our guide, Lawrence, was remarkable inasmuch as he could spot a sleeping cheetah in long grass at 150 metres without binoculars while driving along.

We did a game drive every morning at dawn and, again, an hour or two before dusk. We never tired of getting up so early.

Out here in the bush, the locals were far friendlier and less intimidating than they had been in Nairobi. As we crossed the equator, they wanted to show us how water changed the spiral direction when going down a funnel – although they wanted a tip for the trick. They were also keen on foreign exchange, asking us on one occasion whether we wanted to change our 'useless' English coins for Kenyan shillings.

On our journey back to Nairobi, and in the middle of nowhere, the exhaust became partly detached from our Land Rover. The only sign of life was a small mud hut 20 metres away. While Lawrence was under the vehicle, a couple of small kids came out – maybe seven or eight years old. We were writing postcards home and they just stared at us. Julia then handed the pen to a child, at which point, they ran back to their hut with the pen held high, screaming with delight. A wake-up call to us as to how privileged we really are.

One evening we had a talk from a Masai. He was tall and thin and explained why they have a tooth removed when young – tetanus, or lock jaw, is common as they go around barefoot. With a hole in their teeth, they can still be given water and not die. I remember learning about the bushmen of the Kalahari at school and his Masai stories and culture suddenly made the teachings from the past come alive. Interestingly, although dressed in his traditional costume when he spoke to us, he had travelled to New York on a cultural exchange, so he was wise to the way of the West.

We departed from Nairobi on the overnight train to Mombasa for a week of lying around in the sun and doing very little. The train was known for its luxury but, although fine, it was not quite the Simplon Orient Express. However, it trundled along at 30mph and was comfortable enough.

The dining car had tablecloths and white-jacketed waiters wearing white gloves. A young Dutch couple sat opposite and Julia mentioned that I could speak Dutch. I do not, but I know a few phrases and follow the Nelson Mandela dictum that if you speak to a man in your own language then you speak to his head, but if you speak to a man in his language then you speak to his heart.

So, the Dutch couple insisted that I tried my Dutch. "Hoe gaat het met je," I said. "Sorry," they replied, "say again?". After several attempts at changing the inflections and blaming the train noise I gave up and told them in English what I was trying to say. "Oh, you mean Hoe gaat het met je?" I had crashed and burned in front of my new(ish) wife.

Some years later, in 2012, we took the children to Berlin for a long weekend during the Queen's Diamond Jubilee. Having studied German at school I convinced them to stand aside and let me get the table at a restaurant, as well as order the first round of drinks. It worked perfectly, and our Coca Cola and glasses of wine duly arrived. The waiter then asked me something. After repeating a couple of times, I had to admit that I was British, to which he replied in perfect English, "I am so sorry sir. Your German was so good I thought you were Dutch."

Julia was doing resident-on-call during these years, which meant the average working week could notch up 60 or 70 hours.

If it spanned a weekend, then I would go to the Sunderland Royal Hospital at least once and have lunch with her. Mobile phones were rare items so, if I called her, I had to go through the switchboard and have her paged – or bleeped.

Julia was on call on the August Bank Holiday weekend in 1997 when Princess Diana died in the car crash in Paris. I paged her that morning and she had not seen the news. The world was in shock and the TV channels were back-to-back reporting it. I even called Lisa and broke the news to her. It was one of those events where you remember where you were.

Her funeral was also an occasion like no other, and the nation mourned. Rosh were working at Didot Power Station that weekend but the site was closed during the funeral, which was unheard of.

Lisa's husband Eric, who owned Burger King franchises, including the busy Northumberland Street outlet, closed the restaurant and came home because no one was in Newcastle city centre that afternoon.

The Millenium was another major occasion for many. There were prophets of doom, whose predications that there would be a global IT crash because computers would not recognise 00 as the year 2000 (in double-digit referencing in computer programmes), but instead think it was 1900, did not materialise.

With a 14-month old baby, we stayed home and did not

IAN DORMER CBE

party.

EMILY DORMER ARRIVES

I always wanted children, and although Julia was obviously focused on her career, so children were not the top priority, as soon as Emily arrived Julia admitted it was the best decision she had ever made.

Having our two babies, who are growing up into the most wonderful human beings, is the proudest achievement of our lives and surpasses everything else by a long way.

Julia was still a registrar while she was pregnant, so hospital shifts were tough at times especially as she neared her due date. She had finished her PhD, and her Viva was held when she was eight months pregnant - to much hilarity amongst the examining professors about towels and hot water apparently.

Julia had bought herself a British Racing Green MGF the year before when she went back into clinical work, as a treat. Emily's arrival meant this was then sold for a more practical Vauxhall Astra Estate.

Julia's parents, Heather and Keith, came to help us decorate the back bedroom at The Drive to make it a nursery. The rules of the time meant the hospital was not allowed to tell us the sex of the baby - allegedly someone had sued the hospital after they said it was a boy and it turned out to be a girl, so all the clothes and decoration had to be changed...Crazy world.

We did not care either way, and the nursery was painted in a neutral yellow.

The due date came and went, and still we waited, knowing that nothing more would be done to induce the birth until the baby was 10 days late. As if to order, just before we got to that point, things started happening. At first, Julia thought she had wet herself, and then realized that it was her waters going. At about 04:00am, Julia woke me up and we headed off to Newcastle's RVI. The midwives quickly worked out that the baby was a way off arriving, so sent me home to get more sleep with instructions to return at 09:00.

Julia's sister Sharon (an A&E doctor) and her husband Jon were living with us at the time, having sold their flat before they departed for Australia, where they planned to live and work for a year. I had breakfast with them and then mum took me into the hospital, so I did not have to park my car.

Julia was all fine and dandy, although she was in considerable pain. The gas and air was having no effect, so I was sent on a mission to get her an epidural. Pain-free delivery was the birthing plan - although the midwives always tried to talk mothers out of it as it meant from that moment they were immobile in a bed until the baby arrived, potentially making more work for them.

As I left the ward, I bumped into Peter Blakeman, the

chap who had introduced me and Julia. Bingo. He was excited for us and said he would sort the anaesthetist.

Julia was then wheeled into a private room which was decorated in the style of artist Charles Rennie MacIntosh. Dr Pete Evans duly came in to administer the needle in the back, before recognising his patient. "Oh, it's you, Julia," he said. "I didn't realise. I will get someone else," which was the correct protocol.

"No, you f***ing won't," Julia replied. "I need it now."

The enormity of the pain during the later stages of delivery was to become evident on the trace. The little spikes that it showed at this point would soon become Himalayan by comparison.

Poor Dr Evans: the medical fraternity have a dreadful sense of humour, and his colleagues ribbed him for ages afterwards, that Julia had walked about with a limp following his epidural. He was so relieved when he saw her a year later and she was absolutely fine.

For me, the rest of the day meant a lot of waiting. I bought as many of the day's newspapers as I could as a memento, but most of it was spent watching TV. The film The Third Man from the Graham Greene book was shown in the afternoon, which was great as it featured the Ferris wheel in Vienna that we had been on during our visit to Slovakia a couple of years earlier.

The midwives kept popping in and out until Jayne arrived, telling us that she would get something to eat, and we would get the baby out on her return.

As Countdown started on the TV the pushing and shoving began, and out popped our baby girl who was immediately passed to Julia. I cut the umbilical cord and she was then wrapped up in a blanket. Mother and baby were healthy. Nothing else mattered. It was about 17.30pm, and Emily Jane Dormer weighed in at 8lbs 8oz.

Our midwife said she was a long baby and so she would be tall. Now that she is 22 years old, and fully grown at no more than 5ft 6inches, we can conclude that such assumptions at birth are twaddle.

Emily was our first so Julia was kept in overnight, and I went back the following day for all the training on nappies, bathing, and the like. When you are suddenly given this very precious creature it is in one breath terrifying, and in the other remarkable.

I had seen the grainy picture of her during scans and I had felt her kick through Julia's belly as she developed inside. But now this little baby was dependent on us and we hardly had a clue what to do. There was so much to learn, such as supporting the head and trying to feed her, which was such a challenge. Julia was never going to breast feed so Emily was bottle-fed; her body, her choice, although the midwives and health visitors tried to persuade her otherwise.

The next few weeks were a bit of a blur as people came and went to ooh and ahh. Julia's mum came to stay and help us for a few days and we worked out how to sterilize and prepare bottles with powder and boiled water, with all the kerfuffle that goes with it.

I went back to work the following week, but I was a bit of a zombie. Every couple of hours Emily cried; sometimes more frequently; not because she was hungry, had wind, or needed a nappy change, she just woke us. Her cot was in our room for the first few weeks and she spent many evenings in bed with us. We needed more sleep and tried anything to help us through.

As time went on, Emily moved into her nursery but she still woke us up at night.

Julia went back to work after Christmas, so we needed a system to make sure we could function. In the end, one of us did until 2:00am and then the other took over until morning, which often meant that we were in bed and asleep by 9:00pm.

I also remember the feeling of hearing another cry having already got up five times, only to realise that it was 3:00am, and Julia's turn… What relief it was to be able to roll over and go back to sleep.

But the moments alone with Emily, in the dead of night, were precious to me. She loved to be held over my shoulder and walked up and down. It was just me and her as we cuddled and paced up and down her nursery. Listening to her gentle breathing and holding my gorgeous little bundle was special. All too often though, as soon as she had drifted off to sleep, I would gently roll her down into her cot, only to be greeted by a wail. On those occasions, I had gambled on returning to my bed too soon and should have left it another five minutes.

During the day, she liked to be rocked, so we put her in her car seat and I would swing it backwards and forwards between my legs. If I stopped, she would wail.

I know why only young people should have babies. It is hard, backbreaking work.

Emily's nursery was Elmfield in Gosforth. It was a large house and only a few hundred metres from home so easy for either one of us to drop off or collect, plus it had a great reputation; only the best for our girl. It was open 51 weeks a year from 7:45am until 6pm, and cost about £10,000 a year. You needed a good job to justify the cost but as Julia was striding towards her consultancy post, with better pay and better working hours, it was all worthwhile.

Emily was by far the youngest there, but nursery nurse, Clare, took a real shine to our baby and called her "Buttons". Clare was lovely, so we felt confident that she was being well looked after. They certainly fed the children better than we did, with wholesome food and no sweets to pacify them.

The children learned how to be sociable, while being stimulated and entertained all day. I arrived one lunchtime to pick Emily up, and all these gorgeous faces around a table stared up at me. I struggled to spot my own amongst the bibbed and food-covered faces.

I was also responsible for taking Emily to get her inoculations. It is not pleasant to have your child happily sitting on your lap, only for someone to stab them with a needle that hurts, so that was my job.

However, whenever Emily was poorly, the nursery phoned Julia first, despite the fact that I often had greater flexibility in terms of getting out of work to see to our child.

On one occasion, they called Julia three times, but because she was holding a clinic at the hospital, she had to say that she would be there when she could; the line of patients outside took priority. They finally called me and I went straight over. Emily's body was roasting hot, but her hands and feet were stone cold. It was the strangest sensation, and it was later explained to me that the body was shutting down the less essential bits to save the core.

Julia arrived pretty much at the same time and we were advised to get medical treatment.

So we went home…

I turned to Julia for medical guidance, but of course she could not act rationally over her own child. She called Sharon, whose A&E experience meant she had a great deal more experience of babies etc. She made it clear that we had to go to the hospital, meningitis being the big fear.

We were whisked through the A&E waiting area with our limp child in our arms, and a syringe of orange medicine was "injected" into her mouth and down her throat. We were then hurried up to the paediatric ward where a couple of junior doctors and nurses took over. Thankfully, however, the medicine had started to kick in and our lifeless child began to look around and perk up.

The doctors then started to fill in forms, which included who we were and what we did. When they discovered that Julia was also a doctor at the same hospital a member of the team slipped away and, hey presto, a few moments later the consultant arrived.

By now, Emily was doing fine, but they wanted her to stay in overnight – even though we were sure this was overkill and probably due to having a medical mum.

Julia was meant to be on call that night at the hospital, and although she naturally wanted to be with Emily, having a sick child was her problem and not one the hospital was prepared to be flexible about; her shift still had to be done.

I stayed on the ward with Emily; my first and only night in a hospital, and Julia came to see us around dawn. Later that morning, Emily was discharged, fit and well.

Another time I was less available. I was just finishing a meeting in Dover at 5pm when Julia called to say that Emily had chicken pox and could not therefore go to nursery the next day. She had full clinics, my family were abroad on holiday, and there was no way I was getting home. Fortunately, Grandma Heather came to the rescue driving up from Blackburn to look after her.

Bedtime went through different phases. One of my favourite times was when she would snuggle in my lap and have her bedtime bottle. Draining it dry, all full and warm she just said, "bed now". I would carry her up and away she went.

The nursery used to let them have an afternoon nap, but she got to an age where she did not need it, or rather she did not want to go to bed until 8 or 9pm. Stopping the afternoon sleep helped. We also discovered that the nursery sang "Oranges and Lemons" to help lull them all to sleep. It was like a magic drug. As soon as I started to sing, Emily would go, "no, no, no," knowing that 10 seconds later she would be out for the count. Amazing.

As time went on, we also learned how to be parents. It is not something you instinctively know; you watch others and learn from your own experiences. You need neither a certificate nor a licence to raise a child, which seems very strange, considering you needed a licence to own a dog at the time, and had to pass a test to drive a car. Raising a child is far harder and far more important.

Figure 10: Emily Jane Dormer

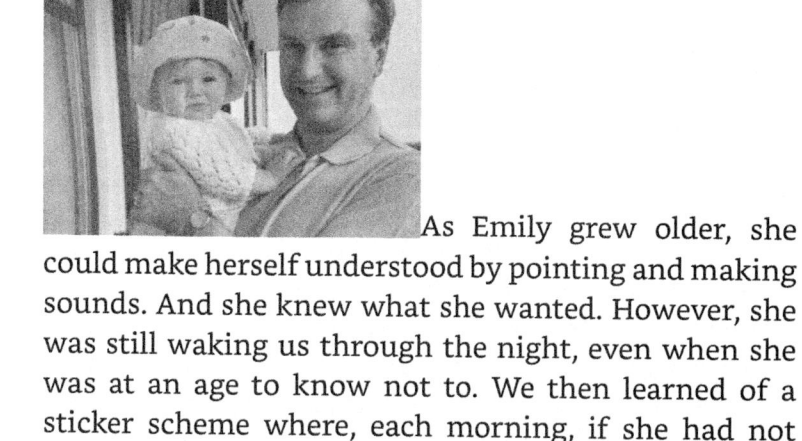

As Emily grew older, she could make herself understood by pointing and making sounds. And she knew what she wanted. However, she was still waking us through the night, even when she was at an age to know not to. We then learned of a sticker scheme where, each morning, if she had not come through and woken us up she got a sticker on a chart. If we went through the whole week with a sticker each day, she got a present on the Saturday. Not many weeks passed before we broke the cycle and the chart became redundant.

She always had a big smile. On one of our early holidays in Greece when she was about six, the kids club had run a drawing competition. About a dozen kids went on stage that evening and a couple of parents were chosen to select the winner: a tough job. Each child was asked to describe what they had drawn. Emily had the biggest smile throughout her time on stage and melted everyone's hearts. When the two parents were asked who was the winner, Emily was chosen, because of her smile.

Central High

When you have been paying £10,000 a year in nursery fees, paying £8,000 for school was not a difficult decision. We looked at Westfield School, and Church High School, but the best was Central Newcastle High School for Girls (later becoming Newcastle High School for Girls).

Julia was very stressed that four-year-old Emily would not pass the selection test. Of course, what she said about what they had had to do during the test added to the stress level. But, needless to say, Emily was admitted.

Emily remained at Central High throughout her schooldays. While there were plenty of the usual falling outs, cattiness, and traumas of growing up, it was a great 14 years for her. We did briefly look at the Royal Grammar School for sixth form, but it was a non-starter.

In Emily's final years, Central merged with Church High, or more accurately took it over. Church had far better main school facilities, so Central school moved into their premises which were a couple of streets away.

Julia and I shared the drop-off and pick-up routines with grandparents from both sides chipping in, in part to help out, but also to have some time with their grandchildren.

I wrote an article for the Guardian in 2015 which described this juggling trick. "Sleepless nights & Compromise: How to Juggle Family and Business"

We attended as many of the school events as possible and I only missed a handful throughout Emily's time from nativity plays through to sports days. Emily never had a starring role in either, but always went about it with enthusiasm.

Musical recitals were similar. Emily tried lots of musical instruments from the ocarina and clarinet, to the violin.

One Chapman House concert we attended was at a busy time for me. I sat down with the programme sheet and was relieved to see under the usual introductory words just 10 recitals, with Emily in the 8th group. It was violin and they just plucked at the strings for four minutes. Not Mozart, but it was my girl and it was wonderful. Just two more recitals, and I could go. Or so I thought. Turning over the programme sheet, I discovered another 25 groups.... and I was trapped in the middle of a row of seats, listening to other people's kids' awful renditions.

When Julia's grandma died and left her a little money we bought a baby grand piano so Emily could learn. I had always dreamt of my children serenading me in my old age. For years, Emily persevered with piano teacher Mr Wood, and did reasonably well, but music was not her forte.

However, performing certainly was. Success at the Ryton festival in her teenage years proved her to be a great orator. She could recite prose or verse with a clarity and a passion that was way beyond her years. She was even chosen to read other students' creative writing at events instead of the authors themselves.

One event, a fashion show, propelled her into the stratosphere but sadly I missed it and it will forever be a hole in my life. Having parents approach me after extolling Emily's performance is a #prouddad time that I will never forget. Fortunately, Julia was there. Emily was co-compering the event but, just as it was about to start, the power to the stage lights went off. Emily's microphone was still working, so she ad-libbed, spoke to the audience, involved them, amused them, and rescued the day.

Emily was never Head Girl, but it was times like this that people commented to me that she should have been.

In her sixth form years, Emily took part in a couple of school productions. Annie was being performed at the Northern Stage Theatre and was very professional and all we knew was that Emily had the role of policeman: a small but speaking part. However, she had saved a surprise for us; she also played President Roosevelt and did so brilliantly. It was a very special moment as she wowed us with her performance.

I am sure she hoped for a bigger role the following year but, again, she was typecast as the policeman in West Side Story.

Debating & Youth Parliament

The natural progression was for Emily to move into debating, and she entered competitions.

Most of the time, she got there by train accompanied by a teacher and other students. She loved the challenge of being given a subject, and no choice of a side to argue, which had not been studied or considered before. With just 15 minutes and no access to the internet or resources to swot up, she had to stand and argue her ground with her natural intelligence, charm and character.

She even spoke at the Oxford Union, and we saw her debate Eton College, where reputedly British parliamentary cabinets are framed.

It was through debating that Emily first set eyes on Alex Yeadon. He was a year older, and a student at Grammar School for Leeds. She fancied him and entered more competitions in the hope that he would be there.

It was, however, an attraction from afar until, a few years later, they met again at Nottingham University. From there on, debating became irrelevant as they became a team and Alex became very much a member of our family too.

Many UK towns and cities have a Youth Parliament. They do not really decide on anything, but they raise issues that are of interest to the younger members of a population and then share these thoughts with elected officials. It is a way of involving young people in our democratic processes, starting with votes in schools for the representative.

Emily stood, and was elected, as one of the Newcastle representatives. While some representatives did next to nothing, Emily (of course) gave it her all.

It was wonderful because it gave her greater exposure to the rich tapestry of individuals that make up our society. She became good friends with one chap, Liam, who lived in Heaton with his grandma as Liam's parents were unable to look after him and his sister.

Emily and Liam went to Canada together for a "Newcastles of the World" conference, representing our city. It was Liam's first time on an aeroplane, at 17, but fortunately Emily could discreetly and reassuringly make sure that the journey was stress-free.

The highlight of the Youth Parliament year is a sitting in the House of Commons during October half-term while the House is in recess. It is chaired by The Speaker, who was at that time John Bercow – someone who was firmly committed to increasing youth interest in politics and the ways of government.

It was broadcast live on BBC Parliament Channel and four debates were held or, more accurately, there were four opportunities for members to stand and speak in that illustrious chamber. Each member was asked to keep contributions to no more than two minutes, and to only stand and seek to be called upon if their part of the country was invited to do so. John would call, "now let us hear from someone from the South West," and then pick one. They were also asked to only stand and seek to speak once.

They all did amazingly well. I lost nearly a day's work as I watched it at my desk, watching Emily bobbing up and down but never getting a chance. When it got to near the end of the last debate, I thought her chance was done. Then John called for the North-East of England and up Emily leapt again. "You, yes you," John said, pointing at her. "You have been leaping up and down all day. You must be exhausted!"

Emily introduced herself from the "great city of

Newcastle upon Tyne," and spoke eloquently and with passion on the Age Pay Gap; not a subject she wanted to speak on, but she did it well.

Then John said, "Members of Youth Parliament, I did not know this was Emily Dormer. I am now going to embarrass her in front of you all. I know her dad. We were at university together, and he is a very clever bloke."

The camera panned-in on the deeply embarrassed Emily: dad job done. But I was proud of her.

That clip from 2015 is probably on the internet somewhere, and sitting on Emily's left is Liam.

The following year, Emily was selected to open one debate from the dispatch box. Although she was allowed notes, she had (of course) memorized it. I can watch these clips back time and time again, and I glow with pride more and more each time.

Emily was keen to get involved in the political world, and I connected her with Lord Shipley who had been on the board of 'ONE North East' with me. She spent the week shadowing him in Westminster, while grandparents Newton stayed at the flat to look over her because she was only 16 years old.

She would phone me up in the evening after each day bursting with excitement about the things she had seen and done. "Dad, I met this lovely lady called Betty in the tearoom today who was really interested and supportive of votes for 16-year-olds. Do you know what she used to be?" I worked out straight away it was former Speaker of the House of Commons, Betty Boothroyd. "How did you know that!!?"

Being old sometimes helps.

She also attended receptions, and John (Lord Shipley) and Lord Stoneham offered her a glass of wine. She replied that she was only 16, to which they insisted she could if she wanted to – in recounting this episode, she made me laugh by highlighting that this was *"peer pressure"* on another scale…

Emily also learned the canape protocol of Westminster at these events. The best canapes always come out *after* the speeches, otherwise people would eat, drink, and run!

Fashion and Young Girl Dreams

When Emily was about 10 years old, all her friends were into a TV programme called, 'America's Next Top Model'.

They all wanted to be models but, being as catty as girls can be, they had obviously knocked Emily down in this regard. I cannot start to imagine how hard this must have been, but Emily seemed to rationalise and resolve this issue in a way that was years above her actual age.

One evening, Emily came to me asking if we could go to the Post Office. "Why?" I asked. "I have these letters to post…" "What letters…?" "Mum knows all about it".

I explained to her that Post Offices are closed at 7pm at night and that I would send in the morning.

When Julia got home from work, I asked about the letters that I now held. She knew nothing about them. One was addressed to a model agency in New York, one in Milan, and one in London. Julia recalled a conversation she had with Emily a week or so before about her owning her own agency if she was not a model herself. However, she had recommended working in the industry first to get experience, and then we would help her set up her own business.

I then remembered having the same conversation with Emily myself and coming to the same conclusion; it is great when both parents are on the same page.

We debated whether to open them but decided no harm could be done so I posted all three envelopes.

A few weeks later a letter arrived for Emily from Sarah Doukas of Storm Model Agency, thanking her for the letter, liking the agency name Emily would have, and explaining that she could not offer work experience until she was 16 years old, but asking her to stay in touch.

As confidence boosts go this was pretty big. Sarah Doukas was one of the biggest names in this industry (having discovered Kate Moss among others) and had written to Emily. Wow.

A couple of months later Emily gave me another letter to post. It was to Sarah Doukas. "What is this about?" I asked. "She said to keep in touch," Emily replied.

So, she was.

A few weeks later a handwritten note came back from Sarah apologising for the delay replying, but pleased to hear Emily's news, and asking if she could email direct in future, as that will be quicker.

A few months later, Sarah Doukas came up in conversation and we realized our little girl was emailing away to one of the icons of the industry without our knowledge.

"I hope you are not bothering her Emily. She will be very busy," we said. "Oh, it is fine," she replied. "If she is busy, she just writes back telling me so."

I admired Sarah so much for this. Emily did a Q&A with her for the school magazine and when I became Chair of the IoD, Emily came to London and videoed an interview with Sarah for an IoD 'Women in Business' conference.

Figure 11: Emily with Sarah Doukas

Emily got the day-off school and we went to Storm's offices in London. Emily was great, but Sarah was amazing. She gave great insights into her business world and added so much value. She picked up Emily's questions kindly and professionally. As an inspiration both to Emily and to me, she was unparalleled.

When she turned 16 years old, Emily did her week with Storm as Sarah had promised she could, but by then Emily had moved on and had other aspirations.

The Newcastle High Newsletter reported:

Emily Interviews Sarah Doukas for The Institute of Directors

Emily Dormer in Year 9 has an ambition to own a model agency. In pursuing her ambition, Emily has managed, by writing regular letters, to strike up a relationship with Sarah Doukas the owner of Storm Model Agency, one of the most successful model agencies in the country (and incidentally responsible for discovering Kate Moss as well as managing Michael Buble!). Sarah gave Emily her personal email address and they now regularly correspond. This prompted Mr Dormer who is the Chairman of the Institute of Directors to ask Sarah Doukas if she would speak at the next IoD Women as Leaders Conference. Sarah initially agreed suggesting that Emily should introduce her at the Conference but unfortunately realised that she is out of the country on the conference date. Eager to help, Sarah Doukas agreed, as an alternative, that Emily could visit Storm and conduct a filmed interview that could then be shown at the Conference.

The filming of the interview took place at Storm"s offices near Sloane Square where Emily met various people from Storm and from The Institute of Directors as well as Sarah Doukas herself. Sarah was charming, natural, and immediately put Emily at ease. The whole interview was completed in just one take and, with Emily's questioning, Sarah gave some wonderful insights to her business and inspirations.

Well done Emily, for being determined and focused in pursuing your ambition. We can't wait to see the interview.

Mama Huhu

Hi, I am Emily.

I am 12 years old, some may say a little young to own a jewellery business! But I find myself with the same entrepreneurial skills as any other stall-holder here at the Mixer Market.

> I decided I would start my business in the October of 2010, whilst on holiday in China. My love for Pandas and Fashion combined created Mama Huhu (Chinese for fashion).
>
> You may think my dad helps out a lot but really he doesn't, he just drives me here and buys the occasional cup of tea. Most of my jewellery is made by myself, but many are from foreign markets.
>
> I also have a segment in my school magazine based on my love of fashion. I called it LabelED and I really enjoy writing it.
>
> I hope to one day to take Mama Huhu global (once I get a driver's licence!) and I will always say Mixer Market is Mama's home.

Originally, Emily started Mama Huhu with a friend, but they lost interest before the market day arrived. So Emily booked the stall herself and made the jewellery.

All I made her do was an Excel spreadsheet for the profit and loss. We gathered together some other bits and bobs to sell (surplus fancy soaps and the like) and had her do a trial set-up, but it was her own doing.

It was a full day affair, held at a Working Men's club in Jesmond and there were dozens of stalls.

She was well supported by family and our friends but still she stood by the stall all day dealing with the general public and at the end made £60 net profit.

A month later, she had another stall and made £25, but the following month she made only £5. She looked rather disheartened at that point; a whole day sat in the stall, and several days' preparation for just £5.

A few days later I tried to comfort her, saying that this was normal in business. Sometimes you win, sometimes you lose. "That is what Sarah Doukas said too," she replied. My admiration of the Model Agent guru grew all the more.

Skiing

Having the Chalet in France boosted our skiing ability.

We had missed one season on the slopes after Emily was born but headed out on subsequent winters.

Emily had been poorly on the first trip so she did not take to classes in Meribel.

In Saalbach Hinterglem, she added some private lessons, which was a great boost, and by Les Deux Alps, she was getting the hang of it.

Morzine, the ownership of the Chalet, and the discovery of BASS ski school changed the world. Skiing four or five weeks every year, with lessons for most of the first few years was transformational.

Eventually, Emily wanted to have BASS sessions not for the learning but because she was so much better than us, that she actually had more fun.

We were once going up the Chamossiere chair lift and saw a group going down the side of a black run (off-piste) from the top. Mad we thought... then spotted Emily in the group.

While Emily is no athlete on the land, she is a ballerina

on snow (forgive the mixing of metaphors). There is nothing I enjoy more than following Emily down the pistes... when I can keep up. It is graceful and effortless. I have to maintain all my concentration though and am often going at my limit. At which point, Emily will decide to change gear and disappear into the distance.

ESSKIA

With skiing very much part of our DNA, Emily and Mark joined the Tigers Ski Club at Sunderland dry slope.

I had skied plastic in my youth and tried again at this time, fell over, gained a bruise on my bum and thigh as big as Northumberland and have not skied an artificial slope again. But they loved it. Having said that, Emily managed to have a major fall while training for a slalom race one evening, breaking her thumb and mashing up her face.

She subsequently broke each of her wrists on snow holidays – once, when snow-boarding – and both times in silly, near-stationary, topple-overs.

There were two other very keen skiers at her school: Milly, who was Emily's age and her younger sister, Lois Jackson. Lois later joined the GB ski team and FIS circuit. You needed three in a school-team, so they were made up.

The English Schools Ski Association championships took us around the UK. The girls easily grabbed 3rd in the country one year and were robbed in Norwich the following year. A small water spray will lubricate the plastic, but they only turned this on after our girls had raced. Our official complaint went unheard.

It seemed like a natural progression for Emily to undertake the BASI ski instructor course with BASS in December 2014 when she was just 16.

I took the week off work and pootled a little on the slopes, although it is no fun on your own, but it was hard graft for Emily. No leisurely lunch stops, and she had classes at the end of the day, followed by homework; this was a proper qualification to teach.

I took another couple of teenagers under our wing who were on their own (a year older than Emily, but still young), feeding them and taking them out for pizzas. One had an apartment in Les Gets and was getting the bus round to the cable car for Avoriaz. Incidentally, his place was next door to TV architect guru Kevin McCloud (Ch4's Grand Designs) who we had seen in the valleys a few times with his family on our trips.

To complete the qualification, they needed to shadow an instructor for 30 hours. Emily completed this over the season and was duly qualified. Not all students did that last bit, and the commitment and dedication were a credit to her, even though she never actually used the certificate - although she chose to do it instead of a Duke of Edinburgh award which involved trekking and camping through the North York Moors in the winter.... So, no fool Emily.

16-18

Emily bagged a great set of GCSEs, and headed effortlessly into sixth form. Emily was always mature for her age, and she was ready for the move up.

Passing her driving test first time was given, although she remains a very slow and steady driver. We bought her a Nissan Figaro for Christmas when she was 17 years old. A cute little car that was only sold in the Japanese market, but they are invariably exported after they are five years old to the UK as there is no second-hand market domestically. They are automatic with a 900cc engine, a removable roof, and are cute. It was Emily all over.

She was adamant she did not want to borrow ID or have fake ID to go pubbing and clubbing before she was 18 years old, giving us as parents little cause for worry as she was so sensible. That does not, in any way, suggest she was not fun. I miss Emily's sense of humour and fun-loving characteristics more than anything, now she is not at home.

She had high hopes of going to Oxford to read PPE, so it was heartbreaking when she did not get a place. Nobel prize-winning Pakistani women education campaigner Malala Yousafzai was at the open day with Emily, and she did get a place, despite admitting her predicted grades were not what she hoped.... but a Nobel Prize trumps a BASI Level 1 badge, for sure.

A couple of hours after Emily had finished her A levels, we headed off on a dad and daughter trip to North Korea, which had started as a joke.

"What are you doing after the exams Emily? Off to Zante with your friends?" No, she said, she was more likely to go on holiday to North Korea.

At the time, tensions were high between the DPRK and the West, with missile-firing and a nuclear programme adding to the strains. But jokingly sending off for information on package holidays to the hermit nation slowly turned into reality and a great week was had by us both.

TV and radio

The DPRK trip led to various radio and TV appearances together from BBC Radio 5 Live, BBC Radio 2 Jeremy Vine Show through to local BBC TV and radio. But Emily has done other media appearances and has always been polished and professional.

The appearance that was the biggest shock happened one evening, just after I had arrived in London. I turned on the TV and BBC's magazine programme, 'The One Show' was in full flight. They had Lord Andrew Lloyd Webber as a guest and had asked people to send in photos of themselves with their musical instrument and the presenter suddenly said as I looked up in shock, "And here, we have Emily Dormer with her violin. Look, Andrew, it only has one string – is that like yours?" And staring at me through the screen was my 12-year-old daughter.

My phone then pinged as friends round the country sent messages about her appearance. Even at home, Julia was shocked.

Emily had just gone into the other room to get her instrument, took a picture and sent it, without saying a word.

MARK DORMER

Having had a painless and straightforward delivery with Emily, Julia said she would happily have another. And nearly four years later, 12 days after the due date, her contractions started.

Julia's mum and dad were by now living across the road in Montagu Court, so they were prepped to come over and stay with Emily.

Julia decided she wanted to watch the end of Coronation Street (probably the last time she ever watched it) before we headed off to the Royal Victoria Infirmary.

Arriving shortly after 8pm, we found ourselves in a queue of women and their partners trying to check into the maternity suite. It was clear that the unit and staff were overwhelmed, and it was the midwife's job to get rid of as many as possible.

As we lived so close by, and contractions were not close enough, we were despatched home at about 11.20pm. It had taken nearly 3 hours to get through the queue. But on getting home, major contractions started in earnest. Instead of just going straight back, Julia insisted on following the instructions given - to call before returning. The screams of pain during the brief call were probably enough for them to agree to her coming back.

It was 11.50pm as I turned into Richardson Road towards the hospital, and I declared that our boy (we knew it was a boy this time) would not be born on the first anniversary of the terrorist attack on the New York World Trade Centre.

One word was emanating from Julia at regular intervals now: it began with an F and ended in a K.

She waddled across the carpark and into the hospital. I found a wheelchair, but she could not sit in it, so she knelt, looking back at me as I ran down the corridor with her screaming, "F**K!". We were lucky it was the middle of the night as we trotted past a deserted café, otherwise we would have turned some heads.

Maternity reception was now empty and, as they called for a midwife, Julia screamed. "I can feel a f***king head…!!"

The receptionist decided to walk (and waddle) us down where we were met by a midwife. By now it was obvious that our baby was on the way out, so we were ushered into a small empty side ward where Julia put her hands against the wall. The call went out for a birthing pack, sheets were thrown on the floor, and at 12.10am Mark Joseph Dormer dropped into this world.

The mayhem of Mark's delivery was quite a contrast to Emily's sedate arrival. My only job for this birth was to get Julia an epidural. I failed, but at least Julia can say she was a proper Earth mother and had given birth with zero pain relief. Because of the carnage of delivery, I decided it was not worth getting involved with cutting the umbilical cord. We had a gorgeous little boy, and everyone was in fine fettle in the end. That was all that mattered.

I went home a couple of hours later and emailed friends about our new arrival. It was funny to get back a couple from the other side of the world instantaneously, yet so many would wake up to our news.

As Mark was our second child, Julia was allowed home the following day – although not quickly enough to her mind. We had Mark with us when we picked Emily up from school, inevitably creating plenty of excitement.

Like Emily, Mark went to Elmfield nursery, but he was a bit older at about four months. It is difficult to know whether he was a better baby or whether we were better, more relaxed, parents. But we lost less sleep with Mark. We were also equally focussed on our little girl so were less neurotic about things the baby was up to. He still deprived us of plenty of sleep but we had learned tricks with Emily that made it much better.

As he got older, having an older sibling created certain challenges, not least in getting him to go to bed. Why should he go to bed when Emily could stay up later? But he had a competitive spirit in him from birth. "I will race you to bed and bet I will win," I used to challenge our little boy. I tried to cheat and get in the way, or hold him back as we ran up the stairs but in the end, of course, he got there first, laughing away.

School

Mark quickly outgrew Elmfield so, when he was still two years old (his third birthday was a week away), he started in the nursery at Newcastle School for Boys

(NSB), or Askam House as it was known then.

He stayed in this group for two years, and thrived. Mrs Donohue was the famed head of the lower years and was a marvel at understanding and getting the most from boys, describing them not as naughty, but curious, or experimental. An interesting analysis, considering Mark had tried to see if a whole new toilet roll would flush down the loo, but only succeeded in blocking it instead.

Mrs Donohue also understood parents. At the welcome evening she explained how we should not believe our boys when they came home and said they played with no-one, did nothing, and ate nothing, all day. For her part, she said she would not believe anything the boys told her, about what they said their parents did.

Mark certainly entered into the mix of school life. One lunchtime, he had done something wrong and the playground duty "carer" (ie a part-time, non-teaching member of staff) asked him his name. He decided to say he was a German boy who had just joined the school and whose English was limited. How could Helmut defend himself? Mark was later found out, but what a canny trick.

As the Royal Grammar School was the best school in the North-East we aspired for Mark to go.

Its first entrance was at eight years old, with a competitive test and all-day assessment, which fewer than 30% of applicants passed. Around that time, NSB had decided to change from being just a prep school to educating through to 18 years old. We were deeply concerned that the NSB report for Mark would be less need to ease up to give me a chance.

Swimming

Swimming is a key life skill and, as I had been a club swimmer, I ensured that both Emily and Mark were enrolled in lessons, and then the Dolphins swimming club in Jesmond.

When big sister does something, little brother wants to follow suit, so I asked Dave who ran the club whether Mark could join. I cannot recall whether he was four years old or five, but he was young and although he came for one session that June, Dave suggested he came back a few months later, in September.

Figure 12: Mark the athlete

The September session started with a "time trial" for all the children – setting a base line for the year ahead, and I was one of the parents who volunteered to man a stopwatch.

The first stroke was butterfly. I looked down my lane and in the middle of the line was Mark. Did he even know how to do butterfly? When his turn came, the whistle blew and six children dived in. Mark dived in a fashion. The little trooper swung his arms over and kicked his legs. He was only a quarter of the way down when the others finished. But he did not give up; he kept on doing his butterfly. When he touched the end all the viewing parents cheered and gave him a round of applause. I pulled him out and gave him a hug. Dave ran over, probably thinking I was being inappropriate hugging a child (only to realise he was my son) but, equally, to congratulate Mark, who was completely unfazed by it all.

Swimming increasingly took over our time in the evenings and weekends as he progressed into the Newcastle City squad.

The team made the national finals in Northampton one year but came eighth. As an individual, he achieved county and regional times and attended galas throughout the north. Many hours were spent by pools in Sheffield, Leeds, and Sunderland, through to Bishop Auckland and Stanley.

These galas always had a 7.30am or 7.45am "warm up in the pool" period, only for the swimmers to then get out and sit around for hours until their race. Whole weekends were spent at a gala for just a handful of races that lasted no more than 20 or 30 seconds. But I would not have wanted to miss one.

I even did school galas in Newcastle and Huddersfield, through to Leeds, and often organised business trips in these cities so that I could go and watch on a Wednesday afternoon.

The RGS swimming pool was 25 yards and was replaced by a new sports centre during his time as a pupil. Mark held 12 school records in the old pool that, of course, cannot now be beaten.

Training started to become six days a week as he hit 13

years old. We only tried the 5.30am sessions a couple of times before deciding that these were beyond the call of duty, but we managed most of the others until we hit a crossroads.

The decision was then made that would change his destiny.

For the last swimming session, we took chocolates for the squad and said our goodbyes. We had spent many hours, if not days, of our lives together. As we gathered in the reception, Mark came out looking like he had been crying and I said as much. My indiscretion was saved by another parent: "the chlorine level was very high in there tonight; I think lots of the kids have red eyes."

As brutal and boring as swimming had become, it was part of our lives and that chapter was closing.

Rugby

In the Autumn 2015, I was walking along Clayton Road in Jesmond to get Mark from school when another dad, David Guthrie, stopped his car to talk to me. David was a seriously good rugby player and, if he had been a little younger, everyone said that he would have been professional player, rather than a policeman. He helped coach his son - who was in Mark's year - at the Northern Rugby Club.

"Can Mark come and play for Northern on Sunday?" he asked. Sorry, I replied, swimming training is all Sunday morning. He then set to convince me to try it once because he knew that Mark was good and might like it. Mark agreed.

Mark loved it, so we tried for six months to run

swimming and rugby in parallel until his swimming coaches took umbrage.

That summer, I went to the South Northumberland Cricket club annual dinner where an All Black (Sean Fitzpatrick) and a swimmer (British female Olympian) were the guest speakers. The contrast was incredible. Sean talked about his commitment to the squad, as well as how he would sweep-out the changing rooms and train hard for the good of the team. The swimmer told us how she would get out of the pool having pushed as hard as she could, and vomit on the side, only for her coach to tell her to get back in and try harder.

It convinced me that the right decision had been made and that I would rather my son be involved in a rugby culture. But I acknowledge that the discipline of the six days/week training regime, and the core strength it developed in him, were positive things in the long run and almost certainly helped him achieve greater heights in rugby.

The big negative was the weather. While hot, steamy swimming pools in June were unpleasant, the driving, freezing-cold rain on windy and exposed rugby pitches in January were miserable. The only advantage I had was not having to run around in shorts.

The Northern Club was run by rugby dads. I was obviously not one of them, having avoided rugby at school; I had not wanted to get hurt by the big lumps that surely wanted to squash me. I did not even know the number of points scored for a try, conversion, or penalty, let alone the complex laws of the game. But they were a really friendly bunch and we had some great times, including a dads and lads tour of Northern

Ireland one year.

The development of these rugby players led to the county selection evening. They had run several training sessions with boys from across the region and we did not really have any expectations, although we did not want our boy disappointed. We had no idea whether he was even in the mix.

We had been told that the successful ones would be given a letter at the end of the session – basically, the decision had already been made. We were stunned when Mark came off the pitch with a sheet of paper and one of the rugby dad's boys did not. We could not squeal with delight or anything like it, but instead slowly headed to the car and home.

Bloomin' heck… he had surprised us again.

Mark went on to play several county games including as Captain for one match. But an even bigger surprise was round the corner.

Sitting at my desk one afternoon my mobile phone rang with an unknown number. "Hello, my name is Aiden McNulty from Newcastle Falcons." I immediately assumed it was a sales call for corporate hospitality, sponsorship, or advertising, but I did not interrupt, and he continued, "We have been watching your son play and would like him to join the Academy. Is he free to come up tomorrow night?" I felt faint. How had this happened? Mark had joined the U16s as one of only two players from his year at school. At that time, NSB had about eight boys with many on a scholarship at the school for rugby (a year or so later, when squad lists came out for the U18s, it was interesting how it featured none of the NSB scholarship boys).

The U16 games were good, but the next level was primarily U18, with only a couple of U17 matches.

Again, our only hope was that Mark would play one U18 game, even if it was just on the bench. Instead, he played them all, starting each bar one. Plus, this was the first year that the U18 squad had made the Academy finals. The games took us to Birmingham, Worcester, Yorkshire, and Leicester.

But the real shock came in early 2020, when Mark was invited to the England U17 camp in Bristol. These were the cream of the crop, and my little boy was in the top 40 in the country. We watched the game, and he did not look out of place - did not try to impress but did his stuff.

COVID interrupted any games and chances to embed his place, but he was invited to the U18 camp that they organised that autumn.

School Rugby

If there had not been an opportunity to play rugby at school, I think it is unlikely Mark would have rugby as his primary sport. RGS is a rugby-playing school with the first team pitch in the centre of the school complex, while football is played on outlying fields.

It was voted Rugby School of the Decade by NextGen XV and its list of professional rugby-playing alumni is impressive.

Mark started to really blossom as a loose-head prop when he was on a tour of Romania at Easter 2015 with the school and led the team out as captain in a couple of matches. We went out and saw a couple of games – in Bucharest and near Brasov in a town called Sacele. The latter were real bruisers, and the whole town seem to come out to watch from their communist-built apartment blocks.

Mark got a major bloody nose from this match, although nose bleeds are not uncommon for Mark, either on or off the pitch.

We missed the last game in Bucharest, but we saw a video on Twitter of him standing in the middle of crouched teammates doing 'the wolf pack'. Basically, it was him chanting and his teammates responding. We had never seen him lead like this before. He was captain of the U16s, leading the team's pre-game warmups and helping them have a great season.

Like Emily with her public speaking, Mark had found his niche. Many parents and teachers approached me saying what a great first-team captain he will make. Chris Ward, a teacher/physio/rugby coach, was so taken by Mark that when he (Chris) left, he bought Mark RGS cufflinks and sent him lovely note, while also sending us a letter.

Dear Mr and Prof. Newton,

I hope this email finds you well. I am emailing in regards to your son Mark. I have taught Mark at school throughout the academic year in both PE and Games, unfortunately however, I will be leaving the RGS at the end of this term. Due to my impending departure, I felt it pertinent to send you an email to let you know that Mark has been an outstanding pupil in every regard. Fundamentally, he has been a model pupil. His commitment, resilience and *determination on the sports field is generally the exception rather than the rule; yet Mark always displays these traits in abundance. He is incredibly well mannered and his attitude to everything is always positive. His maturity in school is there for all to see and he is a role model to his peers. I have spoken to Mark about this in the last few weeks and I genuinely believe he will make a great senior prefect and 1st XV captain in his sixth form years. Perhaps the memory that will stick in my head about Mark, will be his fight and drive on the Romania tour in the final two games. He led the side to win the second half of the second match (despite bruised and bloodied!) and guided us to victory in tricky circumstances in the final game. His love and passion for the school was there for all to see.*

I'll look back on my time at RGS with great fondness and I'll remember the boys that threw themselves into everything for the good of the school; Mark, of course being one of them. I sincerely hope that Mark enjoys the rest of his time at RGS and I'm confident that he will have a great and prosperous future ahead of him; at school and beyond.

Warmest Regards,
Mr C.A. Ward
4-7-18

P.S. I'd like to thank Mark for helping organising my leaving present. The shirt will be framed in due course!

The Lower Sixth

Mark's lower sixth year started badly. In pre-season training he fell badly with someone on top of him and he got in my car outside school saying he had been hurt. I must have said something on the lines of you will run it off, but the pain and disappointment filled reply of "no, it is really bad" struck home. Fortunately, the Falcon's great pastoral care kicked in – and their recommended insurance paid dividends. Falcons, physio, through to scan and orthopaedic surgeon appointment rattled through in days. But no rugby for Mark until the end of October. He missed the big school Derby at Kingston Park against Durham school. In fact, he missed a whole raft of games but he managed to make the St Joseph's festival in Ipswich. As trophy holders it was a tournament with big hopes for them, but sadly they did not win two years in a row.

The rest of the season went well, and propping with U6th Phil Brantingham at school and with the Falcons, paid dividends. Phil switched to tighthead to allow Mark in at loosehead. Phil is an U17, U18 and now U20 England player with a contract for Falcons, Phil's leadership, mentorship and support of Mark is creditworthy.

Figure 13: Mark Dormer - Italy v England U20, February 2022

Skiing

After watching Emily scoot down slopes, Julia and I knew that Mark would want to be on skis as soon as possible so, once he was three years old, he went into the Ski PouPou, or ski nursery in Morzine. When I went to collect him, the teacher stopped me and said, "he is very good."

I'd had the experience of helping develop Emily so I knew that I could take Mark up on a drag lift by fitting him in front of one of my legs (and not on the bar). From skiing between my legs, to holding on to my horizontal ski pole like a bar, he progressed very rapidly, letting go of the pole and free skiing when we had the space to do so.

He soon joined the BASS programme. After each week of lessons, the class were awarded a badge. It started with a snowflake, then a polar bear, then a penguin. Levels 1 to 9 followed.

On our way to collect him after his first week, Julia and I debated whether he would get a snowflake or Penguin. He got a Level Two.

In some regards this was a nightmare, as he progressed through the levels too quickly and was not big or strong enough to get to the next stage. More than one meltdown happened when he was awarded the same badge two weeks running. We had to develop a scheme with the instructor where he got something akin to a Level 4 "double star" to stop him wanting to throw himself off a chair-lift in frustration and anger.

He's now a powerful and confident skier; I just wish I could keep up and follow him off-piste. There is something to having children when you are younger.

Because skiing was such a key part of our lives, Emily and Mark joined Tigers Ski Club at Silksworth dry slope. It was Baltic at times, standing on the sidelines for two hours while they trained in slalom, but it led on to competitions and, as with Emily, we headed-off to races across the country.

Mark became the fastest under 12 in the country when he was nine or 10 years old. It had been a strategic decision to enter a higher age group as we knew the organisers (Lesley Maitland's husband later worked for Rosh for eight years as safety manager) and she tipped us off that the u12s were poor in quality and light in number. But he still skied fastest.

FAMILY HOLIDAYS & TRIPS

Early family holidays with Emily and then Mark included trips to Minorca, Majorca, Cyprus and Greece. These were great in as much as we could chill, and there were always little playmates around the pool, and we added-in the occasional day trip. One of these took us on a tour of the Caves of Drach in Majorca. On our coach was a chap who I was convinced was a doorman at the Institute of Directors. I wanted to go and say hello, but Julia told me that he was on his holidays and to leave him alone.

However, I did not want him to think of me as an arrogant director who ignored him so, in the gift shop, I managed to sidle up to him.

"Hello how are you?" I said, but the man gave no indication that he knew me.

"Don't I know you through work?" I then asked, to which he replied, "What do you do?" I told him I worked for Rosh and mentioned going to the IoD in London.

"I live in Hereford, although I used to be a metallurgist," he explained.

I conceded that we probably had not met through work

but said that it had been nice chatting to him.

"I was an international snooker referee for over 20 years," he then said. Yes, I had seen John Williams putting the balls in place on the green baize for years, so I did sort of know him.

I had a similar famous person interaction some years later on a train to London.

Julia, Emily and I had been to the first of the Take That reunion concerts in 2006. The concert was fantastic, and incredibly, the following day, across and one row in front of me was a member of the band with his manager. I called Julia from the vestibule to let her know that I was on the train right beside Jason Orange, her favourite.

"You have to get his autograph," I was told amid squeals and screams from her and her nursing colleagues at the other end.

I grabbed my chance when the rail staff approached. He was very nice and obliging and, just as I was about to say, "Thank you Jason,"

I saw him sign his name Mark Owen.

The Wonderful World of Disney

I disliked the whole concept of Disney before I had visited it. The thought of spending time in an artificial, glitzy, theme park did not appeal but because Lisa, mum, dad, and so many others had loved it, when Julia and I were in the US on a medical conference, we decided to spend a few days in Orlando.

Wow.

EPCOT, Magic Kingdom - they were fantastic; it was like

being in a movie set. We had a great time, although we did not really see anything that children would enjoy. And then we went again when Emily was still in nappies and wow again. They suddenly seemed to have so much for young children. It was amazing but nothing for older children or teenagers that we could see. You get my drift. Disney's magic unfolded every time and every year.

The staff were not employees but cast members. They were acting every minute of the day, whether they were in costume as Cinderella, or driving a boat on the "Jaws" ride. We bought the children autograph books to collect all the characters' signatures. Again, it was well managed with Winnie the Pooh through to Peter Pan all having discreet minders to make sure the magic was maintained, and they could escape for a break without upsetting their fans. The customer service was amazing on all fronts. Lining up on Main Street for the evening parade, I saw a small child drop its ice cream as it went to sit down on the kerb. Just as it was about to burst into tears a "cast member" rushed over, picked up the mess and two minutes later came back with a fresh ice cream, courtesy of Mickey Mouse.

We were smitten.

We have now visited all six Disney theme parks in the world.

The first to be built was Disneyland in Los Angeles in 1955, and it is clear how subsequent sites took that experience and improved upon it. Alongside Disneyland are neighbouring parks such as California Park and the Studios in LA, which together, add to the whole experience. I took Emily on the "Soarin' over

California" ride when she was only three years old, not realising she was probably a bit young. But she was entirely unfazed as we swooped around in front of the Imax screen, although I spent most of my time concentrating on her, not the ride. I then ran round again on my own, so I could enjoy it properly.

We have visited Disney World, Orlando three or four times, experiencing all the parks over time, including Animal Kingdom, which turns a zoo into a safari, and the water parks such as blizzard beach, which turn a hot day into a surreal snowy scene. The Kennedy Space Centre a couple of hours drive north of Orlando was also a unique experience. There is no way that I would have been a pioneering astronaut in the ramshackle craft which they used to go to the moon. The simulation of the control room re-enacting the Apollo 13 crisis was so well done that it brought tears to my eyes.

We have also visited Disneyland Paris three times, in the summer, October half term when the theme was Halloween, and once before Christmas, when it snowed on Main Street. Well, Disney 'snow'. It looked real but was more like foam bubbles! The French team initially did not deliver quite the same high-quality service levels as their American counterparts.

Whichever Disney park we go to, we always do the Small, Small, World ride. It's naff and dreadfully unsophisticated, but very much part of the Dormer family tradition. When we went to the new Disney park in Shanghai they had a couple of amazing and unique rides. One was the inspiration for the 'Pirates of the Caribbean' film franchise and included massive projector screens which made you feel like you were sailing up to a massive square rigger. The Tron ride at Shanghai was a fast-paced motorcycle ride which I let the children do twice but declined the invitation myself.

We were pretty much the only Westerners at Shanghai and yet, peculiarly, the food offerings were very Western – burgers, sandwiches, salads etc, which meant that the Disney village restaurants were pretty empty in the evenings. China was still in the early stages of opening-up and the Chinese people's exposure to western culture was in its infancy. The state still controlled the internet with platforms such as Facebook completely blocked.

We had heard that the Chinese were bad at queuing at Disney, but this proved unfounded. Disney systems worked well. In fact, the queue is part of the entertainment and considered to be a warm-up for the ride. The only downside was standing behind a Chinese toddler who was being potty trained. They had a flap on the back of their trousers that would be buttoned upwards to show their cheeks, allowing quick and easy deposits whenever they needed to go without soiling their clothes, one supposes. I never saw it in action, but this unusual child-rearing approach was somewhat disquieting.

Tokyo was one of the older Disney parks, so not as sophisticated as Shanghai but, uniquely, Main Street actually had a roof – more like a greenhouse arched cover – and no other park in the world has one like that. Hong Kong was small and, of all of them, the least impressive but because it was on Lantau, and near the airport, we went there for the day (with luggage) prior to our overnight flight back to the UK. It also followed had ever taken. The pilot swept down a gorge with seemingly inches on either side of the spinning rotor blads. I feared one would snag on the rocks, causing us to crash and burn. Needless to say, the pilot knew what he was doing.

We then drove to Death Valley - another amazing experience. We stayed overnight at a lodge in the heart of the valley in 110°F heat. On July 10th, 1913, the hottest recorded temperature at Death Valley topped 134 degrees (57 Celsius) and birds fell dead from the sky. Chatting with the proprietor the next morning I mentioned how we were going to drive over a pass down into Yosemite. "Is the pass open yet?" he asked his colleague. "No, still blocked by snow," came back the reply. We stood at Dante's View in the searing heat not believing we had to take a three-hour detour because snow was blocking our way.

Figure 14: visiting Alcatraz with Emily and Mark, 2008

San Francisco has long been my favourite US city because it has so much character. During various family trips we did the Alcatraz tour, Muir Woods to see the

Giant Redwoods, and Chinatown. But a rarely visited gem was the Cable Car Museum. I discovered how the constantly moving street cables were grabbed by the car operators, and these then pulled the operators up and over the hills.

One year, we took the opportunity to head out to Orinda in the suburbs and meet Mitch, Sue, Emily, Aylsa, and Matthew Cohen at Halloween. It was a wonderful opportunity for Emily and Mark to experience this great American tradition, which involved dressing-up and going from house to house collecting candy with the Cohens. It was a great for us too, because parents were offered such gems as bite-size Tequila jelly.

We then flew from San Francisco to Los Angeles and, with a day to kill, hired a driver to take us around the major sights. The resting place of Marylin Monroe's ashes was a lovely quadrangle space, but only accessed through a small ginnel (alleyway) running between houses, which surprised me. We then did the hand-and-footprint walk and, armed with a map, went searching for famous people's homes.

East Coast USA

Medical conferences also took us to the East Coast, to Boston, which we combined with a trip to New York.

Emily and Mark got a fashionable set of trainers with wheels in the heals – Healy's – which were great in airports and on smooth marble floors because we could just pull them along. Not wildly practical at other times though. While Julia and I had been in Chicago we had seen little girls with bags from American Girl Place. From then on, with our own little girl, we headed for cities with this most unique of doll shops.

October trips almost invariably meant it was Emily's birthday, so we decided to get her a doll in New York. This included matching clothes for Emily, and both the doll and daughter got matching hairstyles in the in-store salon. Mark and I went off to the Fire Brigade Museum during this session but, we all went for lunch in the store's very clever restaurant, which (of course) included a chair for the doll. As a big surprise for Emily, Julia's parents, Heather and Keith, had flown out to join us and met us at the table for lunch – although Emily initially walked right past them, much to our amusement.

Over time we visited American Girl Place stores in Los Angeles (Mark and I went to a motor museum), Miami Beach, and Boston (where we both had to tag along). We also had a cracking week in Washington DC, where we stayed at Kevin's beautiful townhouse in Friendship Heights. Unfortunately, no sooner had we arrived than Kevin had to leave for a business trip to Japan. But he made it very welcoming for us - from leaving rubber lizards and snakes in the kid's bed, through to tear-free shampoo in their bathroom. We also had a tour of the Capitol by a Congressman's member of staff, courtesy of Kevin, and a tour of the White House, which again need a Congressman's sanction.

There is so much to see in DC, so I was able to add more sights, from the Holocaust Museum through to the Treasury where they were reprinting dollar bills. We also managed to get to an American football game to watch the Washington Redskins play (This was before the name was retired in 2020, because of sensitivities over Native American culture, and the team rebranded as the Washington Commanders). Jet lag caught up with the little ones and we had to leave at half-time.

Despite having spent a lot of time in the US, I had never been to a football game, although I had gone with Lindsay to see the Baltimore Orioles play their first baseball game at the Camden Yards a few years before. We had had great seats behind the dugout. I also finally caught up again with Lindsay, after a gap of nearly 20 years.

China

In 2010 we decided the children were old enough to do a more adventurous holiday and booked a two-week tour of China.

Starting in Beijing, it was just us and another extended family from Surrey with our guide 'Kevin'. We had a couple of days on our own before joining up with the tour. Fortunately, we had a briefing from Rosh's QSE manager Phil Sparham's girlfriend who was from Beijing. One thing she taught us was how the Chinese indicate numbers up to ten on one hand – surprisingly useful information which we put to use almost the moment we arrived when we ordered food from a KFC (although chips were not a standard side dish which took us by surprise). But that was pretty much it for Western food during our two-week stay, apart from one other occasion.

We then discovered that, although China was becoming more open, Westerners were still unusual. The children, with their blue eyes and blond hair, drew particular attention and people would sometimes discreetly take their photo. I was lining up a shot of them in front of the Forbidden City when a chap was stood next to me doing the same, taking a picture of my children. Twenty or thirty times over the course of the holiday we would be approached and asked, "Can we have our photo taken with your children?" Once, someone asked us by holding up Google Translate on their phone.

After the first couple of occasions, when it seemed weird, the kids got into the rhythm of it and obliged like seasoned Hollywood professionals. This willingness paid dividends.

We went to see the Bird Cage stadium in the Beijing Olympic Park. It was a £2 taxi ride, which we managed without a problem. However, we encountered problems when we tried to get a taxi back. Every driver wanted to barter for the fare. I insisted that we use the meter (using sign language and monosyllabic words, of course) but each one in the line refused.

During these exchanges, a Chinese family approached us for a photo. No problem of course, and kids went into Hollywood-star mode in a blink. One of the taxi drivers saw this and must have realised we were not that bad. He tapped me on the elbow saying, "Taxi", and took me into the nearby boulevard before waving down a passing taxi. He then had a word with the driver before turning to me and saying, "Meter". It demonstrated very clearly to us that, if we behaved decently towards the locals, they would look after us.

The local silk market was a great discovery, although morally a bit off, as I am sure the designer-label clothes, trainers, ski jackets were not official merchandise. But being able to buy a Spider Ski Jacket for £25 instead of

£250 was too tempting to resist.

The best bit for me and Emily was the bartering, although it was not something that either Julia or Mark enjoyed. Mark was a bit young for this. He wanted a gyroscope and we started to haggle. The trick with bartering is to walk away and then you get your price - but at that point Mark burst into tears, which rather destroyed the gambit. Back then, the stalls were often small; almost like walk-in wardrobes. If you stepped inside the 'wardrobe' and there was a stallholder blocking the entrance, you were essentially trapped. They may typically have been just five feet tall, but they had you.

All the shopkeepers also spoke decent English, using a few key phrases. When I tried to beat them down, they would counter with, "You rob me!" So, I started using that line after hearing their opening offer. It was pure sport and great fun. I managed to get a suit made overnight, while Emily got a lovely silk dress.

Off Tiananmen Square is 'The Hall of the People'. I chatted with Kevin about it, understanding that politics would be a sensitive subject, so I was careful in my approach. It transpired that he had no idea how many 'representatives' sat in their Parliament. He insisted that it was not important to have representation, and democracy was not that good. His argument was that if a road or an airport needed to be built for the good of the nation, then it was wrong to have individual interests get in the way of that advancement. Also, democracy led to people electing leaders like President Bush. That told me.

The Great Wall

Figure 15: The Great Wall with Mark, 2010

It might have been very hot and humid in Beijing, but this was nothing compared to the heat we experienced when trekking the Great Wall.

We had followed local custom and bought small umbrellas to keep the sun off us but, as we headed out towards the countryside, we started to struggle. It was wonderful to be in a completely tourist-free area of the Wall, and seeing it meander through the expansive countryside into the distance was a sight to behold. But, equally, it signalled no end to a long hike in the heat and humidity. Kevin had been joined by 'Uncle Joe', a local guide, for this. Kevin obviously knew nothing about the hike because his answers to questions like, "How much further?" were vague and empty.

When we finally came off the wall to walk through cornfields, and we saw a settlement ahead, we were over the moon. But it just turned out to be Uncle Joe's House. Fortunately, he was able to sell us cans of Coke, 7Up, and bottles of water - I wonder why we went this way? But it did feel surreal to find ourselves sitting on his bed, watching TV with his grandchildren.

The next leg of our holiday took us on an overnight train from Beijing to Luoyang where we saw the Longmen Grottoes – massive carvings of Buddha in the cliff faces of the river bank.

China has a large population, and most of them seemed to be standing alongside us at the station as we carried on towards Xian. And most of them got on our train. It was a massive crush, and Kevin had to work his magic to remove people from our reserved seats but it still meant that all our luggage was piled up on the tables between us. There were hundreds of people in the aisles too but, amazingly, a little chap with a trolley still managed to get through the carriage, selling snacks and drinks.

We were left to our own devices that evening in Louyang so we decided to eat at the hotel. Despite being a big, business-like hotel, the staff still seemed to want to direct us to KFC. Eventually, we convinced them that we were happy with a meal in the hotel restaurant and they took us to a table. The restaurant was quite busy with around one hundred other diners, all Chinese of course. We managed to order food without too much trouble, because the menus had pictures and we settled down for our family meal. We then had an odd feeling as we looked up to the stage at the end of the room. A man had taken to the microphone and was making a speech, inviting a young couple up to join him. All the other tables clapped and laughed. A photographer was going round taking pictures. We were at someone's wedding.

Before long, a young child came up to me and was showing me her English picture book, and we were having our photo taken with members of the family, becoming very much part of the celebratory occasion. I resisted making a speech though.

As we left Louyang on the orbital highway I looked out into the suburbs to see tower block after tower block being constructed. I counted 30 in all, with cranes on top and there were probably many more out of my line of sight. This was happening on the edge of a city which was already home to more than nine million people. China is altogether on a different scale.

The Terracotta Army

Xian is a fantastic walled city, with walls that are 20m high and 10m thick. We hired bicycles and rode around the top. But the main purpose of our visit was to see the Terracotta Army.

Although deemed to be one of The Great Wonders of the World, I found it dreadfully disappointing. Yes, it was remarkable that an illiterate farmer digging his land discovered such an amazing tomb. We even met the farmer, and he signed a picture book for us. But 95% of the army had been discovered in bits and so had been stuck back together for display. Maybe it had been built up to such an extent that it had had too high a bar to jump?

But that evening we went to a park that had huge water fountains that sent water cascading several hundred metres into the air, in time with music that was played over loudspeakers. I had seen a famous (and allegedly the best) fountain display in Las Vegas outside the Bellagio, but the Xian display outdid that ten-fold.

Giant Pandas

Figure 16: Say "Bamboo"

Chengdu was a highlight of our trip because it was a chance to see Giant Pandas in a sanctuary. These seemingly lazy, cute things who could fall asleep on the most precarious of branches were adorable. We had had heard a rumour that for a cash donation of around £100 each, we could hold a baby panda, so I had spent the previous few days running around Chinese cities looking for ATMs and drawing-out funds so we could do this as a once in a lifetime experience. And the rumours were true.

We were issued with polythene bibs and gloves to prevent infection, before we were given a two-year-old panda cub to sit on our laps. The keepers put some honey on the panda's paws and he was more than happy to just sit there, licking away, while we cuddled him.

Food

We had taken both biscuits and plastic forks in case Mark struggled with the Chinese food, but from the start he was fine. Both he and Emily mastered chopsticks, although eating dog was a step too far. On a market tour, Kevin carefully steered us clear of the stalls where dogs were for sale, featuring skinned offerings hanging up on hooks. But he did introduce us to his own favourite dish one lunchtime – 1000-year-old egg. The hard-boiled egg had been fermented or marinated in something that turned it black/dark purple in colour. Mark spat his out, but Emily swallowed her portion like a real trooper. I declined a second helping.

The Karst Mountains

Guilin Province is home to the magnificent Karst mountains, which was the most touristy spot on our travels. But the old streets and buildings were lovely, and our bamboo boat-ride between the hills was amazing. We all had great fun, squirting other boats using a large, syringe-like, water pistol. At one point, we stopped at the side of the river and a bent old lady sold us some jewellery she had made – or more simply, polished stone. Emily got an orange fish that she wore for years, losing it several times and then finding it again in the most unreal places. This made us believe them to be a lucky charm. For example, she lost it at Disney before finding it, some hours later, on Main Street USA. Then, sadly, one day the fish was lost again. We are still waiting to find it and I am sure we will.

The fishermen on the River Li here were made famous by a HSBC Bank TV advert. Traditionally, they went out in their boats at night, using a bright light to attract the fish. They had trained cormorants with a strap around their necks that dived off the boat and caught the fish. They could swallow the small fish but not the big ones, which were scooped out of their mouths by the fishermen. It was an amazing experience but, of course, now only put on for tourists rather than a way of life.

The Final Stop

Our final stop was Hong Kong, which felt dreadfully Western.

We did all the key sights and then had a last-night, celebratory meal at a great restaurant in One Peking called Aqua, featuring staged dining area that looked out over a laser show which was happening on Hong Kong Island. It was the most expensive meal we have ever had, costing around £100 a head, which included a pizza for Mark. However, he spotted Julia's steak, liked the look of it so, as mother's do, he swapped plates.

China was an amazing experience for us all. We packed so much in, from cookery lessons and calligraphy lessons, to bike rides into the countryside where we saw the classic scenes of workers bent double in paddy fields. We never really stayed anywhere more than a couple of days, so it was exhausting in that regard. But, most importantly, the children had learned so much (as had I). The overriding lesson, and one that we still carry with us today, came from Kevin our guide who said, "It is not better, it is not worse, it is just different."

Dubai

I never wanted to go to Dubai; it was too fake and artificial for me, but we went because Julia wanted to ride camels through the desert for her 40th birthday. So, we did just that, and then returned repeatedly over the next few years because we enjoyed it so much. We loved the high quality of the accommodation (Jumeriah Beach Hotel) the quality of the food, and the quality of the service (staff get deported if they lost their employer sponsor). When we mentioned to Reception that it was Emily's birthday, they not only rocked up with a cake at breakfast, lunch, *and* dinner, but there was also a handful of staff with a guitar to sing 'Happy Birthday' each time.

The Wild Wadi Water Park was far more than just a swimming pool. It had rubber-ring rides with jets of water that pushed you up before you slid down a myriad of tubes. Of course, I also had to try what we called 'the death slide', just for the children's entertainment. This was a near vertical 50m drop, where you got a wedgy that was close to a colonoscopy. I hate things like that, but when your children say please, what do you do?

The shopping malls were also outstanding. I once sat next to Gateshead's Metro centre manager and asked how the Mall of the Emirates compared. The Metro Centre's footfall was 5,000 people per hour, while

Emirates Mall was 1,000 people per hour. It seems like a different league, but the key statistic was not that, but the average spend per head. The average spend at the Metro Centre was £94 per person, whereas at the Emirates it was £6,550 per person. Its designer shops were also huge, and obviously the clientele was very wealthy. We even skied the indoor snow dome once, even though it was 80°C outside.

Usually visited Dubai in either May or October, although once we went at February half-term when Mark was playing cricket for the school in the Emirates, and we went to watch a couple of games. The green cricket pitch seemed very odd within the expanse of desert, but we were told by one school team that they played against that the school paid £300/day to rent the pitch. Keeping this patch of earth green meant keeping it watered, at a considerable cost. We also visited in August. We were transiting from the Maldives, and would have required a night at the airport hotel, but we decided instead to spend a few nights at the Jumeriah Beach. It was hot. Very hot. And you definitely needed to be a mad dog to go in the sun at midday. But the bonus was that we were upgraded to the Beit al Bahar Villas in the hotel's grounds. It was pure luxury with our own plunge pool, butler, and dining room with regular snacks and treats provided. We even had our own cabana reserved by the executive pool. Very fancy.

On our first visit, I had been surprised to discover that the sea was warmer than the swimming pools but the pool manager explained to me that they chilled them to make them nicer for guests. The pools were also adorned with dozens of lifeguards; so much so, that it would be impossible to drown. We were once at The Lazy River at Wild Wadi, walking towards an exit ramp, when a man got a bit close to our little group. I looked at him sternly, but he said to me quietly, "Please ignore me, sir. I am here doing a test for the lifeguards." The next minute, he was lying on the floor of the pool holding his breath. Seconds later, the lifeguard whistled repeatedly, then jumped in to save him.

Did they pass the test? It was a very impressive examination of quality control.

Israel

We started in Tel Aviv and it was cosmopolitan, liberal and modern. There was a rainbow beach and scantily clad young beach goers promenading along the sea front. We hired bicycles and pootled up and down the promenade too, wandered around the shops, and it felt like thousands of others cities. At the end of our week we were in Jerusalem after a short tour of the country and despite being under an hour's drive from Tel Aviv, Jerusalem felt like a different time zone.

As we had arrived at the start of the Sabbath our hotel had one of many unique features to the Jewish faith. Not being allowed to work, drive, or even cook, from sunset Friday until sunset Saturday, the hotel was geared around this doctrine. The principles include not completing an electrical circuit such as turning on a light or pressing an elevator button. So one of the hotel lifts automatically stopped on every floor going up, then every floor going down. Such adherences are alien to our lifestyle and a great education on cultural diversity.

Our tour guide, who drove us all week, was a 40ish ex-Mossad operative. He was really perceptive -- from my questions about the lack of security in Tel Aviv – "it is there, you just cannot see it" through to his early question on how religious we were. As non-church goers we asked for a light touch, but we are very interested in the historical aspects. When we later saw some tour groups praying at the stations of the cross in Jerusalem, and singing hymns in Bethlehem, we are glad he checked our level of devotion.

We travelled north up the coast to the lovely city of Haifa then across to the Sea of Gallilee. Again, the religious branding started to appear with the fossilised remains of a boat "from the era of Christ" was on display. Anything vaguely 2,000 years old was given the veil of being blessed by Jesus. We stayed in a beautiful lodge overlooking the sea and the serenity and beauty was palpable. The contrast was stark just a few miles away.

We climbed to a United Nations look out post that overlooked Syria. It stood high on a hill and we were in concrete walkways and pill boxes so were safe, but below across the border we could here gunfire in the Syrian town as the civil war played out. It was the first time I had heard shots in anger. It was chilling.

Our trip was fascinating in many ways but so much because of the familiarity of names from growing up and having Religious Education classes for so much of my education. Jerico, Nazareth, Mount of Olives, Bethlehem are all familiar. The story of Masada was not however. The incredible fortress perched high on an isolated rock in the barren and sandy landscape was phenomenal. The 960 Jewish people who were besieged there by the Romans but chose mass suicide rather than be taken. The Romans had built a ramp to gain access to the walls. We took a cable car.

The Dead Sea followed and the scenes of extremes continued. It is remarkable how you float in the heavily saline water. It is impossible to sink. Although warnings were a plenty about not swallowing any of the water otherwise you would be very seriously ill.

The end of the trip in Jerusalem encompassed everything about this part of the Middle East. A wall and wire separated Bethlehem, and our guide, Yulav, was not allowed to pass across to the other side. But we were sent through and met a Christian guide on the other side, who took us to Christ's alleged birthplace, before taking us back to the crossing (via his brother's gift shop). The divisions continued with the Temple on the Mount being holy to Muslims and Jews a like a fragile peace hangs over the area. Security here was visible and heavy. We went to the wailing wall – women to the left and men to the right, and stood with our hands against the wall as the faithful and orthodox Jews "wailed" either side of us. This was the closest they could get to demonstrate their devotions. We witnessed 4 walking through the grounds of the Temple with four Israeli soldiers guarding them. They were forbidden from praying on this walk but you could apparently hear them muttering as they went past. Yulav scurried us away at this point in case any of the young Muslim's nearby decided to start throwing stones at them. The tension in the air was thick and nervy. Checkpoints entering both the wall and the Mount had made sure we were not carrying religious materials as much as anything more sinister.

Jerusalem had a far greater presence of Orthodox Jews. We were told that if you accidently drove down some of their streets on the Sabbath you could find your car being hit by bricks. The extremes of religious faith were everywhere. Including the Christian community with their prayers and singing. So we were worried we would struggle to find a good restaurant on the Sabbath which also happened to be Emily's birthday. But even the agnostics were catered for. The Old lady owner was a real character too, pulling up a chair to our table to sit and write down our order of food.

We stayed at the King David in Jerusalem. Famous for being bombed out repeatedly, although fine and grand when we stayed there. On our floor the Italian President was staying too. When we left on our final morning for a very early flight we dropped a bag, causing the security guards to jump in alarm further down the corridor. So we nearly got shot in Israel.

Maldives

These beautiful islands are probably among the most stunning holiday areas in the world.

Arriving by sea plane, our island was about 300m x 100m and still managed to accommodate everything we (and another 100+ guests and staff) needed.

There were two stand-out occasions. The positive was scuba-diving with Emily. We had had lessons in the UK before leaving and completed our open-water qualification in the Maldives. Diving down to nearly 40m, to a packet steamer wreck, was magical. The water was warm and clear, and we had many great dives.

The negative was Julia's mum, grandma Heather, nearly dying. This had been organised as an extended family holiday with the four of us, Sharon, Anna, Heather, and Keith. The first night we were there, Heather was looking for the bathroom and, in the dark, missed the door but toppled down the adjacent stairs. It was 05:00am when Sharon banged on our door. Julia was so convinced that her mum would not make it that she insisted I woke-up the children so they could say goodbye as staff carried her off in a stretcher. Fortunately, Sharon kicked into A&E doctor-mode and accompanied Heather and Keith on the two-hour boat ride to the hospital on mainland. There was no way that Heather could have gone in a sea plane.

Meanwhile, the hotel staff were great. They gave the group a wad of cash and a local mobile phone, so we could get updates from Sharon throughout the day, all of which amazed us: no fractured skull, no broken arm, and no broken hip or leg. It was after dark when they eventually got back to the hotel. Heather was black and blue; dazed, but OK. Sharon had exhausted herself that day and, as she handed care over to Julia, she sat down next to me and cried. She had suddenly stopped being Dr Shenfine, and could at last - 14 hours later - be a distressed daughter. Over the next two weeks, Julia and Sharon forced Heather to do various exercises – "wiggle your fingers, or they will have to be amputated" – but she could not walk for days and had to have room-service for half the holiday.

Mauritius

Another beautiful island and one where Mark attained his own open water diving certificate... or so we thought.

A year later, when we were heading off to Australia and planning to dive The Great Barrier Reef, we went for our refresher in a swimming pool and discovered that the man who examined Mark was not qualified to do so. Poor Mark had to do his open water tests in the freezing North Sea in a mad panic before we headed Down Under. But we enjoyed the diving once we got there, including a magical moment where dolphins danced and raced beside us, as we powered along in the boat.

I also took Mark out in a small Laser dinghy. It had been many years since I had sailed and, because there was a good breeze, I managed to capsize a few times. We easily righted the boat, but his confidence in me as a captain was destroyed. Another afternoon, we went fishing in a motorboat one afternoon and, while I caught nothing, Mark and Emily were reeling-in the fish. One game where I could not go too far wrong was golf. There was a free-to-play course next to our resort, so I played many rounds with Mark during our stay. It was lovely dad-and-son time, although it was probably the last time I beat him. The competitive spirit kicked in and, by his later teens, I was well and truly in second place. And happy to be there.

Japan and Australia

The year I turned 50, we booked a three-week trip to Japan and Australia.

We flew into Osaka and headed to Kyoto, where we had dinner with a Maiko, or trainee Geisha; a very expensive, but an unparalleled, experience. Our trainee Geisha was a teenager and, through an interpreter, we learned about the disciplines and training it took to become this most unique servant. She played an instrument to us, sang, and played games with Mark and Emily in our private dining room as we sat on the floor. The 10 course-meal was beautifully and delicately presented, but unfortunately, each included a fish element which none of us ate much of... and Mark ate nothing. Even dishes we vaguely recognised were covered in fish juice. One course was a whole fish, six inches long, and included head, tail, innards, the lot. We were politely advised to eat it all, but Emily was the only one brave enough to do so. I nibbled round the belly.

We rode the bullet train to Tokyo and toured all the key spots but the real highlight was our Teppanyaki meal, which we had on our last night. We sat with a couple of old Japanese ladies as we experienced the theatre of this most amazing fayre for the first time and loved it.

The oddest thing happened that evening though, inasmuch as it was someone's birthday at another table and when they brought the cake with candles out no one sang. Do they not sing happy birthday in Japan? We found the Japanese to be a very polite and formal nation. Taxi drivers wore white gloves and hats. We had to hand over a credit card using two hands rather than one, otherwise it was deemed impolite.

But, on one occasion, their adherence to rules left a sour taste. We were staying at the large Okura hotel, and I asked if we could use the swimming pool showers in the late afternoon after we got back from Disney, even though we will have checked out in the morning. But the answer was 'no' because we would have checked out. Nothing changed their mind – such as offering to share towels – regardless of how many different managers I spoke to. We had checked out.

The contrast was the following day.

We flew overnight to Cairns and drove up to Port Douglas where we booked our Great Barrier Reef diving trip for a few days later. Having arrived, we discovered we needed towels, but because we were about to head up to the Daintree Rainforest, we were not going to be able to check-in to our Port Douglas Hotel before we set off to go diving. Julia was all for buying towels with our experience of Japan still front and centre. But I decided to ask at our Port Douglas hotel if we could borrow towels in advance. The receptionist – who looked uncannily like Dwayne "The Rock" Johnson - had no hesitation and gave us four large fluffy towels.

"Would you like a credit card impression?"
"No."
"Would you like my name?"
"No, you look like an honest-type of guy," he said.

I was pleased as punch, but also mentioned this in many Institute of Directors speeches on customer service, from then on, using this example to show how companies can empower staff and delight customers.

Interestingly the Barrier Reef dive was not the best I

had had. Maybe because it was overcast, maybe because my expectations were so high, but compared to the Maldives and Mauritius, it easily ranked third. Fraser Island was interesting, although we did not see any of the famous dingos. But we did experience landing and taking off at one of the only two official airports in the world which are actually beaches, and we had a circuit over the island. The other airport beach is Barra in the Western Isles of Scotland. From here, we also took a boat trip to see minke whales. What magnificent beasts, whose natural curiosity made them come right up to our boat and poke their heads up to see us. Truly magical.

Ayres Rock, or Uluru, was equally stunning. The massive flat and barren landscape could be seen from the aeroplane, and this huge rock stands out.

We had a dinner under the stars one evening, and an early start another day to see the sunrise over Kata Tjuta, or the Olgas. But the sheer vastness of this barren land dominated. Julia was giving a lecture at Griffin University near Gold Coast, which also happened to be the base for the UK TV show, "I'm a Celebrity, Get Me Out of Here." As a treat, we stayed at the Versace Hotel where the evicted celebrities stay. It was glitzy, but not that special.

Sydney was our last stop and the real highlight was walking across Harbour Bridge. Not on the footpath, but over the top of the arch. The views were stunning, but I was also impressed with how they kitted people out with coveralls, hats, and even handkerchiefs, all of which were attached together so that nothing could drop onto the folk below. The Park Hyatt Hotel offered great views across to the Opera House, but also had a celebrity guest, who we saw in the bar. A giveaway was all the fans and paparazzi outside. Queen were in Sydney for a concert and Brian May was staying here.

Our own claim to fame came on a wet morning on Bondi Beach. We were stopped by a young woman who had clearly spotted we were Brits from a mile off. We were asked to give our thoughts to camera on the costs of data and mobile phones while on holiday. The interview was later used on a Three mobile web advert.

South Africa

As Julia and I had adored our Kenyan safari, we wanted the children to experience the same.

On April 29, 2011, Prince William married Kate Middleton, which gave us an extra Bank Holiday, just after Easter (22-25 April). This meant we had enough public holidays clustered together around the school holidays to give us the chance to go to South Africa without using too much of Julia's annual leave allowance.

It was also a great opportunity for little (and big) boys to have their first flight on an Airbus A380 – so of course, once aboard, we had to do the full circuit - down the front stairs along to the back and up the rear stairs, to get back to our seats.

Figure 17: Kwandwe Game Reserve

Kwandwe was a private game reserve in the Eastern Cape and was the perfect introduction. Our guide, Alistair Lamonte, captured Emily and Mark's interest in everything from lions to dung beetles. We can also now tell the difference between black rhino poo and white rhino poo. There are sticks in the black rhino poo, because they eat bushes, while white rhinos stick to grass.

They thought it was all as magical as we had, even when the wind whipped round from the South (next stop Antarctica) and we all nearly froze to death in the back of the open top Land Rover, despite having blankets wrapped round us.

I had assumed that Africa would be hot, and all I had apart from shirts was a dress jacket. I ended up buying a fleece while we were there - and took considerable grief from the family for my optimism.

We spent some time on the Garden Route before arriving in Cape Town on the day of the Royal wedding. We caught some of the ceremony on the TV screens at the airport and watched the rest when we got to the

Mount Nelson Hotel.

The food quality and quantity on the V&A Waterfront, a major destination located in the oldest working harbour in the Southern Hemisphere, impressed us, but with Table Mountain as the backdrop, it was awe-inspiring.

Figure 18: Table Mountain, 2011

We toured Robbin Island where Mandela had been held and soaked-up the views from Table Mountain.

We enjoyed hearing the local music that was being played in the streets and thoroughly enjoyed our time in the city.

Although not as dangerous as Johannesburg, Cape Town was still regarded as hazardous, although it felt safe to us. We walked through a park much to the concern of the hotel receptionists, and we just took a minibus ride for a few rand into town from Table Mountain... even though it was almost certainly not licenced etc. Were we lucky, or too trusting? We survived without issue and had a great time.

A few years later, we returned to South Africa and I fulfilled one of my lifelong dreams. As boys, Richard and

I had gone to the cinema to see the film Zulu, which told of the bravery of the British soldiers, fighting against all odds as they defended the mission station at Rourke's Drift. Added to that was the honour of the Zulus who in the end let them live and saluted their fellow brave warriors. It was captivating.

We stayed at Fugitive's Drift where David Rattray, one of the great historical authorities on the Zulu wars, had lodges. Unfortunately, he had been murdered by robbers a year or two earlier, but his son, Andrew, continued the business.

The violent problems of South Africa had been evident on our five-hour drive from Johannesburg. We had organised a driver for the journey and, enroute, we stopped at a small settlement for some lunch. It was not much more than a crossroads with a KFC, and nowhere near a big urban centre, but the KFC restaurant had security on the door and steel bars that kept diners on one side of the counter.

Our battlefield tour started with a Zulu guide taking us to Isandlwana where the conflict began. Let me be honest here, the British colonisers had been arrogant and horrible. They went out of their way to pick a fight with the Zulus, who had been peaceful for decades. But 20,000 Zulus slaughtered the 2,500 British with ease, despite having only spears and cowhide shields against the British rifles and cannon. Piles of white stones marked the spots where the soldiers fell, making their last stand. Our guide told the history so well, without prejudice or comment. Mark was so taken by him that, after learning about his family, he suggested (off his own back) that he would like to give his Newcastle football top to him, for his son.

That evening, I asked Andrew, our guide, what time we were departing for the Rourke's Drift tour the following day and he told me it would be 3pm. We asked if we could go at 9am because we will be up. No, came back the reply - the battle of Rourke's Drift started at 3pm, and so shall we. This set the tone for one of the most incredible tours I have ever done. We slowly walked round the site, occasionally sitting for a time in chairs as Andrew described the unfolding battle, including the stories of the individual soldiers at the ramparts. While the setting was obviously different to the film set, the layout, and buildings were all there. It was so moving that tears started to well in our eyes. Mark looked at us, as only a young child can, and asked, "Why are you crying?"

The 100 or so men who successfully defended the mission against the thousands of Zulus on January 22-23, 1879 went down in history, and 11 Victoria Crosses were awarded in the aftermath; the largest number ever given for valour in one battle. Our tour also took place on Emily's birthday. At dinner that night we had a power cut, so we dined by candlelight with 10 other people on one long table. When the pudding came out, I was given one, but not Emily. I kept moving mine to Emily, and the staff moved it back. I then realised why, because they emerged from the kitchen with a special one for her, complete with a candle, while singing Happy Birthday in Zulu. The most memorable birthday rendition that I have ever heard.

We then went on to the beach north of Kosi Bay with the mission to see the giant turtles laying their eggs on the beach. We drove up and down the beach in jeeps each night of our holiday to no avail, until the last night. The giant beast was oblivious to us as she dug her hole in the sand, laid her eggs and then crawled back into the sea. We kept back until she was laying but were able to be right next to her with infra-red torch which illuminated the nest.

India

I had loved my first trip to India 25 years earlier and wanted to share the experience with the rest of the family, but concerns about Delhi Belly, the begging, and poverty etc., made them reluctant. They finally agreed, but only if we flew Virgin Upper Class. Deal! The Virgin lounge is the most innovative I have ever been in, with a pool table (great when you have a bored young lad with you) a nail bar, which was Emily sorted, and even a barber where Mark had to have his hair cut, for the second time in a week. We started in Delhi before heading up by train to Agra and the Taj Mahal. We hired a driver, Sanjay, and a minibus for the week and he drove through the night from Delhi with the bulk of our luggage to meet us at Agra.

Sanjay became part of our family and the kids wanted to take him home. Indian roads are different in that highway rules are optional, particularly if you drive a big vehicle. We would be on a main highway only to be confronted by someone coming the wrong way down our carriageway or find them stationary in the outside lane having their gear box changed.

Potholes were normal, while camels and elephants were part of the natural fabric. But Sanjay navigated it all with ease. A motorbike nudged us once – which upset him dreadfully -- but he was always cool and immaculate. He greeted us on return from a tour of a red fort or historic monument with cool towels to wipe our hands and face, and cold bottles of water. We arrived in India in the run-up to Diwali, the Hindu equivalent of Christmas. As we were heading back to Delhi near the end Sanjay asked permission to stop at a town so he could handover presents to his family. He rendezvoused with a relative in the main street and the handover took less than a minute. He was so grateful. We appreciated that he would have an hour or two's drive to get back to his family on the actual celebratory day, so we organised for him to take us to the airport earlier than necessary. He desperately did not want us to do that, but we insisted.

At the airport, I gave him an envelope containing a tip. Tipping is a key process in India and I had researched the amounts before leaving home. We were very generous with Sanjay. I turned round as we entered the terminal and saw him jumping up and down waving both his arms in glee. Happy Diwali. Once again, Emily was celebrating her birthday on this trip and Sanjay bought her an alabaster elephant (and asked my permission to give it to her). Incredibly kind. We had bought one ourselves from a young lad. We met him as we were heading to a monument, and he asked me to go to his store, which I said we would on the way back. "Ahh, you are English. Mr BBC!" he said. We had a little chat and carried on smiling.

On our return he spotted us in the crowd and came up, asking politely, "Mr BBC, you will come to my shop now?" His shop was off the main drag and being minded by his father, who took the covers off his display as we approached. We bartered for one of his small alabaster elephants, paying £3 or £4, which I knew it was probably a bit steep, but I told the father how proud he should be of his very polite son, and did not mind the premium. I am sure Sanjay paid a fraction of the price.

I was ready to be disappointed by the Taj Mahal. It is rated as one of the greatest sights in the world; surely it would disappoint? But it did not. The majesty and stunning beauty was even better than expected. We were staying at the Oberoi where you could just see it through the haze too. Well worth the premium and a special birthday treat for Emily.

A tiger safari in Ranthambore finally yielded results on our fourth game drive – some families we met did not see any tigers at all. Unlike in Africa, wildlife was in short supply so seeing this majestic and beautiful cat was all the more special. The guides were not allowed radios to communicate sightings between them (again, unlike Africa) so we would stop and listen to nature's way of communicating the presence of the beast, as birds and smaller creatures squawked alarm calls to each other. We glamped in Ranthambore, staying in a tent with a flushing toilet. In fact, everything we did on this trip was of a high standard. Every meal stop or rest stop we heard the retort, "Very clean food and very clean toilets," and they were. All spotless.

Jaipur was a former palace, and had been featured in the drama series, 'The Far Pavilions'. We ate all our meals outside in the courtyard, and at one breakfast a massive monkey jumped onto our table. It was the size of a 3-year-old child and, while we all screamed, it sat there taking our croissant until the staff rushed out and shooed him on his way.

Our second trip to India had a couple of practical purposes. Mark wanted to go to an Indian Premier League T20 cricket match and, with my business connection to paint manufacturer SK Formulations in Mumbai, the trip was logical and my contact, Sachin, was able to organise tickets for us. Julia and Emily went straight up into the Western Ghat while Mark and I stayed one night by the Wankhede Stadium. The seats were not really designed for big fat Westerners, so I had to sit forward while Mark sat back, and every so often we would swap round. The cricket was fast and furious, with Chenai seemingly too far behind Mumbai to win with two overs to go, so we decided to head off and beat the crowds – not least because we were still tired from the overnight flight. But when we got back to our room, we saw the last over on TV with Chenai's batsmen blitzing Mumbai's bowlers to win. What a finish. And we missed it!

Our first stop on the Western Ghat was in an eco-lodge. It was more basic than we were used to, but very dramatic with a crow's nest platform on the roof that offered a view over the surrounding forests and across the hills. We then proceeded to the Hilton, which was more our bag. We spent the last couple of nights at the Taj Hotel by the gate of India. Mumbai had changed since my visit 28 years earlier. There were no beggars, and there seemed to be more wealth. The Dhobi Ghat laundry was the same, and we saw the Dabbawallas delivering their lunch tins, but there were not the cheap clothing markets or as many offerings as my previous visit. We had curry, or Indian food, for lunch and dinner every day for a week and as much as I enjoyed it, I desperately needed a change by the end as I was starting to get heartburn. Unfortunately, I have suffered ever since.

Sri Lanka

Sri Lanka is India done light. Construction workers wear hard hats, but wellies are worn not safety boots. The people are just as friendly and charming, but they are less in your face. Maybe because it is less crowded? One fascinating fact told to us by our guide were the top contributors to the nation's economy. Top of the list were expats sending money home, followed by tourism, tea, and gemstones. We had a lovely week, staying by the ocean near Galle, and the food was extraordinary. The croissants were better than anything I had tasted in France, and the steak just melted in my mouth. It was all owned by the Dilmah Tea family and one day we saw the old gentleman founder, who happened to be visiting. He was patron of a great place.

We went on a leopard safari in the Yala National Park where we saw many beautiful creatures, along with elephants bathing in a creek. One evening, after dark, our guide took us to a small lake by our lodge and shone a big torch over the water. Eyes glistened back: crocodiles. After that, we took up the offer of having a member of staff escort us back to our lodge after dinner. Before our arrival, I had been sceptical of the wisdom of spending two nights at a tea plantation. But it was a stunning stetting, at around 1600m up in the hills, with incredible terracing of tea plantations looking down onto a lake. And the food and service at the former plantation manager's house exceptional. I could have stayed a fortnight.

We did the compulsory tea factory tour, but the moment that touched me the most was when we independently followed a trail through the plantation. We came across a group of old lady tea-pickers having their mid-morning break, so we said hello, only for them to offer us a place beside them to share their food. These ladies were poorer than I can imagine but prepared to share what they had. Humbling.

While Sri Lankan roads were better than many Indian roads, the route up to the plantation was still quite hairy. A bus coming down the narrow windy road would dominate 75% of the tarmac. How we were never pushed over the edge defeats me. Even on the coastal roads, the traffic was scary, especially when one bus decided to overtake another, and they would only just get past while an oncoming bus careered towards them.

Thailand

The Soneva Kiri island is Thai although it looks over to Cambodia. We flew there on the resort's private plane, landing on the private airstrip. Its selling tagline was 'no news and no shoes'. It was a place to chill, and we did. We had a massive lodge complex with different buildings for each of our rooms, a sitting area, and our own pool. Each lodge had been provided with a golf-buggy and it would be mysteriously turned round if I failed to reverse park it, giving us an easy exit.

Our butler, Amp, was most concerned when we did not ask her to unpack our bags or, indeed, do very much for us at all. But this was not our style. Although when

Mark lost his ball under the decking we did decide to call her – and despite reassuring that there was no rush, she arrived within minutes with two others to rummage and retrieve the ball. Bangkok had changed since my visit many years before. The new rapid transit system had made Tuk Tuks redundant and the roads much more tolerable. The MRT station was across from the Peninsula where we were staying; it was clean, efficient, and the staff were terrific. I bought our tickets from a booth before we headed through the barrier, only to be chased down by the ticket-clerk. I thought I had underpaid him, but the opposite was the case and he had run after me with about the 20p change he had not given me.

Our love of great restaurants took us to the highest open-air restaurant in the world – Sirocco. We later saw it in films such as The Hangover, and the views and experience was amazing. But by heck was it pricey. We had a few trips from the Wats, to the Klongs, and a train trip straight through a market where stallholders had to fold back as the train approached. Here our Buddhist guide spotted a fish stallholder about to bludgeon some live fish in a bucket before displaying them. She insisted on buying the kicking fish and then headed to the river and released them.

Singapore & Vietnam

Our final trip to the Far East as a family group included Emily's boyfriend Alex. We started in Singapore, staying at the Marina Bay Sands Hotel with its extraordinary rooftop pool, which spans the three towers.

However, we had an even bigger treat on check-in. The

Marina Bay Sands is a large hotel so we asked the receptionist if our rooms could be close together. He did better than that, taking us to the Presidential Suite. As upgrades go, it was stunning. I ts floor area was probably bigger than our home. The master bedroom even had 'his and hers' bathrooms. Yep, bathrooms, not two basins, but whole bathrooms each.

We had a hair salon, a kitchen, a dining table seating 10, a grand piano, a gym (which Mark used) with sauna, a multimedia room with karaoke, an office.... And picture windows overlooking the city. We happened to be there on Independence Day so had the glory of great views of fireworks and flypasts too.

In Vietnam, at Hoi Ann, we bought handmade shoes and suits at great prices and chilled on the beach. It was a beautiful city, but very touristy. And, despite the ravages of the war which had scarred the nation, the people were lovely. The country is still communist in name, and the war exhibits in museums in Ho Chi Minh were very focused around the atrocities of the Americans during the conflict. We visited the Vietcong tunnels, walking just a short way through them, which was terrifying; how western troops dared venture further was beyond me.

Columbia

The idea of holidaying in Columbia, the infamous drug cartel capital of the world which had also been ravaged by revolutionary guerillas, was sparked by Disney's Andy Bird. He told me how beautiful it was and untouched by tourists. I wonder why. But it was great and we had a marvellous time. There were no-go areas in Bogota, but we wandered the streets and shops near our hotel and never felt at risk. Security was tight, with checks before entering shopping malls etc.

I always try speaking the local language and caused much amusement when I advised a waitress, "Soy un BBQ pollo." I had told her that I was a chicken. Luckily, we could rely on Mark's Spanish to help us out when we were stopped by police wanting to see ID which we had left in the safe at the hotel. And again when we couldn't access the room's safe and we needed the receptionist to come with the master key. We visited Villa de Leyva where we sampled local wine, causing a stir when the little guide found out that Mark (who was also partaking) was only 15.. but twice her size.

There were many other highlights during out holiday. The coffee plantations in Pereira, and the beautiful Cocora National Park, were lovely, with their incredible palm-like trees. Our chill time was in Cartagena. The town has lots of character and was noticeably warmer than our other locations, but there were also lots of tourists. After a couple of nights, we headed out to an island resort. We had been told that it was a two-hour journey, but little did I think we would be travelling on a speedboat, rather than a ferry with a coffee bar.

The resort was not luxury, but it was the best we could get apparently. The WIFI reception was poor, which meant that one morning I was in the lobby trying to get connected along with another young Columbian. We shrugged at each other, sharing our joint frustration, before I was joined by the rest of the family. As we left the hotel, Mark was aghast to learn that I had not known who I was chatting to. He was the famous international Columbian and Juventus footballer, Juan

Cuadrado. His several hundred thousand social media followers probably meant that his need for WIFI connection was considerably greater than mine.

Moscow

The August Bank Holiday weekend was another chance to get away, and we to go to Moscow. Little did we know what a bind it was to get visas. Political shenanigans meant that we had to have our fingerprints taken at the Russian Embassy or Consulate. We were there for just three days, but we still managed to see everything we had wanted to, from the Kremlin to Gorky Park and the communist statue graveyard. Emily had gone online and found a great restaurant, The White Rabbit, but actually finding it in-person proved more of a challenge. When we finally did, we had great views over the city and suburbs and had fantastic food.

Skiing

Before we bought our chalet, we took skiing holidays in Les Deux Alps and Meribel -and had one surprise trip to Saalbach. We had missed the season after Emily was born – too much to contemplate – but by the time Mark arrived we had the hang of travelling with babies, and he was a much better sleeper. We booked to go to Saalbach. Richard had invariably joined us on ski trips, but I was told he had a conference that week so could not join us. On the bus up to resort four-year old Emily told me that Richard was coming. Julia was stunned that she knew but, of course, little ears pick-up all the whispers and miss nothing.

Heather and Keith joined us to look after Mark. Incredibly, Keith had learned to ski aged 62 years old, which meant that he joined us on the slopes every day.

Figure 19: the chalet

Once we had the chalet we would ski for a couple of weeks every year during the Christmas break. I would have a weekend with the boys, plus we would have a further week as a family at half-term and sometimes a week or two at Easter. No wonder the kids became proficient. We went once for Christmas Day, but that was nearly a disaster. We flew out on December 23rd, catching the 4.45pm flight out of Newcastle and landing without incident in Amsterdam. However, there was thickening fog in Amsterdam and looking at the departure board we could see flights being cancelled one after the other. It was inevitable that the same thing would happen to our Geneva flight, so we needed a plan. Realising there would be no capacity on flights to Genea the following day, I ran to the car-hire desk and booked a one-way hire. Fortunately, we only had hand luggage – and we had taken (or more accurately Father Christmas had deposited) many presents in the chalet that summer. We had to get there. We left the airport at about 11pm, with no map, but a cup of coffee. Alternating drivers, we drove through the night and arrived in Geneva to pick up our local car at 8am. We were exhausted, but Christmas was saved.

Over the years we have spent many a night in a hotel at either Schipol or Charles de Gaule Airport, because connections were missed. Once we got as far as Zurich Airport before missing the last flight to Geneva but we still had a pleasant evening at the Raddisson Blue Hotel, where the wine rack was serviced by abseiling waitresses. We also failed to get home after one New Year trip. Up to four inches of snow had fallen on Geneva that morning, and dozens of flights were cancelled including our Easyjet flight home. With so many travellers stranded, it was carnage. They finally got us on a flight which departed two days later. Fortunately, we could easily get back to the chalet and have an extra day's skiing, so not all bad news.

Heli-Skiing in Whistler

Before I was too old, fat, and unfit I wanted to ski deep powder from a helicopter with my children. We got the chance in Whistler over New Year 2016. We timed it well as there had been virtually zero snow in the Porte du Soleil. We spent a few days skiing on the pistes before Emily, Mark, and I went off for the day. We were assigned our guide and, after being trained in avalanche survival and using the transponders, we took off in a group of 10. I later asked our guide if he was worried when he saw a 13-year-old boy in his group. "No," he replied. "I could see he knew what he was doing by the way he carried his skis from the bus." Unfortunately, two of the adults in our group did not know, and after the first descent the helicopter was called to take them off the mountain.

I had been worried whether I could cope but I found my rhythm and had a great time. It was a clear blue-sky day, in the middle of nowhere with pure deep virgin snow. The helicopter dropped us at the top of mountains, and we skied down to the bottom for the helicopter to swoop us back up again. The loading was a slick operation. We all had to crouch down close to where he landed. The reason was because if the helicopter started to sink in the snow, and we were waiting further away and started walking towards him, we could be sliced in half by the rotor blades. By landing within a couple of feet of us, we were safe. The skis were placed a helicopter width away on the other side, and the guide loaded them into the side-box while we all climbed into the back.

We were also witness to one particular highlight during our helicopter trip. We had stopped to have lunch and were looking at the magnificent vista when one of our group, Matt, asked if I would take a picture of him and his girlfriend Amy. I then saw him get down on one knee and bring a ring box out. Oh my God, I thought. This is an important picture... click, click, click!! Emily was in tears of joy next to me. What a surprise for Amy and us.

By the end of that day I was exhausted but delighted to have fulfilled that one dream. Overall, we had a good time skiing in Whistler with their efficient and fair herringbone queuing system for the lifts, and the "sniffle stations" which were boxes of tissues in the queue, as your nose does tend to run when it's that cold. We finished off with a couple of nights in Vancouver before heading home.

Morocco

It is funny how I do not think of holidays without Emily as family holidays, but of course when she was off at university she did not have the same half-term breaks that Mark did, yet we still went away. One lovely week was in Marrakesh. The King of Morocco allegedly likes golf, so there were several golf courses around the town including the Royal Maroc which was very grand and one of three courses where Mark and I played. The atmosphere of the main square was a bit intense with tourist-grabbing locals either wanting your business or asking for money for their street performances. But in the side streets and alleyways it was classic North African Arabic.

ROSH ENGINEERING

Figure 21: Rosh Engineering, the early days

Dad launched Rosh Engineering in May 1981, once it was clear that Remrod Engineering was going down. The company started by doing odd-jobs for customers, such as transformer cooling radiator replacements for NEEB (North Eastern Electricity Board). One here, one there, using Remrod staff if they had nothing else to do.

As Remrod collapsed, Rosh Engineering began in the spare bedroom of Woodmans Way. The name came from Roy and Sheila, the first two initials of my mum and dad's first names.

We had no permanent staff, no assets (a rented van),

and nothing more than a chair, desk, and some letterhead... plus, a typewriter. Unemployment was high, so staff could be recruited for a couple of weeks and then laid-off when the job was completed. These same people were then picked-up again a few weeks later, when another job came in; a two-month run of continuous work was quite an achievement.

It was a couple of weeks here, a week there and slowly but surely, my dad started to make a living; albeit small scale and modest. No premises, no assets, just his reputation and knowledge brought it to the fore.

A regular team began to come together: Joe Cook a welder; then Albert and Billy Parker, painters who doubled up as fitters; then Billy's soon-to-be son-in-law, Gary Cooper, and onwards and upwards.

Occasionally, I would accompany my dad on site visits to look at potential jobs or while projects were going ahead. Little did I know that Rosh Engineering would become so much of my working life.

Dad filled his days, not just making a living but enjoying the work he grew up with, as he headed towards retirement.

I am sure he always aspired for me to take it over, and the hard slog of my London life was what prompted me to join him. He made me the offer after securing a three-year contract to paint transformers for the National Grid in the North East. Either I could take it over, or he would sell, but if I was going to join him, then he needed to know within a year or two so he could teach me the ropes before he retired.

It took less than a year for Elizabeth and me to make the decision and, on 14 July, 1989, I joined the business. Elizabeth focussed on posting invoices to accounts and I started to learn the technical aspects, and how to boost sales.

She joined me on early sales trips but then, after a while, we realised it was best for her to have her own career outside of Rosh and she went to work for Northumberland County Council.

Between us, dad and I were then responsible for the accounts, the wages, the technical, the purchasing and the sales. We had one van and three staff, with summer peaks sometimes increasing our staffing levels up to five, with two vans. Even those three staff were ad hoc. At the time, unemployment was so high you could lay off staff for a month, and then re-employ them three weeks later without any issue; a run of several months continuous employment was a treat for these guys. Unfortunately, winter invariably meant they were laid off but, within a year, I had secured sufficient business to allow us to employ some staff continuously.

Premises

I wanted to break away from the confines of my parents' home and had a bit of a battle with my dad to move into commercial premises.

He was teaching me the importance of controlling costs, managing cash, and good frugal stewardship. But I wanted to grow the business and employ people to do jobs that were easily delegated. I was doing the wages manually using printed tax tables and entering them into a wages ledger each week, often at the weekends, to free up time to grow the business in the week. My dad was comfortable with having a home-based office, but there was no way we could employ someone to work from there.

We wanted to keep our phone number as 4883450, so we tried to find a place in the immediate locality and eventually identified a small starter unit on Swalwell Bank. It was like a big garage, but we built some basic offices inside it that could accommodate four staff, and no more. The rest was of the space we used for storing everything from tools to tins of paint. It was so basic that the toilet was in a small cubicle in the corner of the factory (as we called it), while people washed their hands in a sink elsewhere in the factory. The sink had a table next to it that was set up to make coffees. The water pipes even froze on cold winter nights. But, to me, it was the first key step up that corporate growth ladder.

First, we employed an accounts clerk, which freed me up to do more sales. Before long we had a couple more staff – an engineering student, and Carolyn who had come to us to sell a product for which we had an agency agreement. As it turned out, this product did not fit the UK market so that agreement ended, so she took on more administration work.

We then progressed to the first of two factories in the Sands Industrial Estate in Swalwell. Both were basic storage and offices but increasingly bigger and more practical for our needs. These latter two were rented from Gateshead Council. Neither had outside secure space, plus I always felt that renting premises was dead money: I wanted freehold.

Unfortunately, freehold is hard to find in the industrial

sphere but, in 2005, I managed to buy a long (125 year) lease on the Durham Road in Birtley. This was much more substantial with more than an acre of land, as well as bigger offices and factory space - but no internal crane. This problem was answered by a stroke of luck soon after we moved in, when Baldwin's Cranes knocked on the door asking if they could rent a bit of the land to store some mobile cranes – and they installed a portacabin. This greatly reduced our costs. When they left, we replaced them with a company that bought and sold pallets, until we moved on from Birtley.

Our next move in 2017 to Riverside Court in Blaydon was a major step change. One of our long-term suppliers, JMD Engineering, tipped us off that the freehold for half their "shed" was on the market. JMD owner, Martyn McDine, had built the shed and kept a third for his business. With a 10T overhead crane lifting capacity, it was a proper factory – except that its current occupiers were shot-blasters. The whole place had to be scraped clean and washed down, while the offices had to be demolished and re-built.

The freehold cost £350,000, but it required another £80,000 to make it liveable.

When the two-thirds of the remaining half of the shed came up for sale a year later we grabbed that too, for another £200,000. While we did not need it immediately, we could not let the freehold go to someone else. So, our balance sheet looked good, we had managed to fund the purchases with retained profits, and we now had a substantial facility.

The whole site was finally secured in April 2021.

Martyn had first approached me in 2019, asking if I was interested in buying JMD, but what he wanted, and what it was worth, were some distance apart. Eighteen months and a year of COVID later, his expectations were more realistic and we shook hands on a £200,000 deal for the freehold, machinery and business of JMD.

We now had the whole plot, plus a new line of business manufacturing steel fabrications and three more staff to boot.

Our Staff

Joe Cook, a welder, and single man from Blyth, was an early long-term recruit. He regarded the team and being away as his family, and he never really wanted to retire. But the hard graft of manual labour took its toll on his body and eventually he had to call it a day in his late sixties.

He was a lovely chap and I kept in touch, visiting him in the care home he eventually went into, and attending his funeral in 2020.

Albert Parker and Billy Parker were brothers from the tight-knit South Shields community, and this led to us employing half their street as well as their family. This included neighbours Terry Cocklin, his son Joe, and Jackie Wood and his brother Tanner. We also employed John Burn with his brother-in-law Jackie Ainsley, while Billy Parker's son-in-law, Gary Cooper, was another early recruit.

Albert was the main painter and led those teams, while his brother - also a painter by trade, but mechanically useful – led the mechanical side for the early years.

Albert died at just 48 years old, from lung cancer. He

was a smoker, as so many were in those days, and it was a sad decline. We were very much a family business in those days. I had been to see his daughter in her school productions, while he was so committed to the business that he once cut-up his trouser belt to make some packing for his spray unit in order to get a job finished.

Jackie Wood was a real character who I only saw once wearing his false teeth. He ate all his meals chewing with just his gums. His wife, Gloria, who he later left, would not let him live in the house, hence why he was happy to work away. At home, he slept in the greenhouse in his front garden.

On one occasion, when he was a young man, he went out drinking with his sailor brother in Shields. They had a few, and then went back on board together at the end of the night - only for Jackie to wake-up off the coast and heading south. He did not return for three months. I asked him whether his mum was worried? "No," he replied, "she knew I was with Tanner and be alright." Jackie died when he was about 66 years old from cancer too. How much of that was down to smoking and how much was caused by painting the hulls of ships in the Tyne & Wear yards without appropriate PPE, I will never know.

George Dean was the first painter we employed who was not related to Albert. He is still with us as I write, having passed 30 years' service a couple of years ago. Solid and dependable, I have sponsored his granddaughter's football team and supported George during his wife Jackie's breast cancer treatment.

This latter trauma was interesting in as much as George and Jackie seemed to hate each other. He always wanted to be away on site working, and she wanted it too – even phoning the office one week to complain that George had been on local projects for the previous month, and asking when were we sending him away next? And yet, when she was diagnosed with breast cancer, he sat in my office and cried and asked to only be local for the duration of her treatment. We managed to meet this request, although it included a couple of loss-making jobs so that he could be at home.

George is also a fanatical Sunderland AFC supporter. Once, he got tickets to the Tyne – Wear Derby game, but he was stuck on Shetland - the ferry to the mainland was out of action for 48 hours, and he was in a right tizz. In the end, I flew him home so he made the game. Sometimes football *is* more important than life and death, as Bill Shankley famously said.

Obviously, over the years, we have had many staff; some have stayed, and some have left, but the ones that died always hit hardest. No-one has died in the line of work, although as well as Albert, two others have died from illness.

Gordon Palmer was one of the older electricians who lost his job in the mines and tried and failed to find employment (even as a TV salesmen) until he joined Rosh. Enormously kind and popular, he had a heart attack on-site in Bristol and never recovered despite rapid action by our staff and a prompt ambulance. He was 64 years old. Taking his belongings back to his wife and family was a difficult, but essential, job for me; I have never delegated tough jobs to others.

David Black was one of our first truly skilled craftsmen and our first electrician. He had worked in Africa for

'Help the Aged' and, we later discovered, had a Kenyan wife. He was an intelligent chap (he subscribed to the magazine Marxist Today) who took the business to a new level in the 20 years or so that he was with us, but he fell ill with a mystery illness that involved an expensive infusion every couple of months to restore his strength. He then developed asbestosis-related lung cancer - not an uncommon problem in his profession at the time. He died a few days after I visited him at the hospice and his funeral was a humanist service. His wife, Jennifer, went round the coffin kissing it on each side before the curtain was drawn.

All staff bring issues, and my first challenge was from Billy Parker in the first year. We were still operating from Woodmans Way, and mum and dad had gone away on holiday. I had geared up for Billy, Gary, and David to go and do a job, leaving on a Monday to start on Tuesday. Billy refused to go, saying he had things to do on the Monday and he would decide when they travelled. It was clearly a power struggle. I told him that we had to travel on Monday because the customer was expecting us, etc. He then started to give me back his fuel card and Rosh equipment. "What is this?" I asked. "I quit then," said Billy. I am sure that he thought that I would try and talk him out of it, on the basis he was so valuable. I did not, and I let him go.

The decision privately traumatised me. I spoke to dad that evening and he backed me and said I did the right thing. When dad got back after his holiday, Billy rang him, asking for his job back. "Nothing to do with me," dad said. "You'll have to ask Ian." Billy never bothered.

Making tough calls when people step out of line is

never easy, but always right. Many years after the Billy incident we discovered that three members of staff were falsifying expenses. They were travelling back from Yorkshire and had fabricated receipts for a local hotel (we took over hotel booking after this). It was Jill who sniffed a rat and we called-in each individual, one by one, for questioning. Our own predictions as to how each person would act or respond did not meet reality. One person who we liked, and thought we could get to spill the beans, stuck to their party line; one person who we thought would continue to lie, buckled very quickly. The third tried to maintain the lie, but by then they were done for.

It was the simple questions that undid them, such as where did you have breakfast? The answers varied from, "it was a buffet downstairs," to, "they did not do breakfast, so we went to the café on the corner."

We dismissed all three, but it hit us hard because it was nearly 20% of our site workforce at a very busy time.

The engineers in the office mucked-in and worked on-site, plus we recruited new staff and stretched others. We pulled through, and also sent a clear message: defraud us, and you are out.

But they were not the only ones who tried to pull a fast one. Another lad was stopped by the police while he was selling £40 of copper to a scrap yard that he had stolen from us. He'd been with us for eight years and we had trained him up from nothing. But he threw it all away in stupid act.

Office Staff & Students

I was always keen to have students on placement year.

For one, it gave us a 12-month interview process, but it also meant that we had a regular through-put of keen, young individuals.

The student engineers were a rich variety; some were straightforward young male engineers from Yorkshire, but we also had several first-class women. Heather was glamourous with painted nails, but not averse to donning overalls and boots, and helping sort out steel fabrications on the shop floor. Ravit was a former Israeli tank driver, who had a fiery spirit, and Suppi was supremely intelligent Sri Lankan woman who we sponsored through her final year. She joined us after graduating but wanted to move on after her first year.

We have always been a diverse company, employing a range of religions and ethnicities, ages and recognising the value of women in engineering. It made our workplace fresh and interesting and I learned a huge amount from this cultural variety.

Venkata came as a transformer design engineer, bringing with her experience from India, rather than as a student. She was in her mid-30s and had gained the right to work in the UK, but her citizenship came during her employment. She then asked if she could have one month as a holiday block the following year because she was getting married. Not a problem I replied. She said, "they have not found me a husband yet, but the wedding will be next June." Arranged marriages are alien to us but are so normal in Venkata's culture. She met him for the first time the week before her wedding. On her return we discussed it and she said she was pleased she had a kind man. Siva later joined her in the UK but he struggled to find a job, which worried me because they might have had to return to India, and we could lose her, so I employed him for a year or two as well.

We used the organisation Association Internationale des Étudiants en Sciences Économiques et Commerciales (AIESEC) when we were trying to break into European markets, which led to us employing a succession of Dutch students, and even a Danish student for three months.

We took on fresh graduates, but also 17-year-olds. Jim Butler was one of most successful placement undergraduates after he joined us. He became a real transformer expert in his 25-plus years at Rosh (with a little break to branch out in the middle on his own).

Paul Scott came as a 17-year-old wanting to work in IT.... although we only had one computer. He, too, blossomed at Rosh and eventually became our Engineering Director.

Each of them helped the success of the business, bringing in systems and new ways of working to improve our performance. They were invariably very different to me – which was a good thing. While I had that passion and drive, sometimes a more measured approach is needed, although I am turning more passive as I get older. Having said that, it worries me that I no longer have the same drive to grow the business as I had in those early years.

Our first accounts clerk was also very good, but I learned another simple lesson. She went off sick and I decided I would pay her full pay which was, I felt, the decent thing to do and all that. After a few weeks, this was becoming a significant financial drain on our small business. I then heard that she was running errands for her boyfriend's business, doing deliveries etc. So, not that sick. I called her and asked how long she would be off, to which she replied that she had a sick note for another two weeks. I said, well, after this week I will have to put you on Statutory Sick Pay, which was a big drop in income. She then said she would come back on Monday. No, you won't, I said, you have told me you will be off for two more weeks.

In those days, our contracts and terms and conditions of employment were too vague but as the business grew, we clearly spelt out what sick pay rates were, when staff got bereavement leave, and for who etc.

She left shortly after, and she was replaced by Helen Moor who has worked for us for more than 30 years, moving from accounts to planning, logistics, and procurement.

After Helen had moved from accounts, we briefly employed another, before Jill Statt joined us in 1999, becoming an absolute rock as our Finance Manager for more than 20 years.

That process of developing and supporting long-serving staff has been a great honour for us.

Tom Hornsby was on a similar path, picking up a First-Class Engineering degree via day release, before leaving after eight years. Others arrived as graduates, like Emanuel Eleftheropoulos, who contributed an enormous amount over the next 15 years and became an invaluable member of our business.

On the Road

In the early years I clocked up more than 50,000 miles a year, visiting potential customers and looking at work.

I used to buy second-hand cars with 10,000 miles on the clock and run them for a year before changing cars. I went through about four Vauxhall Cavaliers/Vectras each year over four years.

I used to listen to talking books that I borrowed from the library as I was driving. Long journeys, such as to Dounreay in Caithness, were a great opportunity to get some major tomes such as 'Hunt for Red October' by Tom Clancy, which was a 12-hour listen.

When dad went away, he took mum; it was her pleasure trip as much as anything else. And why not? They stayed at lovely hotels, enjoyed a meal together, and had a great time.

I was much more work-a-day, preferring to stay in smaller, family-run hotels. There were many evenings when I would be sitting in the bar after my meal, and the owner would introduce me to another chap who was staying and we would get chatting. An altogether more pleasant experience and through that, I learned about so many other types of business. For example, the egg trade is fascinating. Eggs cannot be washed before being boxed. They do not have cocks on most sites, so anyone claiming their egg hatched a live chick is unlikely to be telling the truth. There are also the very high standards that Marks & Spencer demand for their hens, which the egg producer referred to as 'a country club'.

When I went to Holland with the Dutch students the

routine was the same, although we hit a pretty low point at one near Maastricht. The bedroom was so small that it had a sliding door, and I banged my elbows if I tried to turn round in the shower.

But occasionally I hit the jackpot. I stayed in a gorgeous Suffolk hotel one summer, with a lovely restaurant, overlooking a river surrounded by weeping willows.

There was no satnav in those days; instead, I relied on a map on my lap and getting directions from pedestrians. Once, when I was heading to Roche Products in Dalry, Ayrshire, (it makes vitamin C without squeezing an orange) I wound down the window to ask a lady if I was on the road to Dalry. She was mystified. Never heard of the place. I showed her on the map. "Oh", she said, "that is not *'Dal Ree'*, it's *'Dall Rye'*."

I now know, off the top of my head, how long it will take me to get to various points around the country having done the journeys so often. But I rarely had time to really appreciate, or visit, the areas I travelled around, often arriving early evening and leaving early morning.

Occasionally, I got a quick stroll around town after dinner; rarely much more.

Once I did 'play tourist'. Heading north of Inverness on the two-hour drive to Thurso, I saw a sign for the Glenmorangie distillery at Tain, which had tours until 4pm. It was 3pm and I had nothing on until the following morning, so I stopped. It was a great tour around a really good distillery. Sadly, I could not sample the fare.

Northern Ireland was another place I marvelled at and ended up staying over weekends. The murals on the end of houses shouted out the Troubles of the near past. In parts of Belfast, traffic lights were protected by wire mesh to stop them being smashed in riots, which had been a regular occurrence not long before. Police stations were built like gun placements, or fortresses, and were not welcoming places to report your missing dog.

Meanwhile, driving through the province, I would go through one town with painted kerbstones, alternating red, white, and blue, and Union flags flying from poles in gardens. But the next town would be painted in tricolours, with murals honouring dead hunger strikers, or demanding "Troops Out."

I knew about these issues from the nightly news I watched as a child, when Belfast and Northern Ireland were known only for bombs, marches, riots, and terror activities. Those locals who I met on my travels regarded the media coverage as biased and unrepresentative. One engineer said to me that he was more bothered about overly fresh teenage boys approaching his daughter on a Friday night out, than any terrorist issues. Just like any father.

I experienced mild animosity once. We were in a Belfast substation where the double wall (both 20ft high and 20ft between) encased the transformers, talking to the engineer, when a few stones started to be thrown over. "Let us move inside," Walter, the engineer, said. "The locals can hear us chatting."

But this was a rarity. The vast majority of the province were friendly and welcoming. The first time that I took Julia with me, we took a taxi with Walter to a restaurant. The driver suddenly said, "is that an English voice I hear there?" Meekly we replied, "yes." "Been to Belfast before?" We replied, "no". "Why didn't you say," he replied, and turned off his meter before giving us a guided tour. Kindness and generosity like this abounded.

Detached Retina No.1

Given all the driving I did for work, I inevitably picked up a couple of speeding tickets. The first was most frustrating. I was driving down the A697 near Longhorsley, one Friday afternoon, in no particular hurry because I was going home not to the office. I overtook a caravan and, having put my foot down for the manoeuvre, just did not slowdown, which resulted in a £50 fine and three points.

Equally, I had no major crashes until January 2015.

Southbound down the A1 near Leeming Bar, the road becomes three lanes. That day, I was stunned to see that the third lane had a thin layer of snow on it, because as the rest of the road was clear and it was a blue-sky day. I span my Jaguar XJ and hit the concrete central barrier at 70mph, before getting some control and steering to the hard shoulder.

I had had my sun visor slightly down and had hit my forehead on this on impact but was otherwise fine. My head started to bleed, but I was grateful that I had not been hit by a 38 tonne truck in the process.

The police and an ambulance arrived and after being breathalysed (clear of course), I sent the ambulance away. The recovery truck arrived after an hour, and I hitched the ride back to the North East. Julia was on an awayday in Tynemouth and insisted on seeing me (I was just going to jump on a train to meet my appointment in Kent). She then sent me to her sister Sharon, who was an A&E doctor round the corner, to get checked over. A few steri-strips on my cut by a nurse, and I was told to take it easy.

The following week I was off to London, because I was Chair of the Institute of Directors. At breakfast, I asked Julia to have a look at my right eye as something did not seem right. She could not see anything, so off I went. I had back-to-back meetings at the IoD but, in between, had mentioned a couple of times about my eye, which was still problematic. The Institute's Secretary, Loretto Levy, tried to get me an appointment at an opticians – but, amazingly for central London, she could not.

I then had an hour or so before dinner with a member of the team, Alex Mitchell, so HR Director Bill Adams suggested that I pop up to Moorfields eye hospital. It was a 15 minute taxi ride, had an A&E, and I would be back for dinner if all was fine. It was not.

A junior doctor took a look, and said, "your retina is detached but the macular is intact. We will have to operate, but it will be in the morning now." My immediate reaction was could I go home to Newcastle, explaining how my wife was Deputy Medical Director at Newcastle City Hospital and I would rather be under her wing and near home. The doctor looked at me and said, "but this is Moorfields, one of the best eye hospitals in the world, why would you want to go anywhere else?"

I called Julia and explained. It was just after 5pm. Having no experience of eyes, she contacted the Mike Clark, Clinical Director for Ophthalmology at the RVI, who said he would look into it. He then called

Moorfields and asked to speak to his opposite number. Derek Ezra then called me into the examination room with nervous junior standing behind him. He had a look at my eye and decided they could operate immediately. "It will be a bit of a trot," he said, "because theatre closes in 30 minutes, but I have a first-class registrar who will do it for you."

Being processed quickly meant that, the next thing I knew, I was having my head taped into a head brace, rendering it immobile, and anaesthesia was injected to numb my eye. With the other eye taped closed, all I could hear and feel was the odd probe and prod that went down to my chest. At one stage, I heard the surgeon ask for SF6 gas to inject. This gas is sometimes used in high voltage equipment and it felt odd to have it in me. Forty minutes later, I was wheeled out in a chair, head down, looking at the floor - a position I was told I had to maintain for the next 12 hours – even sleeping - so that the gas would maintain the pressure on my retina and stick it back where it should be.

I could see out of the corner of my good eye, a couple of other patients in a similar position to me. "I should have been in a darts tournament tonight," said one. "I should have been out for a lovely dinner with a colleague," I said.

"I was lucky," said the other chap, "I wasn't up to much." We chuckled with the gallows humour.

I took a taxi back to the flat, looking down all the time. Julia joined me later that night and at the post-op session the next morning squealed when they took my eye patch off and my bad eye went wildly wonky. The nurse reassured her it would not stay like that and also advised that I needed two weeks off work. Yeah right. I am not a slacker and I had a business to run.

Knowing that I would not be able to drive, I called Emanuel and asked him to collect me on the way into the factory the following Monday but, come Sunday, I realised I was not going to make work. That simple eye operation knocked seven bells out of me.

I did go in for a key meeting on the Wednesday for a couple of hours but regretted it soon after. The medical people knew their job, and two weeks was needed.

Retinal Detachment No. 2

Having glaucoma weakens eyes, and that car accident had been the catalyst for the detachment.

A couple of years later, I again banged my head, this time on the last day of our October half-term holiday to Israel. The following Monday morning at work, I realised I had black spots in my left eye, or floaters. Sister-in-law, Sharon, was consulted and the obvious answer was, "of course it is not normal." Eye A&E in Newcastle welcomed me as they opened and a very diligent ophthalmologist spotted a spongy tear right to one side of my eye.

It was apparently hard to see, so the Consultant asked if they would let a junior have a look. As this poor young doctor was going through the protocols of examining my eye, a retinal surgeon came in and sat down. The young doctor suggested a few things, all of which were wrong, before the Consultant then dropped a huge hint, saying, "there is a retinal surgeon sat in the room too, which may give you an indication of where to look."

Tsveta Ivanova was a Bulgarian-born surgeon, and she

lasered, or 'welded', my retina back where it had been torn. The examination was painful beyond belief as she used instruments to peer into the corner of my eye. I also could not believe how painful the laser zaps to weld it were. Zap, zap, zap, it went, and I was wet with sweat after 10 minutes. I did not want to make her stop thinking the quicker it is all over the better, but after 30 minutes, I could stand it no more and asked for a break. I apologised but explained that the pain was too much to endure. "Some people pay good money to be hurt," she replied in a thick eastern European accent that had a hint of menace in it. Well, that does not rock my boat.

The following February, I had a fall when we were skiing and banged my head. Back home, I knew my retina had detached again, and presented myself at the eye hospital for my Bulgarian surgeon to operate and stitch it back on. Unfortunately, this operation created a blind spot in the middle of my eye.

Hitch-hikers

Having been a hitch-hiker in my youth, I always stopped for them when I was driving. It was great to have some company too, to break up the boring miles that I did. I even had a "visitors book" at one stage to record the different people I gave a lift to. But as the years passed by, their numbers dwindled.

I once had three French lads all in one go – it is quite a challenge to hitch in such a large group. They were all about to join the French Air Force as trainee pilots. Another time I picked up a couple of Italians in Caithness who had cycled from Dover to John o Groats and the bikes were being shipped back and they were hitching.

When a car spots a hitcher, it can take 25m or 50m before it can stop. Usually, the hitcher then runs to the car. One strange lad just meandered when I stopped. He put his satchel and shepherds crook in the back and got in. He was on Planet Biscuit in so many ways, but not on drugs I must add. He was looking for a plot of land to live self-sufficiently. It turned out that he had gone to Gordonstoun, the same school as Prince Charles, and his father was the famous Lotus Formula driver, Innes Ireland. (A rival driver said of him, "He lived without sense, without an analyst, and provoked astonishment and affection from everyone.")

I also picked up one lad who was obviously taking something – but I deposited him promptly at the next motorway junction.

On another occasion, I picked up a religious fanatic in East Anglia. He left me with literature quoting passages from the Bible that proved homosexuality was wrong and a sin, and women were second-class citizens.

Another hitcher was a great artist and he showed me some oils he had in his bag.

There were also lots of trade platers – drivers who had delivered vehicles and were just heading on to their next job. Their pay was low, so saving any train fares allowance that they were given helped boost their wage.

I even once had a lone woman – a rare occurrence - who thought she would be safer with me than a nutter. She was Swiss. I picked her up at Kinross services in Perthshire and she ended up staying at the Drive for the night.**Customers**

While Rosh's customer base was founded around

electricity generation and distribution companies, we also had a very good industrial base.

Going to visit nuclear plants and big coal-fired stations was always fascinating, but some of the manufacturing process plants were equally so. I went to a glass jar factory that was rattling off 2,000 Horlicks jars an hour. They would have that production run for a couple of weeks before switching to a tomato sauce jar run.

There were also paper mills, with massive rolls coming off production lines, which seemed to be entirely devoid of people, through to steel mills where I followed the slab of metal down a rolling line, and watched a 20-tonne slab heated to white hot, before being rolled out and coiled, and then left to sit for a week to cool down.

Sugar beet factories, unfortunately, have a smell that, at times, turned my stomach.

Of all the places that I travelled to, Scotland was always my favourite patch. The roads were quieter, the pace more relaxed, and the scenery simply stunning.

One of my favourite drives is through Glen Coe on a cold but blue-sky morning. No tourists, snow on the peaks, and a great road. Once I was in the Highlands with a customer in his Land Rover going to a hydro station down a single-track road. As we went over a brow of a hill the view that opened up in front was awe-inspiring and I let out a gasp. My customer, Kevan McShea, had never noticed it before because it was literally his workshop.

At the generating station we met a fitter who reminded us there was to be a 90% solar eclipse 10 minutes later. He had some welding screen glass with him so we could safely see it. It only lasted a few minutes but there was a noticeable and sudden drop in temperature.

The great thing about our customers was they were always good at paying on time and we never had bad debts. Well, we once lost £20,000 when a contracting company, which had been owned by Scottish Power, changed hands and went bust in a year. We did not pick up the change.

We had a few scares though. PTS was another contracting business that had grown and we knew well. Their business grew and their debt with us passed £100,000. Then they stopped returning phone calls. Always a bad sign. Christmas arrived, and I was sweating. They eventually settled, but it changed my perspective of risk and reward and I decided we needed a fancy holiday after I had nearly lost so much.

Roy Dormer retirement

My biggest personal challenge at Rosh Engineering was my relationship with my father.

Dad gave me a great opportunity and for that I am forever grateful. He also taught me some of the most valuable lessons of my business life. Turnover is vanity, profit is sanity. Watch your cash, hoard your cash, cash is king. Cash that is in the liquid sense of a business rather than notes and coins. He was frugal and thrifty, and never into vanity symbols, or "flag poles and fountains" as a bank manager once called them. This means we have always had a solid base and have never needed to borrow money. We have had the resources to ride out business cycles and disasters.

All businesses have ups and downs and the robust ones,

or the ones with cash reserves, are the ones that not only survive, but prosper, when the upswing comes.

Moving out of Woodmans Way into our first industrial site was a battle, as was employing engineers, and even getting extra phone lines. I had to battle to take Rosh to the next level because dad was ticking-over to retirement. But then things started to get interesting. Young student engineers, and graduate engineers were seeking his advice and experience. He loved it. While he was still overly conservative, he was driven in the business.

However, I must emphasise that his restraints on me were probably a good thing too at times. He was one to say, "Do not focus on how much we can make, but how much we could lose." And he was right. But if we had taken a few more risks, how much bigger and more successful would we have been?

In conjunction with Lisa, I had organised a surprise 65th birthday party for him, to try and start his exit from the business. We had 150 people to a dinner dance at the Gosforth Park Hotel and a great night was had by all. But he did not choose that time to retire and was at work again the following Monday.

For the next 10 years the challenges continued, until it came to a head. I was approached unexpectedly to apply for the job as CEO of the NE Chamber of Commerce. I was interviewed, and although I did not get the job, the fact that I had considered leaving Rosh precipitated discussions on ownership and retirement.

Exiting your father from a business that was his baby made it a very difficult time. As tough as it was for him, we worked out an exit plan and share transfer. These were originally going to transfer on his death, but I pointed out that - God willing - I could be in my 60s when that happened. He then started to cut his hours at the business, acting as a consultant and eventually only coming in when invited.

Concerned for him, and what he would do with his time, I got him started on his memoires. And I am glad I did. From then on, things got better between us, and Rosh started to grow more.

Islands

Over the years, I have visited many of the British Isles. The Outer Hebrides looks romantic, but on a wet and cold February day there is nowhere bleaker. I cannot say it is much better in the summer.

The first time I flew into the airport in Benbecula, I was amazed to hear all the locals at the airport chatting away in Gaelic. I was looking for the car hire desk, and then resorted to phoning. The terminal was not much more than half a dozen Nissan huts bolted together. "Och, Angus is there waiting for you," said a woman. Eventually, as I wandered around looking lost, a chap finished his conversation (in Gaelic) with a woman, got up from one of the seats in the waiting area and said, "You'll be wanting your car then." No rush, no hurry. Just when you are ready. We ended-up driving together to a building several miles away to do the paperwork before I headed-off to my meeting.

Many of the Western Isles, and even Shetland, have

strict religious codes, such that pubs are closed on Sundays, as are playgrounds, with the swings locked-up. No work can take place unless an emergency. It really is in a time warp.

The engineer on the island told me how, in the 1970s, many children arrived at school speaking no English – only Gaelic - until TV arrived in the islands. But they were a friendly and decent bunch.

I once had to have access to the top of an open terminal transformer to take measurements. Unbeknown to me, this involved turning the power off to a whole settlement. As I stood waiting for access, I was itching for them to get started, until Donald informed me that they had notified the residents it would be at 0900, but he was giving them another 10 minutes to make sure they had finished their breakfast.

There were some spots where the views and scenery were stunning. Coming round a high coastal road in Uist, I marvelled at the crystal blue bay below. Donald MacKenzie explained how he had been scuba diving there and it was gorgeous. "Do you need a wet suit?" I asked. "No," he replied. I was amazed, was it the Gulf Stream that kept the waters warm? "No," he said, "it is too cold even for a wet suit. You need a dry suit to dive around here."

I routinely flew out to the islands but sometimes took the ferry. I have done Ullapool to Stornaway, and Scrabster to Kirkwall, to name a couple. (Ullapool harbour was often crowded with Soviet 'trawlers' bristling with antenna, no doubt attracted by the nearby American ballistic missile base. It also had a reputation as a landing point for foreign spies).

The Orkney ferry left at 6am, which meant a 5am departure from my Thurso Hotel, but with the rising sun as we passed the Old Man of Hoy (the famous needle cliff) and rounded Orkney, it was worth it.

Island engineers were always very accommodating, and the Orkney engineer came to pick me up from the terminal. On arriving at his offices, I was about to lock his car door once parked up. In those days central remote locking was rare, so you would push the locking knob down while simultaneously lifting the outside door handle to avoid locking yourself out of the car. But no, he did not want that. "We do not lock our cars here. Where would a thief take them?"

He then told me a tale of how some likely lads arrived in a transit van from the mainland and went around the unlocked homes stealing TVs, video recorders and the like. When the thefts started to be reported, the police took the call and promised all the residents that they would have their TVs back for Coronation Street that evening. All the police had to do was stand by the ferry terminal for the 5pm sailing and check the backs of a few transit vans. Fingerprints and DNA testing not required.

I telephoned and chatted to the receptionist for a couple of minutes once in Kirkwall and happened to mention how my optician was from Orkney. In fact, I said I think his brother is the optician in Kirkwall now. "Och, you will be talking about wee Bryan," she said.

Many years later we were on a flight to Singapore. The chap next to me was in the oil industry and on his way to Indonesia, but he lived in Orkney. Of course, Bryan's brother had tested his eyes the week before.

Shetland is deceptively long and thin. Sumburgh Airport is in the southern tip of the mainland and it is over 50 miles to the Sullom Voe Oil terminal to the north of the mainland. There are no trees on the island so the wind cuts straight across. The only tree I saw was in the garden of SSE's engineering manager and it blocked the view from his lounge down a loch.

OPPORTUNITIES

Our move to the North East gave me more control over my time, although I still worked phenomenally hard. When we started considering expanding Rosh abroad into the Netherlands, I asked the Newcastle Chapter of AEISEC if they could supply us with a student to do the research. We ended up having several placements over the next few years, and I was invited to Chair their governing committee. We even got AEISEC a slot on a local TV programme, featuring one of our Dutch students, Wouter Stemerdink.

Then there was the time that I was tapped-up to apply for a role on the Further Education Funding Council. I was appointed, although the FEFC was closed just 12 months later. However, I enjoyed the fresh perspective it gave me and the chance to meet a different type of business leader.

The Institute of Directors would open even more opportunities, particularly once I was on the IoD Committee and then Chair. My profile was raised and, as a result, I was invited to the regional annual dinners of ICAEW and Chamber of Commerce, where I extended my network.

I sat on a regional Mencap fundraising Committee for

a few years as well as The Northern Business Forum, which was a collection of business groups and special interest bodies.

Business Link Tyne & Wear

The creation of the Government-backed business support organisation, Business Link, gave me my first bigger board and organisation experience. I joined at its inception in 2000, and in my four years on the board, with two as Chair, I learned a great deal. It grew to employing more than 120 staff, with a CEO who had been a consultant. Unfortunately, although he was very confident, he did not possess all the knowledge and skills for the job. The board had to have a political balance too, and it included: Irene Lucas (wife of John Hays of Hays Travel) who was then CEO of South Tyneside Council; prospective Labour councillor Alex Scullion; and the MD of JT Dove's Builders Merchants, John Withers, which covered the main geographic and political boundaries.

However, I often felt the organisation was more bothered about ticking the right boxes than truly moving our region's small- and medium-sized businesses on to the next tier. They wanted to be measured by how much funding they secured but I wanted to measure them by how many more VAT-registered businesses there were each year in our patch.

It was a large board and I ruled it with discipline. I kept it sharp and to the point and, on my retirement, I was presented with a gavel in memory of my time. However, as a non-executive you must trust the executive to do their job right and fulfil the organisational objectives. The biggest test and greatest lesson I had in the role was when the auditors uncovered a loan to the CEO.

Any company loan to any member of staff needs board approval. It can be done, but only if correctly approved and minuted. Our CEO had just done it, in cahoots with the Financial Director. A phone call from the auditors led to an investigation and although no fraudulent intent was meant, it was wrong. The board tasked me with a formal admonishment and warning. Unfortunately, the CEO took this as a personal issue between me and him, and our relations soured.

The North East says "No"

Some people thought that Tony Blair only agreed to explore the idea of a regional elected assembly to get rid of his Deputy PM John Prescott out of Westminster for a time in 2004.

When the idea was first floated, I was asked for my opinion by BBC Radio Newcastle. I had been a regular on the radio, reviewing the newspapers from 0700hrs-0900hrs with the presenter of Breakfast, Mike Parr, so the added comment was nothing unusual. However, it led to me appearing on a late night BBC national TV panel debate hosted by the then unknown, Nick Robinson. I explained my objection to having another tier of government; the plan was not to eliminate local authorities but to put a "Geordie Parliament" between councils and national government.

Through the IoD and Business Link I had become good friends with a prominent Newcastle-based lawyer, Peter Allan. He was very old school, writing 'thank you' letters, standing up at table if a woman stood up, and generally charming. He also encouraged and supported me in my climb through IoD and Business Link, as well as in many other areas.

Many years later, I had a call from a Clive Allan asking if he could apply for a vacancy we had as a welder, even though he had re-trained in his 30s and not actually had a welding job yet. It was Peter's son. I was delighted to give him a chance. Peter wrote to thank me. I reminded him of an old lawyer who encouraged and supported a young businessman years before: What goes around comes around.

One day, Peter called me and asked if I would join him at a meeting in his Ward Hadaway offices later that week. He would not say who, what, or why. It was all rather cloak and dagger, but I trusted Peter, so I arrived as invited. The Shadow Minister for Regions, Bernard Jenkin MP, and a young bespectacled chap called William Norton were there, and wanted to know my thoughts about the proposed elected regional assembly. William later wrote a book about the campaign entitled, 'White Elephant, How the North East Said No', where he describes this meeting. *"We were introduced to Ian Dormer, the director of an engineering company on the Gateshead/Newcastle border. Dormer was sharp, amiable, and fluent with a wicked sense of humour and a fierce opposition to the assembly. He held a position on the local IoD and on some regional quangos... Here I thought was someone who could inflict a lot of damage to the Yes Men."*

In the book, Peter is just described as 'Mr S'. Peter is discreet and, as senior partner in a law firm with clients of many different views, he could not be seen to take sides.

Together, we formed the business-led 'North East Says No' (NESNO) organisation, not least to try and counter any threat that the National Front would try and form the credible opposition.

The Conservatives knew they could not be involved because it would be the death-knell in a Labour heartland. They did provide some backroom support but certainly no money. There were lots of hoops to jump through to be designated as the opposition, but we succeeded and in the process were given about £120,000. We privately raised another £20,000.

Figure 22: Founding NESNO in 2004

The directors were myself, John Elliot of EBAC, Phillip Cummings, and Peter Olsen, a Teesside accountant. Philip was a former Durham nightclub owner and managed to bring in his nephew, Dominic, to help with the campaign. Dominic (Cummings) famously went on to mastermind the Brexit referendum campaign and became a top aide to Prime Minister Boris Johnson.

Dominic rang me about joining the Brexit group and we

met for a cup of tea at 116 Pall Mall to discuss it, but I was a hard and fast Remainer so declined.

Emily Maitlis later interviewed me for a BBC documentary about Dominic and how he performed at NESNO. Dominic was quite a controversial character in political circles, but certainly an effective operator. Emily, meanwhile, had famously just interviewed Prince Andrew about some of his relationships which was such a PR debacle that it forced him to withdraw from public life.

NESNO had a seemingly impossible task: this was Labour policy in Labour heartland, and we had half their funds and a fraction of the ground troops. They also had some famous names backing the assembly, from Sir John Hall through to Alan Shearer and Brendan Foster.

We kept our arguments simple – devised in no small way by Dominic. Our strapline was 'Politicians talk, we pay' and we used an inflatable, five-metre tall White Elephant to highlight the waste.

Graham Robb, a former BBC-reporter-turned-PR-consultant, also made a big difference in managing the message and highlighted the key themes in the Government's White Paper. One of the great selling points of the proposed assembly was having a unified public transport policy. But Graham could point out there were three pages on transport in the White Paper, but 23 pages about the Assembly Members' expenses. Need we say more?

I did numerous radio and TV slots, having been given the 'air war' to fight. In one debate, the 'Yes' campaigner rambled on for ages but made no points that demonstrated any real benefits. When I was asked to respond and counter her argument, I simply replied, "I do not need to say anything. We just heard five minutes from Julie, offering nothing to the people of the North East. She made my case for me."

In a later BBC TV debate, chaired by Dermot Murnaghan, the opposition kept trying to talk over us as we were putting our points. "Dermot, can you please ask them to be quiet when we are speaking, or are they too frightened to let the audience hear our points, which confirm the assembly is a waste of time?" I said. Cheers from our crowd followed.

Another time, I was driving to BBC Radio Newcastle because Deputy PM John Prescott was going to be interviewed and the BBC requires views from 'the other side' to also be heard on the same programme, for balance.

I was just crossing the River Tyne when I got a phone call from the producer. "You are not needed now we have someone else," he said. I had not heard from any of the team that they had stepped in, so I asked him who it was. "We have a UKiP MEP instead," was the response. I objected, telling him that UKiP had nothing to do with our campaign, we were the official opposition, to which he responded, "John Prescott refuses to debate with anyone but his equal." Was he arrogant or worried his argument stood no scrutiny? No matter how hard I complained, I was not going to win that one.

We even made mock £50 notes featuring our line 'Politicians talk, we pay' message, and ceremonially burned thousands of them for the TV cameras. My daughter Emily even distributed them at school to friends and teachers.

The campaign was short, sharp, and frenetic. But enormous fun. It was a postal ballot, so it came to an end the day before the count. I then went to an IoD Branch Chairman's Awayday being held at an Anouska Hemple hotel in London, directly opposite the garden that features in the film Notting Hill.

The vote count started at 10pm on the Thursday night (why, when it was all postal I have no idea).

I went to bed but slept badly. At 3am, I woke in a cold sweat having had a nightmare in which we had lost by two percent, and I was gutted. I turned on the TV and searched Ceefax and found the news page. We had won, with nearly 80% voting NO. This was not just a victory, it was a serious drubbing of a government plan.

The Government had been sure that its policies would be adopted in its heartland, with plans to roll-out across the UK thereafter. We had put a stop to this.

Later, talking to the team that were at the count, I asked them when they had realised that we had won. Within 10minutes, they said.

As the ballots were opened there was 'No, no, no, no, yes, no, no, no' written on piles all around the hall. John Prescott had been present and used his authority to delay the announcement of the result until after 2am; the deadline for the following day's newspapers. By the Saturday, it was old news and his humiliation was limited to quick soundbites on radio and TV and so it never made the front pages.

ONE North East 2007

The biggest non-executive public sector role in the North East at the time was at the Regional Development Agency – ONE North East. It had 300 staff and £200million+ revenue, so it was a serious role. It was also the first time that I had been paid a fee of £10,000 per annum.

It was openly and competitively advertised, and I had thought that my involvement in NESNO might mean the Government would kybosh my appointment. But, instead, I was appointed.

The board was even more politically balanced – and as a consequence very large. Again, we had to have both political and geographic balance, so members included: the Leader of Sunderland, Bob Symonds; Newcastle opposition and former Leader, John Shipley, a Lib Dem; Peter Jackson from Northumberland, a Conservative; Ian Brown, a former Lib Dem; and Alex Cunningham, Labour, Teesside.

I got on amazingly well with Bob. He was a classic former miner who had worked at the coal face, but ended up in politics. People might have thought we were poles apart but he was decent, down-to-earth chap, who was fun and had the region's interests at heart. He also told some great stories from the colliery days. He was ousted in a nasty internal political coup in the Council, but always had a cheery smile.

John Shipley always impressed me with his understanding of local government and was raised to the House of Lords during his time on the board. He was a star with Emily and gave her the kind of work experience that money could not buy.

The proceedings of the monthly board were covered by the largest board packs I have ever seen. Once, we had two full ring-binders with double-sided papers inside; I cannot believe that everyone read them. I did, but it nearly killed me. It was the classic public sector approach of tell them everything and we will not be in trouble.

However, the organisation did try to help economic regeneration in the North East. I was asked to chair a couple of the subsidiary businesses which were investing in those start-up, or high growth potential, small businesses that banks were reluctant to risk.

Enterprise Development North East had a £600million loan fund for this purpose which we distributed to professional investment houses in the region with clear target markets to help boost the region. It worked on the principle that no one believed that companies such as Apple or Google would succeed when they started, but everyone wished they had invested after the event.

While we were not in it primarily for the direct financial payback, we were for the employment and economic boost it would give the area. We never found our equivalent of Apple during my time, but we did wash our face.

I also chaired a committee which aimed to simplify business support in the region. Over the years, many companies had been helped by funding from various government-supported schemes designed to help grow business. They ranged from one which had a multitude of promotional websites, through to one that helped businesses develop necessary language skills to help develop their exports. A good degree of consolidation was necessary.

I joined the board of 1NG, which started in partnership with Newcastle and Gateshead councils. 1NG was tasked with developing brownfield land sites in the twin cities and building a conference centre on land next to The Sage, Gateshead.

Chaired by Tony Blair's former Attorney General, Lord Falconer, it had quite a heavy hitting board including Graham Wylie, one of the founders of Sage through to the leaders and CEOs of each council.

While we developed a couple of disused factories, the financial crash in 2008 put an end to our aspirations. The financial crisis, and a change of government, led to the closure of ONE North East. It had made a difference, but politics determined it had to go; a Conservative Government was never going to support a Labour quango.

I must have made an impact on all the sub-boards and chair responsibilities I had had, as I was asked to chair the Audit Committee that managed the closure. It was a responsible task that I am proud to say we did successfully, in a clean and efficient way.

INSTITUTE OF DIRECTORS

I received a cold call from the membership team at the Institute of Directors just before I was 28 years old. They were offering a special reduced rate if I joined before my birthday, so I did. I was looking for something that would give me the peer support that I desperately lacked. At Rosh, I was either on my own, or turned to dad.

My first local meeting was a bit like an old gentlemen's luncheon club at a hotel opposite the station. But I persevered and next went to a Dining Club dinner, which was more interesting.

The Dining Clubs were good, and numbers were restricted - no more than 16 or 20 people sat around one dining table at the Northern Counties Club (a gentlemen's club that had only recently started allowing women in during the evenings).

We were treated to some fascinating guests, including Paul Polman from P&G who talked about innovations such as chips on consumables, which, when thrown into the bin would automatically update your next shopping list. Paul went on to be the global head of Unilever and one of the top executives in the country.

We also had Sir John Hall talking about how he bought Newcastle United. He was not a fan and did not have a clue about football as a business, so went and asked Arsenal, Manchester United and others for advice, which they freely gave. Although the teams competed on the pitch, they did not compete as businesses, because their customer bases were entirely separate, plus it was in everyone's best interests to make the game more successful.

I then had notification about an event aimed at 'Young Directors and Europe', which was being held in London. I had already scheduled a trip to the South East around that time and so I decided to attend. It was my first trip to the grand HQ in 116 Pall Mall. There were nearly 200 young directors (under 45 years old), and various proposals were established, including forming a committee, "but do not let it be made up of consultants," someone said.

A card drop at the end for interested candidates was proposed and, with Rosh Engineering on my card, it was not really a surprise when I was told a few weeks later that I had been chosen.

Over the next few years, our committee invigorated the younger members and organised the events that we wanted.

We tasked under 45-year-olds around the UK to approach their local branch committees to get them to have events more suited to our age group. We also had national events – putting together a half-day conference with potted sessions on everything from the legal responsibilities of directors, through to masterclasses in public speaking and presentations.

After a couple of years, I became Chair of the group and had the daunting task of presenting to the then 70-strong council about the need to cater for younger members.

Our downfall came when we were planning an annual dinner and one of our group, Freddie De Lisle, proposed that his friend Kevin Maxwell speak. Kevin was the son of disgraced media tycoon, Robert Maxwell. Robert had robbed the Mirror newspaper pension fund but was found dead in the sea off the Canary Islands in November 1991 before he could stand trial.

By the time we were planning our event, his sons had been personally cleared of wrong-doing but were planning his defence. We had lunch with Kevin and he was nervous about a high-profile speech. He was also not keen on our billing, *'How to Make and Lose a Billion'*. Having been assured that we had approval from the IoD we started the scheduling. Then the members' complaints came in and the rug was pulled. It was just too radical.

My involvement with the IoD at a national level, plus my drive to get younger members events running in the North East, led to the local branch committee inviting me - along with two other younger members - to join them. We wanted to put on breakfast events and 5pm sessions instead of the lunches. We also wanted practical learning sessions. We added a box to invitations saying, 'If it is your first event, tick here and someone will welcome you and introduce you to others'.

I invited the Managing Director of Air UK, who was one of my Flight International connections, to talk about joint ventures and collaborative agreements. They were the feed airline for KLM, and were eventually absorbed into KLM.

While the average lunch would get 10 or 15 members, our breakfast attracted 48. The committee then had to sit up and take note.

About four years later I was invited to take over as Chair. The committee was still burdened with old men, so my first task was to dig into the rule book and retire-off anyone that had been there for nine years or more, which was quite a few. We then had a more dynamic and current business-focused operation.

We held annual dinners which 250 members attended, and a varied programme of events throughout the year. I even managed to get the branch its first paid, part-time administrator. It happened to be my sister Lisa, but she did a great job.

I also scaled our events by working jointly with ICAEW, AMBA and other complimentary business membership groups. The National Sporting Club (NSC) organised dinners with famous speakers. I arranged for 40 or 50 IoD members to attend and so got to meet cricket legends Ian Botham and Bob Willis. We live in a small world. Bob Willis' brother David ran the NSC, and he was married to Maggie Blot, a doctor who had been based in the North East - Julia had done some joint research work with her. It turned out that Maggie's brother, Tony Appleton, had been a supplier of various machinery, from cranes through to plant hire, to Rosh Engineering.

At another NSC dinner, legendary Formula 1

commentator Murray Walker had been invited to be guest speaker. Lisa, Glenn, Julia, and I were some of the first to arrive at the VIP pre-dinner drinks reception. Murray walked in and, of course, knew no one. So I went over and welcomed him and introduced him to our little group. Julia and Glenn were stunned that I did that, but to me, meeting people is a pleasure. Equally, I know what it's like to walk into a room not knowing anyone and to have someone open-up and welcome you in is the most heartwarming thing that can happen.

Over the years I met people like Nobby Stiles, who played in the England 1966 World Cup-winning team, and the troubled Belfast footballing legend George Best. I had an old George Best football album which I asked him to sign at the event, and I was glad I did as he died from alcoholism just a few years later.

Joining the Board

As Branch Chair I had a seat on the IoD's Council. Despite the Younger Members being closed down a couple of years before, my success in the branch and contributions on Council led to an invitation to join the main board of the IoD – or in those days the Policy & Executive Committee, as it was called. This met monthly and was the operations board for the IoD.

It was top table, the like of which I had never experienced before. The Chair was former Government Minister John Butcher, and Lord Tony Newton (the Conservative politician and former Cabinet member) was an executive member.

I was the youngest there by about 25 years.

One lovely old boy, Graham Wheeler, a former PWC

Partner took me under his wing. He was jolly and supportive and was always asking after my young family and checking that I was spending lots of time with them. But I was building my business and had lots to do. I did what I could but surely now was the time to drive hard? Didn't he understand? But his interest hit me hard when he was missing at one of our meetings, and the Chair informed us that Graham's son had died the week before.

The following month I expressed my condolences and Graham re-iterated his oft repeated "spend time with your family." He had also been driven in his early career, going to work before his children were awake, and coming home after they were in bed. He spent his weekends building contacts and networking on golf courses. Now he was retired and had the chance to spend time with his son, only for his son to die of cancer in his early 30s.

Enjoy your children while you can, was a message I took home that night.

Other board members during my time included:
- Sir Hugh Sykes who was Chair of Yorkshire Bank, and a wily old fellow;
- Nicholas Brookes who was Chair of security printing firm De La Rue and, while he was the most charming fellow, he also had a laser-sharp intellect and nothing passed him by - he would always make sure he challenged board members professionally and thoroughly;
- Sir Robin Young, a Civil Service veteran who had a good inside line to the workings of Whitehall and had been at school with Gordon

Brown. He was now Chair of a few private sector companies.

The Barbara Judge Controversy

The Hon Barbara Thomas as she was known, later to become Lady Barbara Judge. A former (American) lawyer, Chair of The Atomic Energy Authority, on the Board of Port Merion, restaurant critic for Forbes Magazine: she had a pedigree but that was it. I did not rate her. Invariably late, failing to turn off her mobile (which rang in meetings), appearing to fall asleep in a session, and clearly having not read board papers in advance. When she was later chosen by others as my replacement as Chair of the IoD in 2015, I expressed my surprise. She was a disaster and was ousted in 2018 after being secretly recorded making racist comments about the Institute secretary and disparaging remarks about a pregnant colleague.

The Guardian reported at the time that she was "understood to have been recorded covertly by the IoD's director general, Stephen Martin" and to have said, "We have three inexperienced people doing a job [on the IoD's secretariat] when one experienced person could do it and they are making mistakes. And so the problem is we have one black and we have one pregnant woman and that is the worst combination we could possibly have. No, two blacks and one pregnant woman. I couldn't believe it!"

In her resignation letter she said, "I continue to strongly refute the allegations made against me and remain deeply disturbed by the gross and conspiratorial mishandling of the process which has led to the damaging circumstances in which I and the Institute are now placed". She added, "My acknowledgment that issues of race and pregnancy could complicate their removal both legally and from the standpoint of public perception is an observation I believe most lawyers would make, and that many non-lawyers also know to be true. I was addressing the likely consequences of their dismissal, not the reasons for it."

Judge was succeeded by Charlotte Valeur.

During my nine years on the board, I also Chaired the Membership Committee for a while. It was a great member-focused sub-committee, but the Chief Operating Officer, Andrew Main Wilson, was not a fan: he did not like the Membership Committee holding him to account or suggesting better ways of doing things. That was his exclusive world.

It all came to a head during my time as chair of the IoD. The Director General, Simon Walker, asked the board for permission to part company with Andrew. The board agreed that Andrew had outlived his time, and I was charged with giving him the news. Because of a poor experience during my time at Business Link doing a one-on-one and the matter becoming personal, I arranged to do it with Nimble Thompson (Vice Chair and former Eversheds partner), and Simon. The Institute was losing membership and revenue was falling. Simon had to instigate change, and although I could question whether some of his ideas and approach were right, change had to happen. Few like change.

I sat down with Andrew on many occasions to see his plans to turn the business around, but all he could do was salami slice. He increased everyone's targets by 10% and reduced their budgets by 20%. I did not feel he knew how to look at each activity and make tough decisions to end them. How much overhead cost was apportioned to each activity also made no sense. For me, the sporting lunches were not good business. Andrew liked meeting the sports stars, but the events attracted fewer and fewer members. He was very London-centric and focused all his efforts on the South East.

The Board agreed to Simon's proposal to exit Andrew, and we tried to do it slowly and amicably. However, in reality this meant that he stewed in the business for weeks, establishing a resistance to Simon and me and the changes we planned. He had a loyal team, to which he added a small group of disgruntled IoD Council members, creating tough opposition for us. One of the Council members, Nicholas Cook, had unsuccessfully applied for the vacant Institute Secretary position. A second member had pitched an investment proposal to the board, but it was deemed out of scope and rejected. They were joined by a third member who had previously helped us with some re-structuring plans, whose motive was ousting Simon in order to become Director General himself.

Simon and I battled on several fronts for more than a year. I received formal complaints about Simon, which I asked an independent committee to investigate. They ranged from inappropriate spending of Institute money, through to him crushing a claim made against another executive that he was inappropriate with a female member of staff. All were found to be false. Even the investigation process was challenged. We were so embroiled in claims of one thing or another we had to get independent legal advice about the process, including constitutional authority. The bill topped £100,000.

I chaired both the IoD Council and the board and so was seen by our opponents as conflicted. I managed to win a vote of no confidence, but the emotional and intellectual energy needed to get through it all was draining. I lost lots of sleep and instead of spending two or three days a month in London, I was spending two or three days a week. We spent time canvassing the 25 council members to make sure we answered their questions and, more importantly, secured their support.

The day where Simon and I finally bagged the decisive votes from Council, which led to the protractors resigning, was a great relief. I had been supported well by Vice-Chair Nimble Thompson and many other board and council members. I had also a hard-working Institute Secretary, Loretto Leavy, who covered every base. But it was not the tenure that I expected.

Another committee I chaired was the Chartered Director Committee. I had been asked to take over from a former NatWest Bank Company Secretary, who was the outgoing Chair. Meetings were scheduled to finish at 5.30pm, but often dragged on until beyond 6.30pm, by which time half of the committee had left. When I took over the regime was different; they were to the point, on time, and productive.

I was not a Chartered Director at that stage which

caused some raised eyebrows, but the improved functioning of the group more than made up for this.

When I was appointed IoD Chair I vowed to qualify as a Chartered Director. How could I convince members it was a great thing to undertake (and pay £12k to do) if I had not done it myself? The first stage was the Certificate, and a week-long residential course that was brutally hard work. Although the exam a few weeks later was multiple choice it was tough. I have never done such a hard test. Everything from good corporate governance through to finance. I still have a cold sweat with the prospect of working out the average weighted cost of capital.

The Diploma was more fun, because it was case studies and more practical boardroom-type analysis and problem solving, rather than learning. The exam was essays and I loved it.

The final stage to becoming Chartered was drawing-up a portfolio followed by a peer group interview. The relief when I passed was enormous. I had put myself out front and centre. Failure would have been embarrassing to say the least.

I kept in touch with other delegates on the courses. We had everyone from an SAS officer through to the Deputy Director of the Serious Organised Crime Agency (SOCA).

We discussed ethical dilemmas on the Diploma and Ian Cruxton from SOCA trumped us all with his tale of following a drug dealer for days, knowing a big shipment of cocaine was about to arrive. Then one afternoon they watched dealer get drunk and climb in his car. Do you let him drive to the drug drop and get the conviction to save countless lives, or break cover and stop him, losing the chance of a drugs bust but stopping him potentially ploughing into a bus stop of school children? We did not have a clue what to do and he had 60 seconds to make the call. But the genius decision was to get the local patrol car to randomly stop him and put him in the cells overnight until he sobered up.

While I was on the board and leading the Chartered Director Committee, I was asked to become Vice Chair of the main board. It was an odd appointment process, where I was asked by the Chair, Chris Beale, if I was interested, and then no vote was taken, nor was there any suggestion of, "please leave the room why we discuss," instead, I just sat there, and everyone agreed. For an organisation that prides itself on process and governance, it was most strange.

Being involved with other organisations made me appreciate that change and turmoil in my own business was normal. Seemingly great staff went from favourites to being suddenly removed. One real character was Ruth Lea, Chief Economist and Director of Policy. She was a firebrand single woman in her fifties who loved cats and always wore a red jacket.

A staunch Conservative, her outpourings sometimes caused embarrassment during the Labour Government years. But Ruth was not for telling. Once she allegedly smashed up her office when someone criticised her.

Inevitably, the day came when a secret meeting of the board was held at a private club in Queen Anne's Gate and her dismissal was proposed. When the Chair and Director General gave her the bad news, she tipped a jug of water over the Chair. She was very bitter but was given a job by one of the board members (who had resigned in protest at the decision).

(Sir) Henry Angst owned Arbuthnot Latham Bank and was also Vice Chair of the Conservative Party. I later had lunch with Henry and Ruth at the bank and she was very pleasant, but those days of the IoD were not mentioned. The reason I had lunch with just the two of them was in, in part, because the IoD invested £5 million of its reserves in the bank and I had just become Chair.

After the board meetings, we often had a guest speaker. They ranged from the head of HMRC through to the Governor of the Bank of England, Eddie George. I subsequently met Robert Carney (who later became Governor) on a couple of occasions and sat next to him once at a small private lunch in Newcastle.

These were sharp and astute individuals. I asked if he could convince the Chancellor to give tax relief on director's loans or retained profits in small businesses, just as they give relief on company debt with banks in businesses. Surely, when an owner director risks her or his own money, it is worthy of some recognition. Carney was gracious in saying no and warned, "the likelihood is they will remove all debt tax relief rather than extend it."

I also sat next to Michael Gove when he was in opposition and was thoroughly charmed by him. He seemed genuinely engaged in my conversation and wanting my thoughts. His turncoat and political opportunism around Brexit was very disappointing.

Many politicians I've met had the ability to make the

person they are talking to feel important. But some turned my stomach.

John Hutton was a Minister in Blair's Government was one such, who was our opening speaker at an event in Pall Mall that I was chairing. He was late arriving because he had wanted to drop off his kids at school. Nice of him to tell us in advance. He then made a fuss about the laptop on the lectern, in a rude and objectionable way. He was arrogant, full of himself, and I did not like him one bit.

Awaydays

The IoD was very London-centric in those days. Very few of the board were from outside the home counties, and most of the Institute's thinking and its policies were focused around this region.

The board's Strategy Awayday did not venture too far either. The furthest it went was Berkshire. I thought this was wrong and proposed we went out to the regions and branches.

Naturally, the first proper Awayday was in Newcastle. I organised a reception with local leaders and the committee, and the fresh perspective worked wonders.

Subsequently, we went to Edinburgh, Exeter, Manchester, Belfast and Birmingham.

Jason Wohura was the young local IoD Chair in Birmingham, and he was one of four brothers behind an enormously successful Indian food wholesale business – East End Foods. He had organised for us a tour of the new Jaguar engine factory in Wolverhampton. What an amazing, fully automated production line that was.

We travelled there in Jason's Bentley, and he apologised as he struggled to manoeuvre it out of a parking space, saying he usually drove a smaller car in the city. Fully expecting him to say a Fiat or Mini, I asked him what car? A Maserati. Rather embarrassing.

The IoD Annual Convention

The IoD Annual Convention was the business conference of the year in the UK.

Traditionally held at the Royal Albert Hall, it attracted world-leading business figures. I never paid to go, having been branch chair and on the board so a free seat was guaranteed.

The private Director General's lunch also accommodated many of the speakers and I got to meet a few in the process. Occasionally you would have a great name that disappointed, and sometimes an unknown that was a real star. The head of Air Miles, for example, talked about the value of loyalty schemes and how many petrol stations drivers would pass until they found their brand, even if they were late for a meeting and low on fuel.

The best line-up during this period was the Centenary Convention in 2006. It had 6,000 delegates and a speaker list that was top-drawer:

- Buzz Aldren, the second man on the moon
- Archbishop Desmond Tutu by video link in South Africa
- Terrence Conran of Habitat,
- Sir Steve Redgrave, our most successful Olympian to date
- And Margaret Thatcher. The former Prime

Minister was not meant to be speaking, just attending the lunch as a guest. But Lord Young, the former Trade Minister, (and IoD President) persuaded her to take a bow on stage. She got a standing ovation. She was clearly an old lady then.

I managed to meet all of these esteemed guests at the lunch, and all were gracious and charming. It was the days before mobile phones and selfies, so I got several autographs instead.

We had a lunchtime speaker for our private session: Dame Ellen McArthur. Dame Ellen had completed the fastest-ever, single-handed circumnavigation of the globe despite being not much more than 5ft tall. She was terrified of having to speak to us, but she did admirably, highlighting the plight of the Albatross.

It was an honour for me to meet her. I had read her book about the circumnavigation that summer and marvelled at the perils she faced and bravery she showed. But she had also impressed many people with her fast lap-driving on the BBC TV Show Top Gear, becoming the fastest driver "in a reasonably priced car" which gave her cult hero status.

Her skill was incredible considering that she had spent so much of her time at sea. She had even asked if she could have another go, because she thought she could drive faster.

Chatting to her about it she said the hardest thing was the producers wanting her to give a commentary while she was driving; she had needed all her concentration to stay on the track. But her clear determination proved she would have been successful at whatever she chose to do.

One telling Convention was just before local elections, and only a few months before a general election was called during Gordon Brown's Premiership.

I had met Gordon at an annual dinner when he was Chancellor of the Exchequer. Gordon had an almost inverted snobbery towards black tie dinners and came in a lounge suit, but when he spoke he was hilarious. The actor and comedian, Hugh Laurie, who followed him said, "hold on a minute Chancellor, I am meant to be the funny one here tonight!"

But at the Convention, Gordon came on stage, stood behind the lectern, and shouted his speech at us. Half-way through, he mistakenly said, "I want to increase unemployment," meaning, of course, increase employment. The auditorium gasped but he did not notice and charged on.

David Cameron as Leader of the Opposition followed and, while he had notes in his hand, stood at the front of the stage, looked us in the eye and spoke naturally and from the heart. But Cameron also made a mistake, saying, "I want to increase government red tape," rather than decrease it. We all gasped. But he stopped, apologised, corrected himself, and admitted it had been a tiring few weeks campaigning.

Meanwhile, the strain of office was clearly telling on Brown and the fact he lost the election was no big surprise on that performance alone.

The year I became Chair, The Convention had moved venues to the O2, or rather a side hall at the O2 arena.

It was not much of a success, so the following year we went back to the Royal Albert Hall.

I took on a 'meet-and-greet role' in the Green Room backstage, and met some fascinating businesspeople, ranging from John Matonis of BitCoin, to Jimmy Wales, the founder of Wikipedia. The latter was very unassuming and really pleasant chap who despite being American, preferred to live in London.

Figure 23: Sir Richard Branson at an IoD convention

We had also booked Sir Richard Branson of Virgin, who seemed quite nervous and almost humble. He had a veritable posse of people with him. "Do all these people have a job with you?" I asked. He looked, almost in amazement at the handful of young and buzzing aids. "I think so," he replied.

Richard was the star attraction that year, so he was on last, and I followed to give the closing speech. But the whole day had run over and by the time Richard went on to be interviewed by DG Simon Walker, we were already 40 minutes over.

I unilaterally decided to cut my 10–12 minute speech dramatically, and was glad that I did; as Richard exited the stage, and I was announced by, 'the voice of God', all I could see was 3,000 of the 4,000 attendees get up to leave.

The following year the IoD gave me the spot immediately after lunch in compensation, which I was very grateful for. I also had a couple of spots interviewing the VP of Google, Dan Cobley, and the CEO of Tech City, Joanna Shields.

It was the first time I had used an autocue which was terrific and I can see why so many do. I had had a practise booked for the day before and, on arriving backstage, I met another speaker also getting ready for his rehearsal. It was Andy Bird, Chairman of Disney International.

I introduced myself and he then introduced his mum who was sitting on a chair to one side. I asked if she had flown over from LA with her son, "no, I live in Warrington," she replied. Obviously, I looked a bit dumbstruck. Yes, Warrington near Manchester, Andy said, that is where I am from.

He was a lovely fellow and I warmed to him enormously, particularly when he was taken out on stage and he turned to his mum, "come on out with me mum, it is not often you get the chance to walk the stage at the Royal Albert Hall."

Andy's presentation with Disney motion pictures and animations playing behind, which perfectly segued with his speech, was inspirational. He also spoke about the impending opening of Disney Shanghai. As our family had visited every Disney in the world (Orlando, LA, Paris, Hong Kong, Tokyo), the prospect of bagging the sixth was an ideal 50th birthday treat for Julia.

A year in advance, we started the planning with time in Bali, and downtown Shanghai, but our travel agent could not book the Fantasia Suite at Disney, no matter how she tried. Desperate - and a rare move for me to call favours from important connections - I dropped Andy Bird an email. At 0800 LA time I had an email back, direct from him. He remembered me and said he would look into it. I fully expected an assistant to follow this through from that point onward. But no, he replied personally, and advised that bookings opened in October. So, one month later we tried, and tried, and again, we failed.

I sheepishly emailed Andy again but need not have been worried. He connected me directly with someone in Shanghai, who then called me the following day and the suite was booked.

When we later checked into the hotel, the manager came out to greet us, the suite was adorned with 'Happy Birthday' balloons and there was a cake for Julia (even though her birthday was two months earlier, the reason for the trip had been noted).

I reported back to Andy how good the staff were, and named a few, knowing this would be fed-back. He was late replying because at the time he was on holiday in Columbia; a trip he recommended to me and one which we followed up on a couple of years later.

Interestingly, I was reading Radio DJ and TV host, Chris Evans' autobiography after all this and in it he described how a kind young producer at Piccadilly Radio in Manchester gave him support, help, and encouragement, at the beginning of his media journey. Chris then wrote how Andy Bird was now doing something big in the corporate world. Same decent chap, and lovely to know that success happens to those who are good from beginning to end.

Boris Johnson, when he was Mayor of London, also spoke at the Convention. He was popular among the young, and Emily insisted that I get his autograph. "I cannot do that," I insisted. It was not the done thing for the Chair to do. But, of course, I did it for my little girl, although I struggled to get a pen that worked. Emily wanted him to write, "I look forward to meeting you when you are Prime Minister," which he was game enough to do.

Chancellor George Osborne also came to the Convention. I met him at the back door and took him down to the Green Room. The senior politicians always had a couple of aids as well as two or three security detail; very discreet, but very on the ball.

I had a chat with George when he came to Simon Walker's retirement party at the IoD a few years later after he had stood down as Chancellor. He was clear that the prospect of Brexit was not one he wanted to be involved in and he thought it would be a disaster.

The party, held in Simon's honour, attracted the great and good of both business and politics, and included a speech by Sir John Major. I had always thought Sir John was a small man, but he is over 6ft and a very thoughtful and charming fellow.

My time on the board eventually came to an end. I had been there 10 years which was as long as good corporate governance allowed, although I continued to Chair the Chartered Director Committee.

It was good I still had inside connections and exposure, and the then Chairman, Dr Neville Bain, suggested I apply for the Chair role when he retired.

Neville had been a great Chair in so many ways. Early on he stood no messing with Andrew Main Wilson, who had always had the habit of rocking up 10 minutes late for the board meeting. It was Andrew's way of demonstrating how busy and important he was. The second time he did that, Neville told him in front of the whole board, "If you cannot get here on time like everyone else, do not bother coming." Andrew was never late again.

Neville also asked me to contribute a chapter to a book he was writing about Corporate Governance – and as I had more knowledge than him on governance in the small and medium-sized business, I did that section.

I genuinely did not think I stood a chance of becoming Chair, although I privately aspired to it.

Neville was a former Cadbury Schweppes, Courtaulds, and Scottish & Newcastle Brewery Director and had also been Chair of the Royal Mail. The Royal Mail was a monolith and with revenue falling, and massive overheads, they needed radical restructuring and change, but after that they would have a future. Getting the Trade Unions to agree to change was going to be a challenge and management feared it would spark industrial action. So, because it was a public body, Neville took the plan (with all the risks highlighted, and a proposed successful outcome three years down the line) to the Labour Government Minister in charge of the Royal Mail, Stephen Byers. His response was, "My likely tenure in this post is six months so I am not having it marked by a postal strike." The plan was therefore rejected and the Royal Mail continued its downward spiral until change was forced upon them.

Neville was very encouraging and supportive of my application to be IoD Chair, even though he could play no part in choosing his successor. I thought IoD Chairs were in a different league, but he highlighted my understanding and passion for the IoD, my ability to chair meetings, and the respect I had from the board members. So, I put my name into the mix.

The Chair

Figure 24: The top job

The interviews for the new IoD Chair were being held during our half-term skiing holiday. Julia thought that they were trying to send me a message that the job was not for me because they knew that I was an avid skier. But I believed it was just a matter of co-ordinating the interviewers' diaries.

On Tuesday 14 February 2012, I headed off at 0630 for Geneva Airport from our chalet in St Jean D'Aulps. I had organised it with the Institute Secretary's PA, Sheila Cannon that I would have a lunchtime interview.

I made it in plenty of time and grabbed a coffee with Sheila first to find out who the other candidates were. Emma Harrison was the biggest threat. She was a multi-millionairess, a self-made business woman, and the politically well-connected owner of A4E; a supplier of services to Government from Business Link Franchises to arrange back-to-work programmes for ex-offenders. Plus, the IoD DG Simon Walker had made it clear that he would like a female Chair.

In I went. The interview panel was chaired by Philippa Foster Back, of the Institute of Business Ethics and IoD Deputy Chair. It included the De La Rue Chair, Nicholas Brookes, Chris Parkhouse from the IoD Council, and Simon. Between them they grilled me and, as charming as Nicholas is, he showed why he chaired such an esteemed organisation because he did not give me an easy time.

I left not knowing how it was going to turn out. I had done all I could but the competition was formidable. Back at the chalet later that evening I lamented my position.

Richard (who always joined us for half term) suddenly piped up, "Emma Harrison? I know that name..." He disappeared to his car and returned a few minutes later with a copy of the Daily Mail that he had picked up on his journey south a few days earlier. Emma Harrison featured on the front page, having paid herself an £8.6 million dividend; money made from tax payer's money. That wasn't all: A4e also paid Harrison and her partner around £1.7m over two years for leasing properties, including their 20-bedroom stately home, to her own firm. It was toxic and she announced her resignation as Chairman of A4e, stating, "I do not want the continuing media focus on me to be any distraction for A4e."

I arrived back at work on the Monday feeling pretty low, assuming that I had not got the job having not heard. Protocol is usually that the successful candidate gets a call the next day. Later that morning I had a call from Phillipa Foster Back, I assumed giving me the disappointing news, but it was quite the contrary: I was to be the new Chair of the IoD.

By this stage, Neville Bain's health was deteriorating. He had cancer and the year before, when I had been on the interview panel for the new DG with him, he had had a massive growth on the side of his neck. He continued to work as much as he could, but sadly he died in the first few months of my tenure, without even being able to give me a formal handover.

Experiences Money Cannot Buy

I was initially given an office on the top floor of the IoD's grand, Nash-designed HQ in 116 Pall Mall. Later, it would be part of a re-development project, enabling us to exit another building two doors along and save money. I could not justify the space and, as most organisations were going open plan, I led from the front and in my final year just used a little glass box of a meeting space whenever I was in town.

Although I knew the IoD well, I wanted to meet all the department heads and key staff and learn about their roles, the stresses and strains etc. I was having one of these meetings during my first day in post when Simon Walker put his head round the door asking me what I was doing at 2pm. I said I was meeting Kate Brackenbury from membership. Simon replied, "Can you re-arrange because I am off to see Ed Miliband (Labour leader of the opposition) and you might like to join in?"

It was quite an introduction to the role, as we walked down Whitehall to Portcullis House and into Miliband's private office. I was in awe of the access we had. It was just Ed, an aid, Simon, me, and the IoD's Director of Policy, Graeme Leach.

The Prime Minister

As time went on, we had multiple meetings with senior political leaders. I had visited 10 Downing Street before when I was on the board, and we had an audience with Tony Blair. I arrived with Lord Tony Newton, who had been in Thatcher's cabinet, so he was able to give me the lie of the land.

I had always been under the impression that the cabinet met at a room in the front overlooking Downing Street, when in fact it is on the ground floor at the back.

Tony told me how he was once late to a Cabinet meeting and called to advise of his train's progress. At that point, the IRA started firing mortar bombs through the roof of a transit van in Whitehall into Downing Street and its back garden. He could hear the explosions over the phone and felt lucky not to be there. Luckily, there was little damage and no loss of life.

Tony Blair was phenomenal. He came into the meeting and made us feel at ease straight away; no speech, he just said, "Ask me what you like."

At the time, he had just made a U-turn on something Euro-related and the first member said he had two questions. Their first question was, "Why did you make the U turn?" Blair had a little laugh, looked at the ground, and said, "What is your second question?" We all laughed and felt the ice break completely. He then went on to answer the first question deftly. We were putty in his hands.

My famous walk up the stairs to the meeting rooms, past all the photos of previous Prime Ministers, was a real moment to cherish. Number 10 is a bit of a Tardis, with seemingly endless rooms. I probably visited six or seven times over the years and had meetings with special advisors as well as the PM. Once we met in a drawing room that took us past the stairway up to the PM's flat (Theresa May's residence at the time). It was small, stark, and really basic; not the grand entrance to the home of the leader of the country which you might expect.

Figure 25: Outside Number 10

My first breakfast with a PM was with David Cameron and there was just a small group of us: the IoD, CBI, FSB, and Chamber of Commerce. It was a good meeting, and he was as charming and disarming as Blair; I understood how they reached their position on that basis alone.

I had asked the IoD's team to survey our members before we met. We ran regular surveys with them on Policy decisions, and this time we ended with, 'What one thing would you like the Chair to ask the PM to do for business?' While there were handful of childish quips, the 2,000 responses fell into six clear categories, from regulations to government procurement. The CBI's Sir Michael Rake liked to dominate proceedings, as if he and the PM were best mates and the rest of us were along for the ride. When said I that we had questioned our members and they had come back six points, it was no great surprise when Sir Michael then tried to chip-in after just my first point. But Cameron stood him down, saying, "I want to hear all six points first." He duly noted them, and I promised that I would give the background to his staff for further reflection.

It was an IoD triumph, and I felt pretty chuffed.

Figure 26: Meeting David Cameron

These were privileged sessions in many ways, but also because Cameron trusted us not to speak about the discussions inappropriately outside the room. I raised the question of the expansion of Heathrow Airport and the decision on a third runway. Cameron admitted it was vital for the future of the UK as a global trading nation, and he supported it. But the political climate meant he could not waste political capital on such a sensitive and divisive issue at that time. There were more important things to get done first.

We prepared equally well for another audience, but this time we took a dozen different businesspeople to a roundtable. Our group included Dame Margaret Barbour; the MD of Komatsu, Peter Howe; Chair of Bonne Mamam foods, Derek Wilson; Panaz's Tony Attard; East End Foods' Jason Wouhra; and several others.

I had a pre-meeting to agree questions and points to raise to keep the session focused and flowing. We also had a couple of IoD Policy staff including Stephen Herring our tax expert. He wanted to ask some complex double-locking of tax and benefits question, which I thought was too technical and parochial and best left to Treasury officials. Stephen pleaded, so I said the classic, "we will see".

Priti Patel began the session, because Cameron was 10 mins late, and very apologetic. We stood up as he entered, but he waved us down and insisted we carry on the discussion. We went through all the questions and, knowing that the PM's time is tight, I was pleased that we had got through all the scheduled points with four minutes to spare. Stephen Herring at this point was waving at me madly, so I relented.

The Prime Minister listened, considered, raised a couple of points on process, and then said, "What a brilliant idea. And if I recall that was first proposed by X&Y in the 1920s and they were Socialists. How can the opposition complain?"

His knowledge of this obscure treasury policy idea really impressed me. Even more so when, a few weeks later, the idea appeared in the Chancellor's Budget speech. I heartily congratulated Stephen, partly on the fact the PM thought he was brilliant but also that the policy had been picked up. He insisted, however, the Government only adopted part of his suggestion.

Kazakhstan

The IoD was sealing a deal with the sovereign wealth fund of oil-rich Kazakhstan to provide Director-level training to companies' boards which the fund had invested in. It was a major deal, and I was invited to join a Ministerial trip. This involved a private jet to the Central Asian nation and included various meetings and events. It cost the IoD more than £6,000 to join the trip (I did not realise that businesses funded such Ministerial jollies). As the date approached it transpired it was not just any Minister joining us on the trip; it was the Prime Minister, David Cameron.

The flight departed the Royal Suite at Heathrow at 7am on the Sunday morning. It was a tough negotiation at home to get agreement to go because I had to travel down on the Saturday, and so lost most of the family weekend.

I stayed with Richard in Slough and a car picked me up just after 5am. The car and driver had to be registered in advance otherwise entry to the terminal would be denied.

I had seen the terminal on a documentary. It stands in a remote spot near Terminal 4 and had a couple of lounges offering some light refreshments.

In total, there were about 25 business people who were part of the trip, from a Virgin Executive, to a Cambridge College Rector, an EY Partner, and a couple of North-East businesses. One, Gary Lydiate, had married into a family that made environmentally friendly aircraft de-icer. He was a major Conservative Party donor. The other chap worked for BEL Valves which supplied into the oil industry. Plus, there were a couple of obligatory journalists.

Lord Stephen Green, the International Trade Minister, led the way and we boarded the Boeing 757 outside. It belonged to a South African-registered company that based itself out of Manston, and had recently flown the Arsenal FC squad out to their Far East pre-season tour.

I had not realised how far Kazakhstan was. The flight to Atyrau took $5^1/_2$ hours, and we approached the city across the Caspian Sea and over blue-roofed houses.

David Cameron was not on this flight because he had left the UK the Friday before to go to Brussels for an

EU meeting. He then flew to Pakistan for a meeting on Saturday, and on Sunday, he visited troops in Afghanistan.

He did not make our first stop in Atyrau where we had a reception with various businesses because the military aircraft he was using had a technical issue.

In the meantime, we had taken a two-hour flight to the capital, Astana (later renamed Nursultan) arriving after midnight, meaning I was goosed. David Cameron arrived separately at 2am and joined us for a breakfast, taking the time during the meal to come round and chat to us all individually. How he looked so fresh after his schedule, I will never know.

More round-tables and presentations were followed by lunch at the Presidential Palace.

To put our discussions in context, President Nursultan (I wonder where they got the new capital's name from) Nazarbayev, ruled for nearly 30 years, winning 98% of the vote at his last election. Needless to say his record on human rights was a pretty low bar.

There were the obligatory speeches – with the President's through an interpreter – and as he explained how Kazakhstan had just 10% flat income tax, 2% VAT, and 20% corporation tax, a smile crossed Cameron's face.

As Nursultan was leaving at the end of the lunch he came over and shook my hand and we had a chat about my visit (through an interpreter). He is probably the biggest despot I have spoken to.

The lunch and the palace were spectacular, as you would expect from a supreme dictator. Having said that, the starter was akin to a meal in an Indiana Jones movie. We were presented with a small urn, including lid. On opening it look like frog spawn inside. But not wanting my tongue to be cut out and my head put on a spike, I ate it all up.

We arrived back at the Royal Suite at about 6pm on the Monday – an exhausting but fascinating 36-hour trip. I was scheduled to be at an IoD parliamentary reception but had pre-warned Simon Walker that I may not make it and texted him to confirm. Simon later mentioned in his welcome speech at the reception that I was away on a trip with the PM, only to be approached by an MP who told him that the PM was back, as he had just seen him in the Chamber. While I did not have a police escort to whisk me in, the fact I felt beyond more work, while Cameron carried on, was telling. He did this every week and I was doing it once.

He did take his tie off on the flight back, but he was working all the way. No Air Force One bedroom to take a nap either. It is a young person's job for sure.

Parliamentary Reception

I attended a few parliamentary receptions for the IoD over the years. At my first as Chair, I made sure I was there early to welcome guests. The first guests to arrive were a bunch of Lords. The author Jeffery Archer (much smaller than I imagined) had a good chat with me and obviously knew Simon Walker. Michael Heseltine was one of the great politicians of my youth and we had a fascinating chat too. His spectacles had obviously broken and he had stuck the arm back on with an Elastoplast. Not what you expect of a Lord.

Opposition politicians were also welcomed but when I challenged a Labour shadow minister Caroline Flint on one of her policies, she well and truly pistol-whipped me.

My local MP, Chi Onwura, was equally challenging. When I introduced myself as IoD Chair and one of her constituents, she told me we would not agree on anything.

"Do you want economic growth?" I asked. "Would you like a reduction in unemployment?" I added. And finally, "Do you want a more skilled workforce?" Yes, of course, she replied to all three questions.

"Well," I said, "we seem to agree on a lot, now we just have to work out how to do this together."

Politicians in General

Some politicians I met impressed me, and others irritated me, without any political bias.

Once, at No.10, I was chatting with Priti Patel (then a treasury minister) and mentioned that I knew the Speaker John Bercow. She was derogatory about him and told me that they were planning to vote him out of the Chair. She did not succeed for years.

By contrast, Deputy Prime Minister in the Lib/Con Collation, Nick Clegg, came to speak at the IoD and was lovely. Even when some numpty asked a stupid question, he handled it with charm and grace.

Former Leader and then Foreign Secretary, William Hague, was interesting and entertaining, and obviously very sharp and intelligent.

Business Secretary, Matt Hancock, was very engaging

and genuinely wanted to try and improve the business climate.

Transport Minister, Patrick McCloughlin, did a great presentation to members at IoD HQ once, and we were honoured with the amount of time and effort he put in. I did not know at the time, but his son was Jimmy McCloughlin who had just joined the IoD's policy unit. I think the hint was in the name. Jimmy went on to work as a special advisor in No.10 for Theresa May. He called me one Wednesday evening at this time asking if I could get some business people together for an hour on the Friday when he was passing through Newcastle. I knew Newcastle University Vice Chancellor, Chris Day, who helped me sort the venue, and within 24 hours I had 12 top businesspeople assembled, from the CEO of Northumbrian Water through to a director at Newcastle Airport.

Chuka Umunna should have gone on to lead the Labour Party, and his openness and warmth seemed genuine. He spoke to IoD members and showed his father's IoD Membership card in the process, which endeared him all the more to us.

I had lunch with SNP leader and Scottish First Minister Alex Salmond before he spoke to members too. A decent enough chap, with little hint of the scandal that would rock his later career in terms of inappropriate behaviour accusations.

We had a good through put of foreign politicians too including the President of Italy to the Prime Minister of Latvia, Valdis Dombrovskis. The latter had been tipped as the next European Commission President until a scandal where he had allowed building regulations to be ignored, causing a building in Latvia to collapse with multiple fatalities, thwarted his political rise. He presented me with a "stone" coin from Latvia as a memento because they were moving to the Euro the following year.

Figure 27: Ian Dormer, Julia Gillard and Emily Dormer

The summer after I retired, I was in London with Emily, and the former Australian Prime Minister Julia Gillard was speaking. We both managed to meet her beforehand and chat about her time as Premier, although she was quite a bitter woman.

UKTi

I joined a working group on International Trade chaired by the minister, Lord Stephen Green. We held our meetings in various buildings, including having one in the famous Map Room at the Foreign Office. This is a grand room where maps of every country, and parts thereof, were kept and it was the first point of call for officials when we suddenly discovered we were at war with somewhere and we did not know where it was, such as the Falkland Islands in the early 1980s.

The central question we were asking was, "Why are

the Germans exporting more than we are?" My simple philosophy was gleaned from talking to IoD members.

The Mivan Construction Executive, Mervyn Mcall, explained how they only traded in the UK and Eire until one of his key customers mentioned how they were struggling to get a company to build formwork on projects in Iraq. That was a pull they needed and before long they were internationally trading in many countries.

Specsavers founder, Dame Mary Perkins, described to me how they realised they had employed dozens and dozens of Australians temporarily in UK stores while the young ophthalmologists were travelling in Europe. These Australians had then gone back home and started up on their own. Specsavers blitzed Australia overnight, partnering with these opticians and establishing the Specsavers brand there.

Panaz started exporting their textiles because they had a connection with a chap in Sweden.

Again, and again, it was that pull that started the international expansion, and a repeated message from other business leaders.

We needed to give UK businesses that connection to create that pull from abroad.

I wanted the UK Embassies to find potential buyers, whether for teacups or battleships, and make introductions through membership organisations like the IoD, CBI etc. Any business leader would jump on the next flight for a really hot lead.

Instead, the UK Government's approach was to push business into markets rather than let them be pulled.

Their sales technique was akin to, "Brazil is a growth market. We will subsidise your travel for you to try and get business." It was purely speculative and, for most SMEs, a waste of time and money.

The German's approach was to set up offices and/or an outreach of the German Chamber of Commerce to give their businesses a base. This was proposed as a model to emulate. I argued that it was a waste of time because we would be several laps behind the Germans and by simply copying what they did, we would never overtake them. However, the UK Chamber of Commerce also sat on the group and managed to convince Lord Green to do a Chamber-led office approach.

We are still just as far behind the Germans.

Business Leaders

Meeting fellow business leaders was so often a privilege, and I do not just mean the very famous like Richard Branson. I learned from so many and was humbled by a few too.

I once introduced Specsavers' Mary Perkins at a Chartered Director Conference at the IoD's HQ. As we chatted before the event, I mentioned to her that I went to Specsavers in South Shields where the partner optician was an old friend of mine. "Ah, Bryan Clarke. One of our early adopters", said Dame Mary after a short pause for thought. The company has more than 1,600 outlets in the UK and abroad, so I was stunned that she immediately knew who I was referring to.

The week before, Emily's headmistress had cornered me to see if I could help secure a successful businesswoman as a prize-giving speaker. I took the plunge at this point and bashfully asked Dame Mary and was ready to receive a polite refusal. However, despite the fact that the event was in Gateshead on a Friday night, and on the eve of the Great North Run when more than 50,000 runners and their families would descend on the city, I received a prompt reply that said she would be happy to attend. My respect for her grew. I even expected her to bail out two months before the event, when I dropped her an email to confirm. She did not.

She and I arranged to meet at the hotel at 5.15pm for me to take her to the Sage Concert Hall where she was due to speak. Naturally, I arrived early, expecting to have to call from reception and wait for her to come down. Not so – she was standing outside the hotel, ready and waiting. Dame Mary is no prima donna.

She went on to deliver an uplifting, beautifully targeted speech and shook hands with hundreds of girls. She explained her motivation for starting her own business, her reluctance to work in a company controlled by men, and her confidence that she would not have to do so. An inspiring story for males and females alike.

On the drive back to the hotel, small talk turned to her journey from her home in Guernsey up to Newcastle. I asked her whether she had flown via Southampton or Gatwick and whether all the Great North runners travelling had affected her trip. She revealed that she had in fact taken the company plane - rather more extravagant than I had come to expect. However, my qualms were quickly dispelled when Dame Mary commented that it was good timing, because it meant that she could give lifts to half-a-dozen of her staff who were competing in the race.

If all this was not enough to cement her place in my mind as a generous and warm person, not to mention a phenomenal leader, the sucker punch came at the beginning of the following week. As I posted a 'Thank You' letter to her, one landed on my desk from her, thanking me for picking her up from the hotel and delivering her safely back.

You do not have to spend long with a great leader to understand why they are so successful. A year or so later I was even more stunned when she sent me a request to be friends on Facebook. She occasionally comments on my posts too.

I attended many dinners and events and met many more wonderful business people. Some of the dinners were very grand, like the Arbuthnot Bank's 202nd Anniversary. (The financial crash made them delay their celebrations by a couple of years). That was a very big affair in The Guild Hall with opera singer, Catherine Jenkins, and Home Secretary, Theresa May, in attendance.

The annual ICAEW dinner in their HQ was equally grand if less lavish, and the De La Rue (money printers) diplomatic Corp dinner at the Dorchester was one of the diary events of the year. As my tenure went on, I started to know more and more people at these functions. It was a certain circle, and one could even say 'an old boys club' but with an ever-improving diversity.

I had the honour of having tea with the Lord Mayor of London, David Wooton, at Mansion House on one occasion, as well as meeting his successor, Fiona Woolf. It is not essential to have a double "o" in your last name to be Lord Mayor, but it is essential to be wealthy because they basically funded their tenure out of their own pockets.

Hosting IoD Events

Figure 28: Speaking at the IoD

One of my duties as IoD Chair was hosting a miscellany of events and I grew to be comfortable with everything that entailed, from speeches of introduction to impromptu 'thank you' addresses.

We had all sorts of speakers at these events. Tony Blair's former press chief, Alastair Campbell, was great value. I introduced myself to him on his arrival and 10 minutes later he still remembered my name, even after he had been introduced to a dozen or more people – while I had forgotten their names straightaway.

Sports stars also spoke at various lunches and dinners, which is how I met England World Cup goalkeeper, Gordon Banks. He was shorter than me, despite having played in a position where being tall was essential.

Gordon's rise to the top of football was fascinating. In his youth, he had had a regular job, which in those days included working Saturday mornings, after which he would usually go to watch Sheffield play. However, one day he missed his bus so he just went to watch his mates play at the local ground. On arrival, they asked him to go in goal as they were a player short. He borrowed some kit and played well. A professional club scout happened to be watching, and signed him up full time.

I also met England player, and later BBC host, Gary Lineker, as well as former Liverpool, Newcastle, and England player, Michael Owen.

On many occasions, a member of the IoD team managed to get themselves along to the pre-reception - if nothing else to try and meet a star who they idolised. Whenever this happened, I made a particular effort to make sure I introduced them, and I think this cemented my positive relationship with the staff at 116.

One of the big events of the year is the 'IoD Director of the Year' Awards and, on one occasion, that starstruck person was herself recipient of the 'Lifetime Achievement Award', Dame Margaret Barbour. I was in awe of her, as the person in charge of the iconic and successful Barbour brand.

When her husband died, Dame Margaret left her job as a cookery teacher to try and save the business - and took it to global success. When I mentioned to her that Michael Portillo was the compere for the event, she was all a flutter.

Michael hosted many events for the IoD, and I had even shared a platform with him at other business events, so I knew him quite well. Interestingly, I discovered through a chap at Rosh that Michael's brother was a postman and lived in Tantobie, County Durham.

Michael was a great speaker and would have been an interesting Prime Minister, but his fame - and the love from Dame Margaret - came from TV documentaries of his travels by train. He was game enough to try anything on these shows, and always wore the snazziest clothes, such as purple blazers with bright yellow trousers. But he was a real gentleman too.

Margaret was worried about going up the steps up to the stage, so I took Michael to one side and suggested that he might offer an arm to his adoring fan when the time came. Michael delivered in buckets, and Dame Margaret seemed to have the best day of her life.

Journalism

The IoD prompted me to write many articles during my time, from features in the Director Magazine, through to CEO Today, and even the Evening Standard. Most were business- or leadership-focused, although one for the Guardian was about work-life balance.

I also had a few written about me and managed to get some good relationships with everyone from the Deputy Business Editor of the Sunday Times, Andrew Lynch, through to the Editor of the Sunday Telegraph's business section, Kamal Ahmed.

Kamal gave me the opportunity to write a column each Sunday for several weeks in the paper, although once the CBI saw it, they muscled-in on alternate weeks. Kamal later went on to become the BBC's Economics Editor. On one of his first days, I agreed to comment on behalf of the IoD about the corporate governance at the Co-Op - and who should turn up with the film crew, but Kamal.

Prince Charles

In my last year as Chair, we hosted a campaign led by Prince Charles to encourage big corporates to improve their environmental performance.

The evening before, I attended a drinks reception at St James's Palace which was attended by the great and good. But the big day for me was the next day.

Figure 29: Hosting the Prince of Wales at the IoD

We were sent a briefing pack and met his staff about

what was planned. Charles was going to walk the length of Pall Mall from St James Palace to the IoD; the presence of police cars and limousines raises more attention than a couple of chaps walking down the road. His protection officers told me that although bystanders and pedestrians do a double-take, by the time they realise who it was, the Royal party are usually well down the street.

I was to greet Charles on arrival, and my briefing clearly stated that I should just bow my head (not a full waist bow), call him "Your Royal Highness", and then after that just "Sir". I should not reach out to shake his hand; if HRH wished to, he would offer his hand for me to shake.

I briefed IoD reception staff 10 minutes ahead of his arrival and then stood in the lobby, chatting with a protection officer. The officer obviously had an earpiece as he quietly advised me, "they are on their way." A few minutes later, he said, "60 seconds." I went outside to wait on the pavement in front of the building on Pall Mall. Charles arrived, exactly on time. I bowed my head, saying, "Your Royal Highness, I am Ian Dormer, Chairman of the Institute of Directors. Welcome." And as I did, I instinctively held out my hand to shake.

The Tower of London is only a few miles from Pall Mall and, after my transgression, I wondered which way they would take me?

However, a few years earlier, I had had lunch with Charles's brother, Prince Andrew. Again, we had been given a briefing on how our plate of food would be taken away as soon as Andrew finished his meal. But Andrew was obviously not hungry and put his knife and fork together very early on. As plates started to be removed, Andrew stopped proceedings, and insisted we finished, decrying the "old Victorian ways."

Fortunately, Charles was cut with a similar cloth and reached for my hand too, to give it a hearty shake. Still cringing, I led him up the grand staircase to the Burton Room where he met some pre-selected groups before entering the Nash Room for his speech. Rather cleverly, he held a cup and saucer (pre-supplied by the Palace) while circulating the room, which tied up both his hands, and eliminated any further need to shake hands... or have contact with smelly and infectious plebs...

I chatted with one of his protection officers, learning how they had a week to prepare and scout the venues for his visits, then a week on close protection. One of them even sits all night in the corridor outside Charles's bedroom. I asked if he skied too. Yes, he skied, but not with Charles. HRH is too good, and they have a special military detail do that. He also said it was the best job he ever had and would never be able to do another as good. He seemed to genuinely like Charles. As we stood there chatting, every so often he would move us along; a photographer was capturing Charles with the groups and there was no way the officer was going to be snapped too.

I spent most of Charles' speech cringing in my seat from the faux pas of shaking hands and I vowed not to repeat my mistake on his departure. Once it was over,

I escorted him down the stairs. He asked me about the history of the building, and I was able to tell him how it was built on the site of the Prince of Wales's home until the mid-18th Century – and of course he knew who that was. John Nash later designed the current building, which became the United Services Club before it folded and was taken on by the IoD in the mid-1970s. The earlier history was the reason there were so many military paintings but also why we were custodians of one of the only busts of Admiral Nelson which was believed to have been done while he was alive. It sits on a piece of timber from HMS Victory. I pointed this out and this was captured by the photographer.

Charles seemed really interested in it all and asked lots of questions as we walked to the door. His valet magically appeared with his coat and we stepped back out on to Pall Mall. "Mr Dormer, thank you so much for welcoming me to the IoD today. It was a real pleasure," he said. He then offered his hand for me to shake. Partly in relief, partly with a sudden affection for the man, I shook his hand with earnest.

Commander of the Order of the British Empire

The IoD proposed me for an honour after I retired as Chair, which ended up as a trip to Buckingham Palace. As protocol dictates, I did not know of the nomination, although Julia had been tapped up by the IoD for key people to help support it from the North East.

The notice arrived in a brown envelope not dissimilar to that usually reserved for a tax bill. It does not say you have an award, but asked if I was to agree to having one, in which case, my name would go before Her Majesty who would then decide if I was worthy. This process weeds out those who politically object to Royal honours. It also instructed me to say nothing until the announcement at New Year (just in case...).

Inside the envelope, there was a reply card and postage-paid envelope which I promptly signed and sorted. My biggest shock was the level of the award. Honours start with the British Empire Medal, progressing to Member, (MBE), Officer (OBE) and then Commander (CBE) of the Order. Above that are Knighthoods and elevations to the House of Lords.

That New Year, we were heading off to Whistler in Canada to go skiing. I decided to tell my parents before we left but we only told the children when we arrived at Schipol, before our trans-Atlantic flight.

The day of the announcement, I went heli-skiing with Emily and Mark, deep into the wilds of the Pacific Mountains. On our return towards Whistler in the minibus my phone picked up reception and started pinging away with messages. Julia had stayed back at the hotel and was delighted to see all the messages arrive during the day. Our travel agent Sian Oakley saw the announcement and contacted our hotel asking them to send up a congratulatory bottle of champagne.

The IoD announced, *"Ian Dormer thoroughly deserves this recognition for his contribution to the British business community. During his time as Chairman of the Institute* of Directors, and through his ownership of a successful engineering firm in the North East, Ian has represented the values of integrity and enterprise which define success in business.

"Whether it was taking IoD members to meet the Prime Minister, or drumming up support for UK exports on overseas trade missions, Ian's efforts as Chairman of the IoD stand tall and I am delighted to see them rewarded in the New Year's Honours."

They asked for my reaction and I said, "Doing something you love and believe in is usually reward enough, but to be recognised in this way has truly touched me."

Over the following week, I received dozens and dozens of emails, texts, tweets and letters. I even had a letter from the US Ambassador, whom I had never even met.

Some messages were funny. A swimming dad wrote, "Congratulations on your award. But if you think I am going to bow and exit a room backwards, then think again".

Because Julia had to give two months' notice to cancel clinic at the hospital, I emailed the Central Chancery office to see what date I would be given at the Palace rather than wait to be told. By chance, it was Friday 11 March – a day that we had already planned to be in London; Mark and I, along with Richard, had tickets to watch England play Wales at Twickenham.

I hired a morning suit for the occasion, and we booked a room at the Ritz: a once-in-a-lifetime occasion deserved to have the boat pushed out. The service at the Ritz hotel was exceptional. While they had a dress code, residents were granted flexibility, and we could wear jeans in the bar for a quick drink ... and order burger and fries when we arrived about 9pm. However, the rooms were quite small.

The plan was for Mark and I to stay just two nights at the Ritz. The whole family would go to the dinner dance on the Friday night, before Mark and I headed over to stay with Richard in Slough for the rugby. Meanwhile, Julia and Emily booked tickets to the theatre and organised one extra night's stay at the hotel, in luxury.

I had previously been to a Palace Garden Party with Julia about 10 years earlier. How, or why, I had been invited is a mystery, but as 4,000 attend it is quite large occasion. You do get to pass through a bit of the Palace but marquees in the back garden serve a delicate selection of sandwiches, chocolates, and cakes on a plate which doubles up as your saucer, allowing you to hold both your food and drink in one hand. A military band provide the music.

We had the opportunity to walk around the grounds, down to a small lake. Her Majesty the Queen and HRH Prince Phillip walk down a central avenue created across the lawn and designated individuals get to chat to them before they retire into their VIP tent. Our particular group made the headlines because just as it was time to head back to Kings Cross station, the heavens opened with a torrential downpour that surpassed even tropical storms.

We sheltered in the Palace and watched the quad become a massive pool of water. Eventually we had to head off and literally waded through puddles ankle deep in Green Park on the way to the tube.

I knew some previous award winners, so I had a few inside tips for the day of the investiture.

Although the gates of the Palace would not open for us until 10am we were advised to be there in advance, so we got there at 'Dormer Time' of 09:40am. Seating was first come first served, and although there is more than enough, you do not want to be at the back.

Less than 10 minutes later we were allowed through the front gate through the quad and into the Palace. We had to deposit phones and cameras in the cloakroom and then I was directed one way, while Julia, Emily, and Mark, went another. My gang were first to take their seats and secured front and centre.

I was also first in my waiting room and learned from staff that I would receive my award from Prince William, Duke of Cambridge, who was officiating. Next to arrive was Prof Andrew Wathey, Vice Chancellor at Northumbria University and an old chum. What a coincidence. It was then I realised that the CBEs and Knights were considered a step above the OBEs and MBEs, because we were in a separate room.

A chap called Jamie came and introduced himself and explained how he was there just to help Her Majesty. We later discovered that he was part of the investiture team, and himself a Lord rather than simply a mate.

We were given our briefing of what to do, where to stand, to step backwards after the conversation was ended with a handshake, turn and exit stage right. We then had to loop round after getting the medal boxed and sit at the back of the ballroom.

One of the other Commander recipients was footballer Denis Law. He was very nervous, and worried he was going to say or do the wrong thing. As we lined up in the correct order prior to our entrance, he moved forward to look through into the ballroom to check what he would be facing, and of course ended up out of order, which sent him into another tizz. Considering the stadia that he had played in, and the number of TV appearances he had made, I was quite surprised.

One of Mark's friends was watching Sky Sports News and not only saw Denis get his award, but he also managed to take a photo of Mark sitting in shot right behind him. Afterwards, Denis was lovely and not only had his photo taken with Mark but also took our family photo with a Beefeater.

The first stage of presentation is a walk up to a Wing Commander who stands just shy of the dais. He was good at his job, particularly knowing that people would be nervous, discreetly and quietly asking, "Have you any one in the audience with you today, Sir?" I replied, "Front row in burgundy, my wife, daughter and son." To which he responded, "Wow they managed to get good seats!" And then he paused as the cue for me to move forward was nigh.

When my name was announced, I walked forward as the citation was read. I gave a small bow of the head, had the medal draped over it, and the conversation began. William asked how we had managed to gain so many more women members at the IoD during my tenure, which I answered in a dithering way but ended with the point that we had welcomed his father to the Institute the previous year and how he was enthralled by the history of the building. "He would have loved all that history," he joked.

Figure 30: Investiture with Prince William

We were told the ceremony would take about an hour, and with military precision it did. The family had been sitting there for two hours and were really only interested in my two minutes of fame, and although the actor Idris Elba and popstar Damian Albarn of Blur were both getting their OBEs, which added some interest, it was still a long morning for them. They came away really impressed and charmed by Prince William.

We had agreed to meet outside, where the official photographers were, as we had heard the queues could be long if we dilly-dallied. A standard set of pictures are taken, and we were professionally whisked through each set-up - but Emily suggested one more. On the count of three, we all pulled a pose... not regal, but fun. The photographer had never had anyone do that before, but it is my favourite of the day.

The event is discreetly videoed with individual families identified by clever facial recognition software, which was then available to buy on DVD: A great memento.

MOVING ON

I knew that I could only serve one term, as good governance dictates you lose your independence if you stay as a non-executive for an extended period, and I had now served more than 12 years. Nimble had hoped they could find a way of proposing me for another three years, because he felt that I deserved three years of peace and glory, after two years of hell and upheaval. He was gutted, but I assured him that if the IoD was there to promote good governance to others, we should live by the rule too. But it was a kind gesture by him.

The Institute gave me a lovely retirement dinner, which Julia, Emily, and Mark attended. Spending so much time in London at the IoD had certainly been harder on the family than me, with pick-ups and drop-offs only possible if one of us took responsibility, or with the help of grandparents, or other families.

It was only when Emily and Mark came to London for the day during the school holidays, and visited our offices at 116 Pall Mall, that they realised the grandeur of the Institute's headquarters and the size of my role. As we approached the grand staircase, ten-year-old Mark gasped, "Wow dad, this is really impressive. I did not know this was what the IoD was like." But really, for them, the IoD represented just three letters - and dad being away for extended periods.

Mark then spotted a portrait across the landing of Admiral Lord Collingwood, saying, "We have that painting at school." Lord Collingwood was an old boy of RGS Newcastle, and Nelson's No.2 at the Battle of Trafalgar. I told him that all the paintings belonged to HM The Queen, and that the IoD's picture was the original, while his school had been given a copy. But as we wandered up to the grand portrait, I was humbled to see that, in fact, it was the IoD's picture that was the copy. I share this story whenever I showed anyone around, and it always raises a laugh.

The building at 116 Pall Mall has some great history. Aside from being on the site of a former Prince of Wales's home when it was built, there was a disagreement between the builder and architect as to where the entrance should be. This is why the grand staircase heads towards Waterloo Place, while the entrance is on Pall Mall. Nash was the architect, and he also designed the Brighton Pavilion.

It has been filmed as the set for several films and TV series. The Nash Room – our largest function room – doubled as the Vice-Roy's room in the film 'Gandhi'. Meanwhile, scenes from the series Downton Abbey were also filmed at 116, as was the pool room scene in 'Batman', which starred the late Heath Ledger.

A corner of the Carlton Room has a plaque and is

known as the Norwegian Corner. This was where the exiled Norwegian Cabinet met during World War Two, when the building was still the head office of the United Services Military Club.

Ian Fleming, the author of 'James Bond' and 'Chitty Chitty Bang Bang', used to work in Whitehall and would have lunch here every day. The building also houses portraits of every British monarch over the last 200 years, and a grand chandelier gifted by the King to the United Services Club after victory at Waterloo.

EATING CAKE WITH CHOPSTICKS

And other tales from the tour of the DPRK

$20^{th} - 29^{th}$ June 2017

I t all started as a joke.

"What are you going to do after your 'A' Levels Emily? Going off to Zante with your friends?"

"I am not much of a Zante girl. I would be more interested in going on holiday to North Korea"

Google then delivered a specialist tour company – Regent Holidays – based in Bristol that ran holidays to North Korea. The link just *had* to be shared with the family including relevant comments and encouragement. It just progressed from there....

17 January 2017

Dear Mr. Dormer,

Thank you for your email through our website regarding your interest in a possible visit to North Korea. As you may well know, Regent Holidays has been operating since 1970, and has been sending tourists to North Korea since 1985. I have personally managed all aspects of our tours to North Korea since 2004, clocking up over seven months of travels in the country over approximately twenty trips. If I can be of any assistance at any time with regards to your proposed trip to the country please do feel free to call me.

From that point onwards finding out more information and getting a quote just flowed, despite Kim Jong-Un testing war missiles to launch nuclear warheads to the US and anywhere else he could hit. Imprisonment of a US student who was visiting the isolated nation hit the headlines and did add a certain frisson to the idea. But a quote for a bespoke tour came in. Total £3,280 for us both ex-Beijing. It was looking good.

By now we were into fine detail. Emily finished her last A level exam at 11.30 on Tuesday 20 June. It meant we missed the Newcastle to London flight that picked up the direct BA flight to Beijing so took the 15.30 NCL-LHR to get the overnight 18.40 from LHR – Hong Kong and then onwards up to Beijing.

The Application

But the months leading up to departure involved getting a multi-trip Chinese Visa as we were going to Shanghai as a family in July & filling in questionnaires before submitting our visa application for the DPRK. Part of this included "are you a journalist?" Which I was 25 years earlier and had written some articles in the meantime for the national press. Carl said this was fine fortunately, particularly as it was all business related. I did have to trawl through my Tweets… Friend Lindsay Lloyd worked for the George W Bush Foreign Policy Think Tank and had Tweeted some anti-DPRK things which I had liked and shared. My history was purged before our application went in.

NORTH KOREAN VISA

To obtain your North Korean Visa authorisation the process is a rather laborious one. The visa procedure is roughly as follows:

1. *They will investigate your application here in the UK. After they are fully satisfied that you are a genuine tourist your application will be stamped with their approval and faxed back to me.*
2. *I will then fax this approval to Pyongyang, and advise them that you would like your visa to be authorized to be issued in London. It then takes up to 30 days for the full authorisation to be arranged in Pyongyang for you to visit.*
3. *Once your visa is ready to be issued I will then contact you and request you send me*

sign..?? Were we being told not to go….?

I then watched the North East located film *"I, Daniel Blake"* on the flight and spotted my good old friend Michael Milligan in his bit-role. I had also known the lead actor, Dave Johns for 25 years through Michael.

We stayed at the Langham Place Hotel at the airport as we needed to be checking in about lunchtime for our DPRK flight. The hotel was good and a burger in the bar and a couple of drinks saw us through until we crashed… not waking until nearly 10am resulting in a rush to breakfast where we were the last allowed in.

Thursday 22 June
Check-in was like any other. Although maybe with a few butterflies in our stomach, in reality we were going, and that was it. A calm before that bungee jump. Confusion at the boarding gate nearly saw us heading off on a delayed flight to Chicago. These passengers were all boarding through our gate onto a bus at the same time as we were scheduled to go. None of the announcements for our flight had been in English. We couldn't understand the Chinese announcements so we did not know when we were boarding but all the North Korean passengers were very clear because of their badges of the Kim's and their very plain clothing so we just followed them.

A couple of men had seen us checking in at the Air

Koryo desk and gave us a smile of encouragement to let us know that we needed to be boarding with them. That was very friendly, I thought. They were going through an adjacent door to a bus – and so we were away. There were 3 American women on the bus to the aeroplane. Emily so desperately wanted to ask them "this is the Chicago flight isn't it?" just to see their reaction.

We were in row 23, and 45 minutes after our scheduled departure time we took off in heavy rain. Was this another sign "don't go... no you idiots... don't go..." For context, Air Koryo is widely recognised as the worst airline in the world. Europe banned their flights some years earlier due to safety concerns...

We were the last row taken and then there was a curtain. We peered back through the gap and saw another empty half of the plane. Was it left like that to give the impression it was fuller than it was? Our section was only just over half full. It must have made the centre of gravity for flying awkward. I then took the opportunity to have 40 winks.

The inflight entertainment was rousing military music & singing by patriotic choirs. Something that would pervade throughout many a TV screen over the next week. It was fun to watch for the first flight but would later become quite grating throughout every meal (we could probably sing along by the end) – can't even imagine a life time of it.

We declined the inflight food offering having heard that the "meat" in a bread roll was always the same and pretty low grade and of marginal providence. It was also only a 2 hour flight. We were given a magazine promoting the country which was interesting.

A chap from the row in front started a conversation with us. He was good at English and very friendly telling us how he had attended a maritime conference in London. He knew I was her father he said, as we looked the same. Not saying that is racist, as it is true… Then a young flight attendant came and sat with us. She asked us questions about our trip, but was obviously trying to practice her English. Every question took her a while to generate and our answers a few minutes for her to compute. She told us that she did not get any British on this three times a week flight. She had been doing the job for 2 years and only flew the Beijing route. She pointed out a photo of the Supreme Leader in the magazine we were given. She also pointed out her apartment which she lived in with her parents near the main square (clearly an elite family). We then showed her photos of our home on my IPad and our Supreme Leader… Julia…

I have filled in some landing cards in my time but DPRK went one further. Apart from the regular customs and health questions they also wanted to know about reading material – how many books were we bringing in as well as details of phones and electronic items. We desperately wanted to make sure we got it right to ease our entry.

Pyonyang

Pyongyang airport was sparkling and new. There were five other aircraft lined up on the runway – but they were going no-where soon. Engines and wheels were covered over for storage. The first check point wanted health forms, the second wanted passports. It was the first time we had faced militarily dressed North Koreans. They were friendly and fine about the mistake I had made – I thought the city box wanted where the visa was issued – but it should be our home city. We had quite a wait for bags. Most of the North Koreans had large boxes wrapped in a red, white, and blue striped hessian/ sack wrapping. Obviously bringing in scarce supplies from China. We, and the other three westerners, appeared to be the only ones with conventional suitcases or bags. We then went to check point No.3.

We had to remove all our books and electronics from our bags before they were X-rayed. At this point we realised we had made another error and wrongful declaration. We had six books not just five. Oh heck. But this was soon corrected on our form. After that it was pretty light touch. They flicked through the books, asked if we had memory sticks (we did not) and through we went. The memory stick issue we were warned was because some Missionaries try to smuggle in copies of religious material or seditious literature this way. Similarly, with laptops, and we were briefed by Regent Holidays that they had great technical capability at finding hidden files. I was also warned that a telephoto lens for my camera may be confiscated. It would be receipted and returned on departure -- amazing in some ways but with only 200 passengers a week not difficult I suppose – but again this was no issue.

Another thing I spotted as we were exiting was a duty free type shop jam packed with Scottish Whiskey. Often a favourite in the Far East and certainly popular here by the look.

Exiting into the terminal we were met by our guides. With only five westerners on the flight – the other three being women I suppose we were not hard to spot. Pak was older, maybe 60, and Han a twenty-something. Pak admitted she was a little concerned about how long we had taken to come through. We gave Pak our Passports. We would not see them again until we were ready to depart....

Before we left Emily asked if she could go to the toilet, this was the first time of many that Han would go with her to the toilet. We were then loaded up into our mini bus by driver Lee. The car park at the front of the airport was empty. And I mean empty. Our mini bus and that was it. Surreal.

The drive into the city was quiet. The odd vehicle but not many with a check point on the outskirts of the city. The check point was one man and a gun so not that intimidating. There were people working in the paddy fields – just like we had seen in China and other far eastern countries on our travels. Han was somewhat surprised that machines were not used in paddy fields in China....

Pyongyang was bigger than expected with big wide boulevards, tower blocks and large monuments. One point we suddenly slowed down. The 2 large bronze statues of the leaders could be seen round the corner – but Lee had not slowed down for us to see this but out of respect for the nation's founders.

We went straight to a restaurant for dinner. A BBQ we were told. It was a lovely sunny evening and I was looking forward to this. The reality was slightly different. We had a windowless private room with a hot plate in the middle where the meats were cooked in front of us – with some veg and rice on the side. It was very good and tasty. We all had beer and shared stories with our two guides who were charming and interesting. I asked them to teach me a couple of things in Korean:
Thank you is *Kamsa Hanneda*

Cheers is *Choopey*
What more would I need?
Emily was still seriously nervous at this point and really didn't like any moment where the conversation turned to her studying politics at school so settled for 'social sciences'. But as time went on we discovered there was no need to be overly cautious. They told us that we were quite a unique client, not many young people still at school visited.

We then proceeded to the Koryo Hotel - a Twin Towered hotel where we would stay on the 19th floor. Pak very gently asked us not to leave the hotel. It was really a "you will not leave the hotel without us" but said in a way that said the same but was non-threatening. "please do not leave the hotel at any time without us".

I bought a beer and 4 bottles of water to take our room -- €3. Bargain. Throughout our stay Euros and Dollars were all they wanted. The room was a time warp from the 1970s. And this was the luxury option we had chosen. The twin beds with bedspreads, a very plastic olive green en-suite bathroom almost like it had been dropped in a prefabricated box in the corner. The bath squeaked and groaned as I stood and showered in it. But we were provided with all the standard hotel amenities from soap and shampoo through to a nicely boxed toothbrush.

A little anti-room filled the space the bathroom "box" did not fill with a couple of chairs and a picture window looking onto the city. I sat there one evening and for a laugh thought I would see if I could get any wi-fi, internet, or phone reception. I had to try to see if the rumours were true. They were.

The hairdryer was pretty pathetic so most nights Emily went to bed with wet hair – She had also forgotten her hairbrush so had to use a comb. For a couple of days she did her hair in plaits and Pak was so impressed. There was a TV with international channels including Al Jazeera, this was clearly unique to our room as Han and Pak would often ask what we had seen on the news that morning - Pak was particularly interested in what was said about Donald Trump.

The other tower blocks around us had few lights on in the night. Those that did were dim. We were warned that our bedroom lights would be low wattage, so we had brought head torches to read in bed. We were glad we did. Emily also became under a bit of pressure from Pak near the end of our stay to finish the romantic novel she was reading as Pak really wanted an English book. The book was duly donated on our last day.

City Tour Day One - Friday 23 June
Looking down on the street the next morning we

were surprised how quiet the roads were. Virtually no vehicles at all. There was an underpass for the road outside the hotel and despite having no traffic people were walking through. Why? It was not a highway, and there were no barriers to stop you just walking across…

Finding the restaurant for breakfast was a bit of a challenge. We found a number of rooms that could serve as restaurants. But with so few residents they used a small room tucked away on the first floor. The tables had been set for the number of guests in residence. Over the days we stayed there I counted at best 20 guests in a hotel that could probably take 1,000+. We discovered two were Germans – one coaching the men's football team and one the women's. There was another chap who we saw heading off one morning with a set of golf clubs over his shoulder. He did not have a guide with him either. Quite bizarre. The others were Chinese or North Koreans.

We had been told that as we had booked a premium level package for our trip we could get a cup of coffee for free with our breakfast. There was a man guarding the coffee pot. Fortunately, as we arrived the Maître D realised our elevated status and when the Coffee guard asked for €1 he trotted across to say we could have it for free. The Coffee pot guard had no English apart from being able to say "€1", so the intervention was essential as my attempt at an explanation was not getting anywhere. A couple of days later when the golfer arrived and he just took a coffee it caused much consternation and distress for our man. He had left his post for less than a minute. He was probably sent to a gulag thereafter. Coffee is obviously a very rare and precious commodity in the DPRK – almost certainly imported and with so many trade embargoes on the nation it is very hard to source. Every single station had a person stood by it, every lift had an operator, most of them doing nothing. It had more staff than guests.

The rest of the breakfast was sliced bread – a fried egg on request – and some yoghurts and meats and a little fruit – in particular water melon. Not a great selection but enough for us to start our first day.

We headed off sightseeing and went past an amazing sight. A troupe of 30 or 40 women—all in matching outfits with small drums slung over their shoulders - were singing and beating time on the corner of a street. We went past 2 or 3 of these in different guises. They were motivating and cheering the workers on their way to work we were told. They were all volunteers and doing it daily for the good of the nation. A theme that permeated in so many things. Volunteers, but you would not ever, never, not volunteer here.

up to the Square and is behind where the leaders stand for the parade. We went to the top and a balcony / veranda and enjoyed a spectacular view across the square, down to the river and across to the Juche Monument. In the Study House, fundamentally a library, we were shown the variety of books they had. Although they were requested at a counter and popped out on a tray. We did not get to browse the shelves – but they wanted to demonstrate to us they had English books available to all. The book that they delivered to show us was about Chickens…?!? Similarly, in a "music" room where they presented a Beatles cassette tape and played it at a great volume. While we saw very few people in the study house there were a couple in this room. We felt we disturbed them rather rudely with this music.

The awkward aspects of many of these demonstrations was when you could say "ok, seen that, had enough, let us move on". They were trying to proudly show us what they had. We were keen to be respectful and show a keen interest and awe at what they had. Emily's stock comment was "amazing". It covered all the bases of interest, and awe. But how far through the Beatles *Please Please Me* album do you listen? It was also day one.

We moved on through the beautifully adorned Mansudae Fountain Park. The cooling effect was lovely as it was sunny and well in the 80s and pretty humid. Everywhere was immaculate without a weed, spec of rubbish or blemish anywhere we went. Yet they would still have someone sweeping up nothing as we walked along.

We called in on an artist's studio and saw a number of artists at work painting everything from noble Korean fishermen bringing in the catch to historic sights and wild animals. It was around this time we realised that Han had a great sense of humour. As we marvelled at some of the wild animals such as bears and leopards that they had native to the country we came across a magnificent painting of an Elephant. How wonderful it is that they have African elephants too in the DPRK Han said with a smile – then cracked, laughing. With so much propaganda that we are fed in the west how the people are lied to, and believe anything, we really did not know where this line was drawn. But they were not such all believing puppets after all.

Arriving at our lunch stop we were treated to another display of many dishes. There could be up to a dozen small dishes each in front of us, and often they were lukewarm at best. We never saw anyone else having lunch in the restaurants we stopped at. Except once when we arrived early and the staff were eating to hurriedly clear away and serve us.

Rooms capable of seating 70 or hundred would only have the 4 of us – and occasionally Lee the driver to make it 5. All the waiting staff would be dressed in magnificent traditional costumes – as were the specific monument guides that showed us around.

We did not choose off a menu but a variety of plates would be brought out which we would graze from. The first day included a bowl of cold noodles, and pretty much every meal had a dish of kimchi – a Korean dish which looked a bit like a lasagne without the tomato sauce and mince - and made from cabbage.

After lunch we popped into a supermarket. Again, you would never have known it was there as there was no major sign outside. There was actually quite a lot of people (comparatively) in the supermarket, and they all gave us a good stare as we walked around. There was aisle after aisle of sweets and biscuits – right the way through to a tank which had small turtles swimming about in it. But it was not pet's corner. Emily had wanted to buy a hairbrush having forgotten hers. But in this store we needed North Korean currency, which we were not really allowed to have. We changed some Euros and bought what we needed and had a couple of notes left. Although this caused a little bit of a stir, I squirrelled it away, with a "do not tell anyone" nod from Pak.

Other sights included a stamp museum. Not a highlight, although we did see they had produced a stamp to commemorate the wedding of Prince Charles and Diana which seemed quite bizarre. This led to us telling them how I had met Charles and showed them pictures later on. They lost their mind over this somewhat. They really thought I was important.

The Fatherland Liberation War Museum and the USS Pueblo was a more significant stop of the afternoon. The atrium of the museum had a large statue of Kim Jong Un dominating. With a starry pale blue background and very clear distinct features, with music playing that made me think so clearly of DisneyLand. We were walked through the history of how the Great Leader had led the Korean people to victory after the aggressor Americans had started the war against their peaceful nation. Emily nudged me at this point and in a hushed tone asked:

"I did not know the Americans started the Korean War?"
"I did not think the North Koreans won the war?"

But of course, if that is all you are told is the truth

then it is the truth. How do we know our version of events is correct -- it is just different? At this time more than any other I thought of George Orwell's book *1984*. I also thought what a great lesson it was for Emily before she went off to University to study PPE. The ability to question what you are told and not just accept it all is so important.

One of the many times we heard that DPRK had the "biggest and best" was here too. An indoor panorama which highlighted Korea and simulated the war was the largest panorama in Asia. It was very good but not that good...

The museum tour was led by a female soldier in military uniform. We were put with two other westerners -- from Switzerland and Italy who worked for the Red Cross. They were very surprised to see us. We walked along past an exhibition of captured and damaged American military hardware with graphic images of dead and dying US military personnel until we arrived at the captured USS Pueblo.

This had been patrolling a little too close to the DPRK shore and was nabbed. The crew "all confessed" to the crime of spying of course. And repented wanting to be part of the Great DPRK... What a great achievement by their dear leader again.

We then went to a school in the city. We saw some of the resources they had such as a natural history room with stuffed animals but we saw no children in class rooms as we walked along the corridor and then up the stairs. We then entered a stage or small theatre room at the top of the building and were invited to sit down. There was just us and another couple (Chinese?) … But by chance a show was about to start. What luck.

On stage came the teenagers playing instruments (loudly) and singing (even more piercingly). After 20 minutes we gave them a round of applause and they came off the stage and lined up in 2 rows. In the middle of the back row they left a gap for two people. Seems like they had done this before, as we were invited into the space for a photo with them. It felt dreadfully contrived, but it was just another day in the DPRK.

We had stopped at another coffee shop during the day and when we got back to the hotel Emily realised she had left her sunglasses there. No worries, Emily said, I can manage. No, Han said she could go and get them. We did not realise that it was literally across the road from our hotel.
Five minutes later Han re-appeared.
"Sorry Emily someone has taken them, we'll have to find you some North Korean sunglasses".
Never mind Emily says.
"Just joking … here they are"
Han's wicked sense of humour surfaced again. I doubt anyone would dare steal sunglasses in the

DPRK....

Dinner was at a large establishment (although the only diners in the restaurant again). On the way in we heard a party going on in a side function room where music was playing. Having seen a bride and groom having their photos taken at the war memorial earlier in the day Pak poked her head into the room and beckoned us – it was a wedding party.

We had to go right in and look round the corner to see the top table and bridal party in all their traditional finery. We did not want to intrude and were craning our necks but suddenly an aged Aunt grabbed Emily's hand and started dancing with her to the music. Before we knew it everyone was clapping and cheering. Emily was then taken up to the top table to meet the bride and groom. We felt amazingly welcomed with the smiles and claps from the guests. This touch of normal North Korean life made us realise, despite all the horror stories around the political situation, people still fell in love, still got married, still had babies and were decent human beings.

I wrote in my diary:
If you go somewhere looking for negativity you will leave remembering bad things. If you travel looking for positivity you will leave enriched.
A Few Beers Loosens the Tongue

After dinner that evening, we went to a micro brewery for a beer. Orientation was a bit off at times and because we climbed in and out of the mini van and not paying a great deal of attention or having a map I had no idea where we were when we climbed out into the dark and went into the bar.... For that was all it was really. But in reality we were right next to our hotel – in fact pretty much part of the structure of our hotel. Again we were the only other people there. We had a few beers with our guides which loosened things up quite a bit. Emily does not really drink beer, but as that was all we had offered she drank it readily.

We showed them photos from home and explained a bit about our life in the UK. Dishwashers fascinated them. An alien concept that we put our dirty crockery in a machine which made them clean. "But do you then have to take them out and dry them?". No "Does the machine put the plates back in the cupboard?"

We also learned more about them. Pak was the daughter of a diplomat. She had lived in Romania, East Germany and the Middle East as a child. She had a grandson who she was very proud of, and on seeing a picture of him with Disney items proved to us she was very much from a privileged class.

Han was the daughter of an army officer... so very similar but had never left the DPRK. Their English was very good and Han's humour expanded as we plied them with beer. When we were told we had two guides we first thought that it was one for me and one for Emily. Increasingly I thought Pak was keeping an eye on young Han.

We did not intend to raise politics. But this evening Pak did.
"Were you afraid of visiting?"
No. We trusted that they would look after us
"What about the risk of war?"
We do not think your leader wants War was our diplomatic answer.
"What can we do to make sure this does not happen??"
We suggested talking is always good, and maybe China could help as a mediator.
"China does not like us anymore" was Pak's reply.

Pak also quizzed us about the young American who had died. When was the news released? Was it Sunday? or Monday? – difficult to remember due to the time differences etc.
"What did our newspapers report about his death?"
We danced around this awkward situation quite a bit not knowing how deep we should get into such politics. Han did not engage on these sensitive areas.

I was keeping a diary for our trip and pulled it

out to write up the correct names of the places we had visited that day while we had our guides with us. Pak asked to have a look. Fortunately, my handwriting is pretty poor, and at this stage I had not put many thoughts outside of plain facts in the book. But she was obviously looking in a professional "minder" type way. When I was showing her photos on my iPad, again she took control at one point and skipped through frantically to see what I had. There was nothing that would excite the watchful eye of DPRK officials.

The beer was good after a long hot and busy day. In Britain we may have a pack of crisps or a bowl of peanuts with our beers. They had dried fish. One bit of local flavour that was less appetising. Tearing strips off the mother load you chewed on this very dry fishy almost straw like cardboard. Having just one bit seemed rude so I managed to swallow 2 or 3 helpings. Pak and Han lapped it up....

Three things stood out in Pyongyang.
1. All the women wore high heels
2. They all had fancy sparkling umbrellas to protect from the sun
3. Outside tower blocks people came out in the evening to tend the grass.

This last point was the strangest as they would be there with buckets, or old plastic bottles or receptacles to water the grass, which was patchy at times. It was neatly trimmed and weedless, having been tended with scissors. Yep, regular household scissors, and not garden shears or lawnmowers as far as we could see. The intimate care and attention they gave these verges and public grassed areas was all for show. They were demonstrating their commitment to the community. Pak explained they did not have to do it, they did it for the love of the nation.... Yeah right.

In terms of things our guides said five things stood out.

1. The American's were referred to as "Imperialist Aggressors"
2. South Korea was always referred to as the "American side" or "American Puppets"
3. The victory in the war was due to "the wise leadership of Kim Il-Sung
4. The Americans always "tricked", "lied" and "broke the rules" (in the DMZ)
5. The Americans still want war.

A Late Start - Saturday 24th June

In the night Emily picked up our travel alarm clock from the table between us. In the process pushing down the alarm button turning it off. Next thing we know is Han calling us from reception waking us up....

Quick shower. We decided to skip breakfast, but as we got in the minibus we were given a bag with some bread & butter, (thick and not really spread out...) fruit and a yoghurt. Very kind.

We had another full schedule so off we went – first the Three Revolutions Exhibition... can't remember much about there...

A planetarium where we sat, in 4 isolated chairs away from about 50 school children, and had a show of planets and stars...
As we were leaving the planetarium there was a line of school children – maybe 5 or 6 years of age lining up to go in. They looked very cute and then one bowed at us. Followed by another, and within seconds the whole line of children was repeatedly and respectfully bowing low from the waist. It was charming. But they all nearly knocked themselves out with their dramatic bowing. We felt honoured.

The Martyrs graveyard was similar to a British war graves site in many ways although each tombstone had the photo of the soldier buried there. The Korean war permeated the culture and being of the people of the DPRK enormously. It was what bonded them together.

After lunch on Liberation Road (where else) we headed off for some more museums. The Science and technology complex was another opportunity for our guides to try and demonstrate how advanced their nation was. Proudly showing banks of PCs that the people could freely use ...

but no one was using them. We even wondered whether they worked. There must have been 500 or 600 terminals. And you certainly could not get on the world wide web... I did asked about that and the DPRK has their own equivalent intranet. Controlling what you learn and know being the key feature.

There were some good interactive exhibitions for kids both young and old. We had fun green screening. At all the sites were little place cards where Kim Jong Un had sat – after finding out that I was famous because I had met Prince Charles they joked that they should do the same for me.

The birth place of Kim Il Sung was next. The stable like building stood in a park and was Disney-esk in its fake-ness. Including subtle music playing throughout the park. But of course, as it is the place where the liberator of the people came from it was holy ground. The entrance to the park was opposite a fun fair entrance... maybe that influenced my Disney thinking... although the funfair was not open that day. The North Koreans work 6 days a week and only have Sunday off. Holidays are also an alien concept. Apart from days to celebrate the Leader's birthday and the like.

As we were getting back to our mini-van I saw some 2 or 3-year-old kids sitting on a little wall waiting for their mum. They were so cute I asked permission to take a couple of pictures of one.

Another little girl then seemed to get upset and uppity that I was not taking her picture. I had to oblige -- she was so cute too. Again, we felt the warmth and normalcy of the people aside from the political headline maker.

Built in a year, for $1million, and seating 150,000, the largest arena in the world -- our guides were proud of the May Day Stadium. What great achievements the Dear Leader has given the people of the DPRK. I had no way of validating the first two claims but I can count. A quick totting up of seats per row, times the number of rows, times the number of blocks. I may be out by a few thousand either way but it did not add up to 70K... unless of course they sit on each other's laps?

The pitch was astro-turf. Emily made it her mission to make the North Korean's laugh, even though they sometimes did not speak English, so she had to get creative. She pretended she had just scored a goal, running round the pitch arms in the air. It was a resounding success.

The sports hall indoor practice area was pristine. No scuff marks on the walls or anything. The changing rooms spotless. We signed the visitor book and as we were leaving Emily asked to use the Ladies toilet. Popping in to the nearest one under the stands she later told me that there was no water and the plumbing was not connected. The veil of achievement and success was very thin.

The needle-like Juche Tower represented the ethos of the State. There were plaques of followers from around the world which was very surprising. This hermit state had admirers for the way it did things... including in the UK. Our guide surprised us at the Juche Tower as she had a Yorkshire accent. When we asked if she had visited the UK, she said that she had never left the DPRK. How did that happen?

From the top we had magnificent views over the city. The residential blocks in one direction had all been painted in different colours under the instruction of the Leader to brighten the place up. It was certainly different.

At the bottom was a classic Communist type Statue – A worker, a Farmer and an Artist raising their arms in salute with their respective tools of the trade. It was enormous and Emily was dwarfed at the bottom when I stood back to take a picture.

The symbolism was replicated at the Workers Party Foundation Monument which was by another museum.... Here we learned about Mount Paektu, and its sacred and symbolic significance to North Koreans. It regularly features in artwork and in particular as a backdrop to the Kim's photos or portraits. The Mountain is on the northern border with China.

We had the opportunity to go to a bowling alley and could have played, but as we were tiring decided to give it a miss. Pak told us she used to play a lot and I quietly got the impression she had hit a few strikes in her time... the old dog. By now it was close to 6pm but there was only one lane in use in the 30 or 40 lane centre. Another white elephant?

Dinner was another BBQ... like our first night but in a basement private room attached to the bowling alley. Again, no other diners seen going in or out.

North Korea's Day of Rest Sunday 25th June
We had a later start. At first we were not sure why and they avoided spelling it out but later we discovered that the Korean War started on the 25th and there was various parades going on. Keeping us out of the way was the policy it seemed.

Pyongyang has an underground and we tried that out next. Only 2 lines but this 1970s built metro had a feel of another era with grand chandeliers as lights... as well as the compulsory statue of a Kim on the platform.

Display carrousels on the platform also had pages from the newspaper. The last time I saw that was in communist Bulgaria when I was a teenager. We saw quite a few commuters on the train, who all enjoyed staring at us. We did not travel far (about

4 stops) but exited at the city's triumphal arch. Just like the one in Paris. It was imprinted with 70 azaleas to mark the 70th birthday of Kim Il-Sung. In the adjacent square some of the soldiers from the parade were corralling. Singing songs to a marching band. A song of victory and unity.

We had asked on several occasions when we were going to see the big bronze statues of Kim Il-Sung and Kim Jong Il. Our guides were evasive and unsure whether this was possible.

But today we were able to go. Stopping at a flower stand on the way up we bought our offering. Emily thought they saw us coming and made us buy a big dramatic bouquet. She was sure there were smaller ones on offer...

We had decided that we would always show respect for our hosts and the country's traditions. We would have been offended if someone came to the UK and was disrespectful of our cathedrals, or the monarchy. Just as we heaped scorn & derision on President Trump when he was seemingly disrespectful with the Queen on his visit to the UK.

They are magnificent statues. Emily took the flowers up to the base with Han while Pak stayed with me. I was videoing Emily's approach and Pak became quite agitated as I was cutting off the heads of the leaders on my screen. You must always have them in their entirety. The full image, and no less than the full image. When we lined up to have our photos taken I had sunglasses on. Again, they need to be taken off for the picture with the Dear Leaders.

The walk to and from the statues had piped operatic music to set the scene on the approach. A bit like a Disney World but just a bit more sombre… or was it meant to be stirring? There were very few other people at the site although there were some wedding couples paying homage.

Before lunch we had a lovely walk through Moranbong Park. With grassed areas and streams and small lakes it was pleasant albeit quite quiet.... And it was their one day of rest.

South to the Border

We then headed off south to Kaesong and the famous DMZ and border point. Well border point in as much as where North meets South, but no one crosses this line... I sat in the front with Lee but it was still an incredibly uncomfortable ride due to potholes and the uneven surface. There was nothing on the road at all – in $2^1/_2$ hours I saw seven other vehicles – which included both directions – and two of those were JCBs. There were no road markings but it was either a 2 or 3 lane highway each way. At times it seemed obvious that the road would also double up as a landing strip for aircraft, if airfields had been taken out during war. But it was bumpy. All the way. The countryside and hills were beautiful and the villages we saw on the way south seemed very pleasant. Simple as you would expect. We passed no industry.

We went straight to a UNESCO World Heritage site on arrival. A brief look at pre-Korean War history.

The 14th Century twin Tombs of King Konmin. His wife was buried there after giving birth, but he wanted her to rest somewhere with an amazing view. It was a beautiful location chosen by a man who was immediately killed by the King so he would not give it up or something. It was quite a trek up the steps to the top. Pak had often bailed out of such strenuous tours but Han was a sport and raced up there with us. You knew it was going to be a busy day of walking if Pak was wearing her Sketchers Emily noticed.

We then had a short tour around a very old and characterful Kaesong Minsok hotel – the rooms opened up onto a courtyard with a stream through the middle. Alas, we were not staying there.

Our Janamsan Hotel was more functional in appearance and a bit less so in quality and character. After checking in we headed off with our bags to the lifts... But they had to send a man down to the basement to turn on the power before we could use them. I have never had that happen before.

Our room was a two-room suite... well we had 2 rooms one with a couple of chairs my grandma may have had... and thrown out 40 years earlier. A fridge, a proper ground standing white fridge, a portable black and white TV with a very grainy picture, lino floor, and 2 beds that were hard as nails, covered in a loud bedspread with a farm animal pattern. The bathroom was large but the electrics were marginal. I watched a bit of TV before going down for dinner and it was some

North Korean soap opera-like saga... Until a power cut stopped my engrossed viewing. It was the first of six power cuts that interrupted our evening. We continued watching the programme in the reception area with some other North Koreans and they seemed to love it when Emily reacted dramatically to the storyline. Language was not a barrier.

We decided to pay for an upgraded dinner in the hotel. Again, in a private dining room we had Ginseng Chicken. Pak was pretty obsessed by the healing properties of Ginseng and was most disappointed that we did not want to fill our cases with it for our elderly grandparents back home. This was a seriously luxurious dish, but the chicken was not the plump fat ones we were used to at home. Pak and Han did not want to eat what we had bought but we encouraged them to have has much as they wanted, and Lee as well. This was clearly a gesture that they appreciated – it is probably the equivalent of offering round a bottle of Dom Perignon and caviar back home.

Looking at the American Side Monday 26th June

Cold fried egg for breakfast was a bit of a first for me. I did not know it was cold until I tucked into it too. Meals always had a selection of small bowls or dishes each which we chose from. The food was always plentiful – maybe trying to demonstrate that the famine was a myth – but the reality was if you had sharing plates you could have avoided the stuff that looked, or was, rank. The way we had it made that tricky. We never wanted to be rude, and always tried to eat as much of the food as we could but it was pretty much the same every night and it was often quite difficult to leave something uneaten.

A walk through the old town after breakfast, including an ancient bridge over the stream or rivulet and a quick spin round an old royal monument and an old Confucian university. We then headed off for the border.

We had to leave our bus at the entrance and take a military provided transport after passing through a gift shop and history wall on the way. The 10 minute journey to the Armistice Hall seemed a little dramatic with a soldier up front with his helmet and rifle. The driver wore quite a substantial military helmet too which was a bit concerning -- should we be wearing one of those too, Emily asked?

They were at pains to point out that there was no artillery or guns pointing south in the fields either side as we headed along the DMZ. The Armistice Hall had the original table and chairs but little else in a very large hall. But here the line was drawn and the end of the war agreed. Or more accurately, the cessation of fighting.

There was another tour at the same time full of Chinese tourists from Macau. One old lady apparently fought in the War. Our military guide had good English, as they all did. He referred to the Southern side as the American side throughout. The opposing building on the other side had lots of cameras trained north. We were told not to wave or signal to anyone in the south.

We were then told we were lucky enough to be able to enter one of the blue huts. Apparently, the South has priority. With armed soldiers guarding the Southern door we entered and stepped from North Korea to South. Tables straddled the line and I took a photograph of Emily in the South as I stood in the North. Our military guide was very friendly and happy for me to take lots of pictures of him with us.

We had lunch in town... again the only ones in a

dining room for 60 or 70. Metal chop sticks were another strange feature that we used several times that I had never had before.

They were quite tricky to use as they were quite slippery. They came to quite a point too, although they were not used for spearing.

But at every meal they always gave us a knife, fork and spoon to the side. We never needed them but they were very considerate in that way.

We then headed back to Pyongyang along the deserted highway north. We briefly stopped at the reunification gate—which is more like an arch. It shows a Korean woman from the south reaching over to a Korean woman in the north.

Emily was asked:

"Can you see the difference between the two women"

No....

"Exactly, we are one country..."

Emily thought that was very good. It is also clear throughout that there is a common goal between South and North Korea for reunification.

That evening we had a special meal at the Diplomatic Club. It was the first time we actually entered somewhere where lots of people were eating. Although in reality there were a large number of foreigners. Two of which we had briefly met at the War museum. They worked for the Red Cross and were on a fact finding mission of sorts. One was Italian the other Swiss. Outside there were a number of cars with little flags in the front wings.

We had a private room again and had a lovely last meal. Pak's daughter had baked us a cake. It was huge with loads of cream. How do they eat a slice of cake. With Chop Sticks of course. A first for me. Eating cake with chopsticks… They also didn't leave it for dessert, Lee ate it alongside his main course.

Heading Home Tuesday 27th June
With a 6am alarm we headed out for our 0820 flight to Beijing. We had spent our last night in exactly the same room as we had stayed in the previous nights in Pyongyang. Emily had written a postcard for home and gave it to reception to post. It did eventually find its way to the UK. Pak gave us our passports back and we checked in.

We gave Pak, Han, and our driver Lee the last of our Euros as tips. They had been great guides. The departure lounge was quiet with 5 other westerners and the rest Korean / Chinese. There were two other flights – both domestic – out of the capital's airport that day. Heathrow would despatch that many in less than a minute on an average Tuesday. There was even a business class lounge. But no one in it. We had a coffee and boarded the flight which took off on time.

Reflections

What an amazing experience it was. Partly *George Orwell's 1984* and at times like being in the movie "*The Truman Show*". We did see the real DPRK on occasions, but we were shown the grandeur mostly. If we had guests visit Newcastle, we would show them the great and wonderful buildings and history we had, so in many respects we should expect no more or less. We would not take a visitor to the run down and ropey parts of our city. We could see some smoke billowing factories in the distance from our Pyongyang hotel but never got close. The big vanity buildings, monuments etc were what we were shown. They were even building a new pyramid styled hotel in Pyongyang for tourists. Pointless considering our 32-storey hotel was empty. Our hotel was well staffed too, with 4 or 5 bell boys and always 5 or 6 reception staff.

Pyongyang was certainly a bubble, and all the high heel wearing and suit clad residents were certainly not representative of the nation as a whole. But even in Kaesong we never saw poor or destitute people.

Loyalty to the leaders was paramount. They were referred to as "wise", "benevolent", "brave" or "talented". The minibus even slowed down as we passed big posters of the Kims.

While the roads were deadly quiet, and underpasses were used seemingly unnecessary, the average North Korean had pretty poor road sense and on several occasions, we nearly saw someone get run over. When there is so little traffic you get little practice, I suppose.

We never had a hard stare or felt in the slightest uneasy despite the anti-American rhetoric. And let us be honest – how can you tell the difference between a Brit and a Yank... We all look the same. We even had a military truck draw by us at traffic lights once and the soldiers in the back waved and smiled at us.

Beijing

Delighted to be back in relative safety we tried to post our exit from the DPRK on Facebook to discover this social media platform is banned in China... so maybe not so safe yet. I texted instead. We stayed downtown at the Jianguo Hotel and headed off to the Silk market. We had deliberately booked a hotel close to the market. It had changed considerably since our visit 7 years earlier and was less market and more glass fronted stores. Many had signs saying "no bartering" .... Until one shop keeper dismissed this and we then realised that old ways die hard.

Filling our bags with items wanted by us, Mark, and friend Ben back home. Trainers, T Shirts – all designer labels for just a few pounds. Two Canada Goose Coats for £25 each. We haggled like veterans and had a great time. After dumping our wares at the hotel, we then headed down the couple of stops on the underground to Tiananmen Square for a quick wander and photo for the album. It was a really hot day and we took in some shade in the underpass. There we passed some white people and did the obligatory smiles you have to give other white people you pass in Asian countries, then feel guilty for being so obvious.

A Good steak dinner was essential after a week of oriental chop stick food. The Fairmont Hotel was 10 mins away and had one of the best steaks in town Emily said. The waiter had an absolutely massive pepper grinder but did not find it funny like we did... It was over 4foot long and hard for the little chap to carry. The meal cost a fortune but was worth every penny. Filled up with goods and food, bed beckoned before we flew home on the 11.15 flight to Heathrow the next day.

<u>Home</u>

As Dad and Daughter trips go it will take some beating. It was wonderful to share this unique experience with someone who not only had a genuine interest and fascination in this very different place, but also someone who made it fun and special. We did not argue or squabble the whole trip. Emily even tolerated my snoring... We learned a great deal about the DPRK and each other. Emily summed up why it was important to go to the DPRK even though many thought we were either mad, or even wrong in seemingly supporting this totalitarian regime:

But if you do not travel and actually learn first-hand what places are like you will always be filled with the prejudice you are fed. By opening doors and seeing for yourself you realise the people of North Korea are no different than any other. They fall in love, get married, have babies. And want the best for their cherished ones.

A few weeks after our return BBC Radio 2 's Jeremy Vine Show had a segment asking "why would anyone want to go to North Korea on holiday". Tipped off by a friend who was listening I suggested Emily call in. Live to the nation she explained eloquently why, what she learned, and how this is the best way to reduce tension and fear. She then had a call from BBC Radio Newcastle journalist Anthony Day who was listening in. She had been introduced as Emily from Newcastle and Radio 2 passed on her number. Would she go on the Breakfast show the next day? Anthony then asked… "you are not related to Ian Dormer are you?" As a regular contributor, they knew they had to have me along too… BBC Radio 5 Live's Nicky Campbell Breakfast show then booked us… Media tarts all the way.

The next morning we sat in the studio with Alfie & Anna and were on good form bouncing off each other and reliving the great father & daughter trip we had.

Nicky Campbell then followed in one of the smallest studios, or more accurately cupboards the BBC had in Newcastle. The "down the wire" interview is always a bit harder as you cannot see the other person's expressions and feedback. He was a bit more challenging too... although as he once told us when we met him on TV's "The Big Question", he is "a proper journalist".

As we went back to the reception a producer from BBC Look North evening TV show came out. "Could we do the same for the news that evening?" I was off to Chester with work in the afternoon, but Emily could... In the end they booked a recording of us that lunchtime. They came to our home and filmed with Mark Denton interviewing us. When it was broadcast that night they included some of our pictures and video but it started with library footage of missiles launching and military exercises in North Korea. It was very much "why would an 18-year-old want to go on holiday here... or in fact why would anyone want to go on holiday to the DPRK?

Hopefully you now know why, and agree it was a great trip.

AFTER THE IOD

I was told that I would be much sought-after after I retired from the IoD, and although I did not believe or even really want a role (as I had just had the best job going), that is what happened.

The first opportunity I was offered was to chair the Health & Safety Executive (HSE). I had a keen interest in this area through Rosh. I had also chaired a sub-committee years before, jointly set up by the IoD and HSE to promote leadership in health and safety. I had spoken widely at conferences and events on the subject so was very interested. But I think the interview came too soon after the IoD. I was not as fully engaged mentally as I might have been and my interview performance for that level was not as good as it should have been. The chap that was appointed was a good, steady, and safe choice.

The next was to chair OFSTED – the quango that inspects schools and colleges. This was much more left-field and, although I was on the board of my old school in Whickham, I was not really an educationalist and told them so. But my contact at the Department for Education (DfE) said that an educationalist was not what they wanted - they wanted someone from industry who could run the board; they had a Chief

Inspector of Schools who specialised in the educational aspects. Despite my initial scepticism, he convinced me to apply and helped craft my CV so that I could be shortlisted.

The interview was scheduled for the Friday before Christmas, and I had to advise them that unfortunately I had booked a weekend away skiing with the family so could not make it. "Can you do Monday?" they asked. They obviously really wanted me in the mix, so I rearranged my return flight, stayed at Richard's on Sunday night and was at the DfE at 09:00hrs on Monday.

The panel of six interviewers included a woman who just stared at me for 45 minutes and asked one very brief question. She was the No.10 representative, and really quite spooky.

I got a call during the first week of January. The Secretary of State for Education, Justine Greening MP, would like to meet me at 17.18hrs (yes that specific) the following Wednesday at Portcullis House. I duly arrived and, with an aide at the far end of a conference room, the two of us had an amenable chat for about 15 minutes. It was not probing or demanding in any way.

There was no further contact for a couple of weeks, during which I was getting increasingly frustrated as I had also been offered the role to chair the board at Newcastle College. The college was very patient (wanting to be onside with their supreme leaders) but being in limbo was annoying; a point I made to my contact at the DfE.

It was well into February before I was told that the

Permanent Secretary at the DfE wanted a chat. He quizzed me about my opinion on grammar schools for 45 minutes. But I have no opinion on grammar schools. I explained that I had gone to a comprehensive, while my son was at an independent school. The Prime Minister, Theresa May, was a big supporter of grammar schools and he was sounding me out. I had also read that the previous Chair and Chief Inspector had been at loggerheads, and each had made contradictory speeches and statements about education policy. So I tried to reassure The Permanent Secretary that I had no opinion either way; all I would be doing was chairing the board, reiterating that I was not an educationalist.

By Easter, I was well and truly sick of it all.

The Permanent Secretary finally booked a call to speak to me when, again, I was again away. I realised it was a "no", but relieved that I could now move on.

Despite all their reassurances that they did not want an educationalist as chair, they then appointed a former university vice-chancellor.

Newcastle College

This news then freed me to take up the chair's role at the college; I had no idea what I was walking into.

The college was part of the NCG group, led by Joe Doherty, and I was in for some initial surprises about its governance. Joe would not let the board look at the college finances and, as far as I could see, refused to allow us to make any decisions. And he did not like my challenge on either of these matters. Meanwhile, the college Principal, Tony Lewin, kept his head down fearing for his job if he raised it.

The Head of Finance approached me privately with her deep concerns about Joe's bullying tactics, one of which was to tear up the college budget and give the board his own calculations with no consultation or due process.

Several difficult weeks then passed, during which I discovered that Joe had previously been accused of bullying by one of his fellow NCG executives. I also heard rumours that the conference room video cameras could be controlled and used by Joe to remotely eavesdrop our conversations.

I highlighted my concerns to the new NCG Group Chair and, although he took his time, he eventually saw Joe for what he was. Joe liked the limelight and having his picture in the media within college success stories, rather than the staff at the front end. He had also bought a vanity training business which was bleeding the Group dry, but refused to admit he was in the wrong.

Joe was eventually removed by the NCG board. By that stage, he had lost so many of the Group executive team that the longest-serving member had been there for just nine months.

I had had no confidence that they would oust him so, in the meantime, I had handed in my notice and accepted the role of Chair of the Primary Science Teaching Trust, which (as it turned out) began the week of Joe's departure.

I stayed on for a few months for the handover to my successor, although I would have stayed longer if I had known. The whole organisation breathed a sigh of relief on Joe's departure, and I saw Tony Lewin smile for the first time.

Primary Science Teaching Trust (PSTT)

I had regularly spoken to delegates who had completed the IoD's 'Role of the Non-Executive Director Course' in London, alongside the head-hunter, Peter Reichwald.

Peter asked if I was interested in chairing the PSTT, a charity set up to improve teaching of science at primary schools, funded by a £20 million bequest from Astra Zeneca in 2000. It did great work through providing resources and sharing best practice with schools around the UK.

My first job after I was appointed was to turn it from a cosy chat among a bunch of old chums into a proper functioning board. But, having done that, I then realised that there was a bigger problem. The charity's CEO, Prof Dudley Shallcross, was a great atmospheric chemist at Bristol University, but no good as a part-timer in his CEO role. Our investments yielded an income of about £1 million per annum, but he was spending close to £2 million. He was also incapable of either putting together, or delivering against, a business plan.

I lost a couple of great trustees because of their concern about the way the business was run. This left us with a group of Dudley's friends and a couple of others who had good intentions, but not the bottle for a fight.

I had hoped that Dudley's contract would not be renewed but I lost the vote by one, after a key ally missed that meeting.

Meetings became frostier until finally, in the middle of lockdown, I set an ultimatum. My concern about his competence was considerable, so it was me or him. I lost.

I reported my concerns to the Charities Commission to cover my back but the charity still had £17 million in the bank, meaning that it would be fine for a while.

Herbert Dove Trust

One of the nurses who worked with Julia was married to Ashley Wilton, a law lecturer and Chair of an historic builder's merchants.

As two non-medical people, Ashley and I would seek each other out at the hospital staff Christmas parties to chew the fat over business and the world in general. So, I felt honoured when he asked if I would join his board.

JT Dove's had been put in to an employee benefit trust by Herbert Dove because he had no children. It used the model adopted by his friends at the Bainbridge store which later became part of John Lewis. While Dove's had an executive board, the Herbert Dove Trust oversaw the business on behalf of the staff.

Over the years the business had been through some major ups and downs, but I joined as it was prospering – opening more branches – up to 20 at the time – plus a thriving online offering.

I had a wonderful time with the IoD, and after I left, I continued to stay in touch with the team, writing articles, commenting in the media, speaking both at conferences and to delegates at the end of the IoD's 'Role of the Non-Executive Director' course.

I liked and respected the staff and tried to get around

to see them all at Christmas, taking several boxes of Celebrations to each department, handing out the chocolates, and wishing them all well.

I remember grabbing the mail from my desk and running to the station on my first Christmas as Chair, intending to open the mail on the train home. The first card that I opened was from the Prime Minister, David Cameron, signed from him and Samantha in person. Wow. I know he must send thousands of cards, but I felt the biggest ego boost.

But the next card I opened was from Sulari Fonseka and the Front Desk team at 116, which they had bought with their own money and individually signed. In it, they thanked me for the time I had given to them to listen to their thoughts and ideas. My eyes welled-up.

That second card meant so much more.

WHILE I REMEMBER

I have been really lucky in my life. I had parents who were devoted to me and Lisa, who loved us and cared for us so well, no one could have done it better. My dad used to say to me that he "loved me more than all the tea in China". I feel guilty about those teenage years and early years working together when I battled with him too much. It may be the natural way of the alpha male animal instinct to exert their claim to the throne. But when I see it happening, with my own son, I understand the process and feel no ill towards Mark.

To have a couple as role models, where their devotion to each other and to the family is paramount, is extraordinary. I hope I come just halfway. I have also been lucky having a sister that believes in that family bond. She stood by me through thick and thin and carved a way that made me going out to the pub and clubbing easy to pass by the parents. Lisa is totally different to me in so many ways. When I was thirty something and single, she tried to fix me up with some of her friends. It was very kind, but I was not one for the glamourous girl.

We were all delighted when she found her soul mate with Glenn. I was even more touched when he asked me to be his best man at their wedding. He asked as we carried back a set of ladders he borrowed from us, so that Adam could fix a fall pipe at their house. (Adam had put a firework rocket of the pipe but it exploded before exiting at the top, bringing half the gutter down). It was a great honour, and a great celebratory day.

What has motivated and made me happy? Being loved was the greatest happiness giver. Fear of failure has certainly motivated my professional life over the last 30 years. You are only one step from losing everything.

I could be regarded as an early tree hugger, as I am keen on recycling and hate waste. I have loved the magic of my composting bin in the garden where I pile in vegetable cuttings and the like and with a bit of turning and watering every so often, it magically turns into beautiful rich soil. I am sure I am annoying when I pull cans out of the bin and put them into the recycling... probably with a sigh or a tut that others are not as diligent. But hoarding memorabilia from the past and collecting things as "they may come in useful one day" must be extraordinarily annoying. The loft is full.

While I do my little bit for charity, I am passionate about organ donation and giving blood. While we can make more money and give more to charity you cannot make more organs to donate or manufacture more blood. These have to be given. I should hit 100 pints donated before I am 60.

Life has ups and downs. I had a few, but without any doubt I had opportunities and experiences that many do not have. We often debate how much is luck. And how much you work hard for your good luck. But there is certainly an element of seizing the day (with apologies for all the cliches in there...)

When I was hitchhiking with Richard, we spent a lazy afternoon lying in a Paris park, drinking wine and chewing the fat with a couple of girls from Glasgow University. Tandy Taylor was from Beamish, County Durham (small world) and she professed to be a psychic, palm reader etc. She predicted a few things:

- I would be married and then get divorced
- I would re-marry and have 2 children. A girl & a boy
- I would not be a millionaire but would be comfortably wealthy
- I would live until I was 75.

She was right on the first three points and only time will tell on the last.

In case she is wrong, and I depart this world sooner rather than later, I ask only a few things for my funeral and beyond; Get the cheapest coffin. It is going to be burned 10 minutes later. Use the money you save to buy everyone a few drinks.

I do not mind if it is a vicar or a humanist who sends me on my way. If there is a heaven, then bringing in a vicar at this stage will not undo any impediments I may have created on the way. I have been to services by both that have moved me. It is the thoughts that count and I am happy to have whoever will bring comfort to those I leave behind, who cared about me. Funerals are for the living not the dead.

But if I have a say in the music to be played, start

with Rachmaninov's *Rhapsody on a theme of Paganini*. It was played at my father's and I want it at mine. It is beautiful.

But please depart with Louis Armstrong's *What a Wonderful World*.

Remember. The glass is not just half full. It is re-fillable.

I was an ordinary chap, but I feel I have had an extraordinary life.

When I come to the end of the road and the sun has set for me

I want no tears in a gloom filled room why cry for a soul set free

Miss me a little but not too much and not with your heads bowed low

Remember the love we once shared. Miss me, but let me go

Let Me Go; Christina Georgina Rossetti

Figure 31: The Rosh team

ACKNOWLEDGEMENTS

So many people have encouraged, supported, and influenced me on my journey through life. I hope I have done them all justice in the pages. Making that narrative clear and understandable from the brain dump that my writing started out from fell to Andrew Vincent. His own memoires and beautifully crisp writing had filled me with awe. His gentle editing and suggestions have moved my words forward appreciably although it is tough to make a silk purse and all that.

Over the length of my life my parents will remain that constant, solid, and amazing role model. My sister, Lisa has always been there through thick and thin, and despite being different characters we are from the same mold. Similarly with my closest friend Richard who has always been my brother from another mother.

Most importantly are my children Emily and Mark. They are everything I ever dreamt of and inspire more love and joy in me than I can ever have imagined. These memories are for them and their children in the generations to come.